COLONEL THEODORE ROOSEVELT, First United States Volunteer Cavalry
The former Assistant Secretary of the Navy, wearing the uniform of the Rough
Riders, poses as their gallant leader.

PLATE I

Who Rush to Glory

The Cowboy Volunteers of 1898:

Grigsby's Cowboys
Roosevelt's Rough Riders
Torrey's Rocky Mountain Riders

By

CLIFFORD P. WESTERMEIER

973.89
W

The CAXTON PRINTERS, Ltd.
CALDWELL, IDAHO
1958

Printed, lithographed, and bound in the United States of America by
The CAXTON PRINTERS, Ltd.
Caldwell, Idaho
79495

To my brother
Dr. Richard F. Westermeier

PREFACE

EVERYBODY has heard of cowboys, and most everybody has heard of the Spanish-American War. WHO RUSH TO GLORY is the story of that war and cowboys—the Cowboy Volunteers of 1898.

In the late nineties the American public had the roseate hue of blood in its eyes and wanted war. Everywhere, on street corners and in clubs, the same question was hurled into the air: when would the United States move upon the enemy—an enemy who had been made more tyrannical, treacherous, and monstrous by the "yellow pen" of American journalism. From Boston to 'Frisco, an anxious and curious nation awaited news that poured from the thundering presses, boosting circulation with each lurid and fantastic tale.

There is no doubt that this "newspaperman's war"

also had a strong psychological impulse which hastened to pave the way to conflict. Throughout the country the idea of a war with Spain was popular because young America wanted war. The rich fare of chivalrous, romantic, high-spirited deeds in Scott's tales, enlivened by the glamor and valor-filled narratives of the Civil War told at a grandfather's knee, obscured reality. Youth did not want to be impoverished; its reason was lost in the mist of false heroics; its growing mind was entranced by the spell of war. Propaganda, emotion, and a mission—the "white man's burden"—were all that was needed to precipitate the crisis.

Now, more than a half century after this "short war," as it was called (115 days), its most colorful and memory-provoking aspects are probably Admiral Dewey's great naval victory and Teddy Roosevelt's Rough Riders. The course of the Rough Riders is enshrined in the pages of history, and they still ride through the impressionable minds of the young. History tells us only part of the story of the Western horsemen and their rendezvous with destiny; the young remember only their heroes in the heat of battle and the flush of victory. Due to the passage of time, the fickleness of humanity, and the neglect of narrators, facts become burdened with legend and realities are obscured. Many men of glory are ignored.

The Cowboy Volunteers of 1898 consisted of three regiments. Colonel Theodore Roosevelt led the First Volunteer Cavalry Regiment, while Colonels Jay L. Torrey and Melvin Grigsby commanded the Second and Third Volunteer Cavalry Regiments respectively.

Recruits, in the main, came from west of the Mississippi River—the states and territories of the Great
Plains and Rocky Mountains. Some few from other
parts of the country joined the ranks and were enthusiastic with patriotism, entranced by the prospects
of immediate action in Cuba and enchanted by the
lure of horse and saddle.

Among the "classics" concerning the Cowboy Volunteers of 1898 are *The Rough Riders,* by Theodore
Roosevelt; *The Story of the Rough Riders,* by Edward
Marshall; *The Cuban and Porto Rican Campaigns,*
by Richard Harding Davis, and *Grigsby's Cowboys,*
by Otto L. Sues.

Research has not revealed any particular study of
the Torrey regiment. Two souvenir booklets in the
files of the State Historical Museum at Cheyenne,
Wyoming, appear to be the only accounts. In the
pamphlet, *Wyoming Volunteers, Seven Companies of
Second Regiment, U. S. Volunteer Cavalry, Torrey's
Rough Riders,* no author, publisher, or date is given.
The booklet, *Torrey's Rough Riders, Historical and
Biographical Souvenir of the Second United States Volunteer Cavalry,* is a general survey of the organization
and membership of the regiment. A United States and
a regimental flag carried by this regiment; Colonel
Torrey's gun, sword, and belt; and photographs of
the troops are among the relics preserved at Cheyenne.

While much has appeared in books, magazines, peri-
odicals, and journals about Roosevelt's Rough Riders,
the important source of information for the three
cowboy volunteer regiments for this volume has come

from a nationwide examination of the newspapers published at that time.

So often books concerning war are written to portray the conflict as witnessed by the participants or immediate observers. WHO RUSH TO GLORY contains the same record of death and heartbreak, of bravery and courage, of thrill and exaltation, and of humor and pathos as is found in stories of war. However, it is not written from a military standpoint but is, rather, the day-by-day account of a war as it was read by the nation as a whole and, particularly, by the relatives and friends of the men in service. There were no radios and television to report every move of the regiments; letters were slow in arriving, so those at home eagerly awaited the appearance of the newspapers.

The Spanish-American War was the last conflict on the part of the United States in which the press of the nation carried intimate and personal comments and anecdotes, as well as major happenings, about the man in uniform—war was still garbed in the shining armor of glory. The journalists and correspondents of the great newspapers and writers for the local daily and weekly sheets strained to bridge the gap of separation and to bring the story home.

It is within this framework that the story of the Cowboy Volunteers of 1898 is found. In a period of nine months the regiments were organized, fulfilled their mission, and then passed into oblivion. This short span of time, it would seem, is not sufficient to produce any lasting results, but such a supposition does not take into account the nature of the adventure or the character, spirit, and strong personalities of the participants. It does not take into consideration the men who bannered the fame of the volunteers in bold black ink on newsprint. The combination produces an adventuresome narrative full of enthusiasm, ideals, courage, hope, joy, sorrow, disappointment, tragedy, war, sickness, and death and—more important—immortality. Brief though their glory, the Cowboy Volunteers of 1898 ride in the annals of American history as gallant heroes, stalwarts of their Western heritage.

Research for this book took me many places, particularly to the centers of recruitment and to the cities and towns through which the volunteers traveled to the encampments. The rural and urban newspapers of these communities, as well as those of the surrounding areas, were the richest source of information. In addition, the collections of historical societies and universities, in various states, made a notable contribution. As is frequently the case with newspaper research, proper names are often misspelled, and old-timers, though they recall the same names, are not able to remedy this situation. Names of prominent figures were found in reliable sources, but those of ordinary troopers could not be located for orthographic correction.

In these travels I met many thoughtful and courteous people who deserve mention because of their assistance. Especially able and understanding were Miss Ina T. Aulls and Mrs. Alys Freeze, Western History Department, Denver Public Library; Miss Frances Shea and Mrs. Agnes Wright Spring, State Historical Society of Colorado, Denver; Mr. Forrest Blackburn and Mr. Nyle H. Miller, Kansas State Historical Society, Topeka; Miss Edythe L. George, South Dakota Historical Society, Pierre; Miss Lola M. Homsher, Wyoming State Archives and Historical Department, Cheyenne; Miss J. Vivian Hedgecock and Mr. William S. Wallace, New Mexico Highlands University, Las Vegas; Mrs. E. Deane Hunton, Laramie, Wyoming.

Also, I had the good fortune of visiting with people related to, or closely associated with, the three colonels, and to them I wish to express my gratitude for bringing to life these illustrious leaders. In Sioux Falls, South Dakota, Mr. Sioux K. Grigsby, an attorney, spent an evening reminiscing about his father, Colonel Melvin Grigsby, and also presented prints of photographs, some of which are used in this volume. Previous to the annual Cowboys' Reunion in Las Vegas, New Mexico, I spent an enjoyable afternoon with Harman H. Wynkoop, one of the few survivors of Teddy's Rough Riders, who also provided photographs. Mr. Wynkoop has lost none of his charm and wit, nor his skill of expression, in the passing of years, as was displayed in the many letters and news items he wrote for the *Santa Fe New Mexican* during the War of 1898. In West Plains, Missouri, Mrs. Jay L. Torrey, widow of Colonel Torrey, a charming octogenarian, in whose home the spirit of the Colonel still lingers amid the many photographs, books, and mementos, patiently answered many questions and corroborated several statements. In this same town resides Mr. Wallace B. Hodge, a trooper in the Torrey regiment and a lifelong friend of the Colonel. Mr. Hodge loaned me Colonel Torrey's personal signed copy of *Torrey's*

Rough Riders, Historical and Biographical Souvenir of the Second United States Volunteer Cavalry, which contains, in Torrey's handwriting, a "Roll of Deceased Patriots" and marginal notes.

Others to whom I am indebted are, Dr. Robert H. Burns and Dr. and Mrs. Ralph D. Law, University of Wyoming, Laramie; Mr. and Mrs. L. Eugene Peterson, Fort Collins, Colorado; Mr. and Mrs. J. K. and Mr. L. B. Stengel, Boulder, Colorado; and Margaret A. Aber, Santa Fe, New Mexico.

I also wish to express my appreciation to the University of Arkansas for the grant-in-aid which provided financial assistance to complete this book.

CLIFFORD P. WESTERMEIER

University of Arkansas
Fayetteville, Arkansas
May 1, 1958

CONTENTS

Chapter		Page
	Preface	7
I.	The Call	23
II.	Colonels Three	32
III.	We Are Coming!	49
IV.	Recruits and Rendezvous	63
V.	Texas to Tampa	74
VI.	Roundup in Wyoming	88
VII.	The Hunt for Horses	104
VIII.	Grigsby Moves Southward . . .	115
IX.	Torrey's Tragedy	124
X.	God Bless the Ladies!	136

Chapter   *Page*

XI. SING THEIR PRAISES TO THE SKY . . 145

XII. CUBA LIBRE! 170

XIII. TORRY SOJOURNS IN THE SOUTH . . . 185

XIV. IN CAMP WITH GRIGSBY 201

XV. TORREY'S CAVALRY OF WOE 218

XVI. HAIL AND FAREWELL—ROUGH RIDERS . 234

XVII. RETROSPECT 252

BIBLIOGRAPHY 262

INDEX 265

LIST OF ILLUSTRATIONS

Colonel Theodore Roosevelt, First United States
    Volunteer Cavalry . . . . . . Plate I, Frontispiece

Following page 144

Cowboys Become Rough Riders . . . . Plate II

Off to San Antonio . . . . Plate III

Remembering the Maine . . . . Plate IV

Brass at Ease . . . . Plate V

Colonel Jay L. Torrey and Staff, Second United
    States Volunteer Cavalry . . . . Plate VI

Farewell, Cheyenne, Farewell . . . . Plate VII

Frank W. Eggleston Pharmacy, Laramie, Wyoming,
    1898 . . . . Plate VIII

At Camp George H. Thomas, Chickamauga, Georgia Plate IX

Horse Corral, Camp George H. Thomas, Chicka-
    mauga, Georgia . . . . Plate X

Rough Riders on Parade. First Reunion of Rough
    Riders, Las Vegas, New Mexico, 1899   . . . .   Plate XI

Interested Spectators, First Reunion of Rough
    Riders, Las Vegas, New Mexico, 1899   . . .   Plate XII

Governor Roosevelt at the First Reunion of the
    Rough Riders, Las Vegas, New Mexico, 1899   Plate XIII

The combat deepens. On, ye brave,
Who rush to glory, or the grave!

THOMAS CAMPBELL

WHO RUSH TO GLORY

CHAPTER I

THE CALL

THE NEWS that the Congress of the United States had declared war on Spain came to the city of Santa Fe, New Mexico, early on the morning of April 25, 1898. It was not a typical spring day in the City of Holy Faith; although the sun shone brightly in a cloudless, blue sky, it was abnormally warm. The sharp, cold wind, usually prevalent during this season, did not sweep down from the snow-covered Sangre de Cristo Mountains which stand eternal in the background. The narrow, torturous streets were quiet, and the usual miniature beige-colored tornadoes of dust and sand were absent. The peace of the city was not disturbed by nature's seasonal frolic or by the booted and spurred horseman who rode toward the plaza. The Santa Feans had already received the initial shock several weeks earlier when, on February 16, they had heard the news of the sinking of the battleship *Maine.* It came as a blow to these Spanish-Americans of the city and the territory. They were aware that serious trouble had been brewing for months between the United States and Spain, but the remoteness of their lives removed them from the daily excitement of, and contact with, the yellow press which made the Spanish-American problems a more active reality for the East.

On the heels of this naval disaster, almost immediately, ugly rumors spread that some of the people of New Mexico were not loyal; other reports stated that New Mexico sympathized with Spain.[1] Miguel Antonio Otero, governor of the territory of New Mexico, quelled these rumors and the inquiries which grew out of them with a strong affirmation of loyalty on the part of the territory and, in response to an inquiry made by the New York *World,* he wrote in part, "In anticipation of War, the New Mexico National Guard, in many localities, are drilling night and day."[2]

Still the minds of the citizens were not at rest. Rumors persisted that all was not well along the lower Rio Grande and actually, during the middle of April, a plot to invade Texas was uncovered. Dr. Joaquin Marti, the alleged leader of the lawless expedition, and eight of his followers were captured near Carrizo Springs by the combined skills of a local sheriff and the Mexican authorities. The culprits were lodged in the jail at Nuevo Laredo, Mexico, and were to be tried for violation of the Mexican neutrality law.[3] Following this abortive venture, the governor of Texas and the adjutant general received several letters from residents on the Mexican border, expressing their fears of attacks by marauders in case of war. They asked for immediate protection.[4]

The Marti raid, which was nipped before maturing, was the first eye opener as to the seriousness of the Cuban situation. A second jolt came when the infantry on the border was ordered to New Orleans, leaving but two companies of cavalry and one of Seminole scouts to protect the Mexican frontier. Captain Wash W. Shely, the stalwart sheriff of Starr County, expressed his opinion to a correspondent of the *San Antonio Daily Express:*

The government, if it does not send us more cavalry to replace the infantry that has been sent to New Orleans, will leave a large stretch of territory unprotected and subject to incursion for plunder by lawless men under the guidance of just such fanatics as Marti. The single company of cavalry at Fort Brown, that at Fort Ringgold and the company of Seminole scouts at Ringgold will not be able to look after the border. The State has no ranger forces available and it is certain that some kind of additional protection will be needed on the Mexican frontier.[5]

Evidently the fears held by the sheriff of Starr County did not affect a fellow Texan, Colonel Ed Anderson, of Austin, who was at the time in Washington, D.C. Upon reading a newspaper story that Spanish citizens of Mexico had organized to raid the Texas frontier, he remarked:

If the story has any basis in fact, it is one of the funniest items that has crept into print in many moons. People who are ignorant of Texas and the Texans may not see the humor of it, and perhaps it would be hard to explain to a tenderfoot or to a pilgrim "green from the states." However, if all the Spaniards who inherit the land of "God and Liberty" should take it into their crazy heads to cross over the Rio Grande on a hostile mission, what few of them that ever found their way back would cross the river sadder and wiser men.[6]

Scoffing at the idea of an invasion of Texas by Spanish sympathizers, Colonel Anderson suggested that the cowboys might better turn their Winchesters on the dons than to spend their time rounding up steers, and concluded his remarks with historical facts:

Away back in 1836 Texas suffered an invasion by way of the Rio Grande. The bones of 75 per cent of the invaders were left to bleach on the prairies of those whom they made so much braggart talk of subduing. A handful of patriots did the work and today the descendants of these same men —pure American stock—can lick the whole Spanish outfit that could touch on Texas soil, by land or sea.[7]

The bravado of one so far removed from the immediate danger did not mitigate the worries of the border inhabitants. In compliance with complaints and in the hopes of allaying all fears and any movement looking toward invasion, all the state rangers were ordered to proceed at once to the Mexican border for the purpose of thoroughly policing the area.[8] A scoffing dispatch from Mexico City ridiculed the hotheaded and impetuous Spaniards in Mexico who believed that, if they would be allowed to enlist a few regiments and invade Texas, the southern states would welcome them and agree to give back to Mexico her lost territory. This derision, however, did not assure the citizens of the borderlands.[9]

Already, early in April, war with Spain was evident;

and Governor Otero offered the Secretary of War, R. A. Alger, the immediate service of a full regiment of cavalry, "nearly all of whom are of Spanish descent, and that more will follow if needed."[10]

Still there was apprehension of more immediate trouble. The tension mounted, especially when the *Daily Citizen* of Albuquerque reported guerrilla bands on the border and the capture of twenty-five of the desperadoes by the Mexican troops.[11] At the same time the *Citizen* assured the territory that there was no need to fear Indian uprisings in the districts from which the troops were being removed. Thus a new terror was injected in the prevailing fears. Indian uprisings! Having spread the virus of fear, the editor of the *Citizen* expounded with self-assurance, "If one comes the cowboys, organized as a militia, can take care of it. Indians have a wholesome fear of cowboys, who are not restrained in their fighting by considerations of state."[12] Yet, as far north as Nebraska, stockmen worried about keeping the Indians in check; if hostilities should break out, cattle-stealing would be the first outward sign. Therefore, plans were made to organize the cowboys like Texas Rangers, with rifles and revolvers.[13]

To subdue these fears, Governor Otero suggested by telegram to the Secretary of War that Forts Bayard and Wingate be garrisoned with New Mexico volunteers and that the border be patrolled. He described his men as follows: "Our volunteers are excellent horsemen, first-class marksmen, and are all accustomed to hardships of camp life, and a large proportion speak both Spanish and English. They will be ready on short notice and are anxiously awaiting orders to go wherever sent."[14] The Honorable H. B. Fergusson, delegate to Congress, was instructed to bring this notice to the attention of Alger.[15]

That other movements to use cowboy volunteers were afoot is evidenced in an interesting item which appeared in the newspapers several weeks before the statement made by the Governor. This came from the adjacent territory of Arizona and may have been the impetus to the later action of New Mexico. The item, under the heading of "Western News," read:

A movement is underway for the formation of an independent cavalry regiment, composed mainly of frontiermen well skilled in the management of horses and arms, and embracing a large number of cowboys. Companies are being organized at Prescott, Flagstaff, Phoenix, Globe, Solomonville, Tombstone and Tucson. The intention is to be no wise a part of the territorial militia, but an independent command ready to go to the front at once. The enrollment is expected to reach 1,000.[16]

On April 24, in the late afternoon edition of the *Santa Fe New Mexican,* the following headline boldly loomed the territorial reaction toward Otero's suggestion: "VOLUNTEERS GALORE. OFFERS FOR ACTIVE SERVICE POURING IN ON GOVERNOR OTERO FROM ALL OVER NEW MEXICO. RECRUITING THE MAXIMUM. NATIONAL GUARDS READY ON CALL—TWO THOUSAND MEN COULD BE HAD ON SHORT NOTICE—"[17]

J. H. Tiffany, of Silver City, requested the authority to raise a troop of cowboy cavalry in Sierra and Grant counties and suggested that the men be mustered in as United States volunteers for service in Cuba or wherever they might be needed.[18]

All this excitement, the scares and plans, actual and imaginary, had conditioned the Santa Feans to the fact that war was imminent and their relationship within the community, the territory, and the nation would, in turn, be conditioned by their response to the call when it came. The answer to the enthusiastic appeal to create a cowboy cavalry from the New Mexico volunteers on that spring morning of April 25, 1898, came with the official declaration of war between the United States and Spain. That same morning, the Governor received the following telegram from Secretary Alger:

WASHINGTON, April 25, 1898—The president directs that Captain Leonard Wood, United States army, be authorized to raise a regiment of cavalry as mounted riflemen and to be its colonel, and has named Hon. Theodore Roosevelt as lieutenant colonel. All of the other officers will come from the vicinity where the troops are raised. What can you do for them? Answer immediately.

R. A. ALGER
Secretary of War.[19]

The territorial executive answered immediately:

R. A. Alger, Secretary of War
Telegram arrived. Have full squadron of cavalry ready for service. Prefer to send them as cavalrymen but probably can transfer as mounted riflemen, if necessary. Can raise battalion of mounted riflemen in about a week. Can you take squadron of cavalry and battalion mounted riflemen in addition?

MIGUEL A. OTERO
Governor.[20]

Later that day the Governor received another message from Secretary Alger informing him that the cavalry would serve as mounted riflemen "equipped and armed by the United States for this special service." At the time, only 340 men could be used, although extra men might be needed.[21]

Thus the beginnings of the First United States Volunteer Cavalry Regiment—the first of the cowboy volunteer regiments of 1898—began to take shape. Later, it became popularly known as the First Volunteer Cowboy Cavalry Regiment.

Santa Fe was in an uproar of excitement. Governor Otero had already anticipated the trend and made preparations to organize the squadron—the enlistment and muster of men to take place in the capital city.[22]

Under the heading of "Minor City Topics," the *Santa Fe New Mexican* commented, in tune with the season and the hilarity, "There is talk around town of organizing a bock beer brigade for service in the War with Spain. They could certainly be the loudest fighters in the army."[23]

NOTES* TO CHAPTER I

* Unless otherwise indicated, all research material from newspapers is of the year 1898.

1. Miguel Antonio Otero, *My Nine Years as Governor of the Territory of New Mexico, 1897-1906* (cited hereafter as Otero, *My Nine Years as Governor,* etc.) (Albuquerque: University of New Mexico Press, 1940), p. 35.

2. *Ibid.,* p. 36; "Indignant New Mexico," *Rocky Mountain News* (Denver, Colorado), April 26; "Unjust to New Mexico," *ibid.,* April 27.

3. "Quiet on the Rio Grande," *San Antonio Daily Express* (San Antonio, Texas), April 16; "A Hitch in the Movements," *ibid.,* April 18; "An Absurd Spanish Dream," *Sun* (Baltimore, Maryland), April 18.

4. "Texas Rangers Ordered Out," *Sun* (Baltimore, Maryland), April 20.

5. "A Hitch in the Movements," *San Antonio Daily Express* (San Antonio, Texas) , April 18.

6. "Texas All Right," *Daily Oklahoma State-Capital* (Guthrie, Oklahoma) , May 4.

7. *Ibid.*

8. "Texas Rangers Ordered Out," *Sun* (Baltimore, Maryland) , April 20.

9. "An Absurd Spanish Dream," *ibid.*, April 18.

10. "Cavalry from New Mexico," *Fort Collins Courier* (Fort Collins, Colorado) , April 14.

11. "Outlaws on the Border," *Albuquerque Daily Citizen* (Albuquerque, New Mexico) , April 25.

12. [News Item] *ibid.*, April 27.

13. "To Control the Sioux," *Daily Oklahoma State-Capital* (Guthrie, Oklahoma) , April 25; "Cowboys to Be of Service," *Chicago Daily Tribune* (Chicago, Illinois) , April 22.

14. [News Item] *Santa Fe New Mexican* (Santa Fe, New Mexico) , April 22. See "Fear Indian Attacks," *Rocky Mountain News* (Denver, Colorado) , April 23; "New Mexico Asks Protection," *Denver Republican* (Denver, Colorado) , April 26.

15. [News Item] *Santa Fe New Mexican* (Santa Fe, New Mexico) , April 22.

16. [News Item] *Fort Collins Courier* (Fort Collins, Colorado) , March 3.

17. See "A Cowboy Company," *Denver Republican* (Denver, Colorado) , April 26; Otero, *My Nine Years as Governor,* etc., p. 39.

18. [News Item] *Santa Fe New Mexican* (Santa Fe, New Mexico) , April 24.

19. *Ibid.*, April 25. The *Santa Fe New Mexican* commented, [Leonard Wood] "is a captain and assistant surgeon in the regular army. . . He is said to be a physician and also a man of superior military education and ability. It is understood that he is the attending physician at the White House." See "Commander of the Cowboys," *Rocky Mountain News* (Denver, Colorado) , April 26.

20. [News Item] *Santa Fe New Mexican* (Santa Fe, New Mexico) , April 25.

21. *Ibid.*

22. *Ibid.*

23. *Ibid.*

CHAPTER II

COLONELS THREE

"REGIMENTS OF WESTERN SHARPSHOOTERS AND COWBOY
ROUGH RIDERS." This headline of a dispatch from
Washington, D.C., in the *Denver Republican*, April
25, 1898, heralded the news in the capital of Colorado
and in the Rocky Mountain Empire. From that time
on, the words "Rough Riders" were tagged to the
Cowboy Volunteers of 1898. The same newspaper announced that, according to orders from the Secretary
of War, this regiment was to be recruited from the
whole West and that "this regiment of unequalled
fighters will be absolutely separate from the state quota
of the call to be made by the President for 125,000
men."[1]

The three regiments of cavalry were to be commanded by Colonels Leonard Wood, Jay L. Torrey,

and Melvin Grigsby. Torrey was to recruit his regiment in the Northwest, Wood in the Southwest, and it was intimated that Grigsby's men would come from the District of Columbia and Maryland. "The qualifications of the men will be that they are physically sound, of good character, between the ages of eighteen and forty-five, and frontiersmen who are horsemen and marksmen, but not of necessity cowboys."[2]

Both dispatches came from Washington three days apart and contain inconsistencies, but more important than the immediate variations is the fact that there is no mention of Theodore Roosevelt. In the months to follow, however, the terms "Rough Riders" and "Roosevelt" become synonymous, and the name of Colonel Leonard Wood becomes less significant in its relation to the First Volunteer Cowboy Cavalry Regiment. Friends of Roosevelt, then Assistant Secretary of the Navy, were aware of his desire to resign from that position in order to enter military service and join the Cuban venture. According to news from Washington, Roosevelt highly recommended Leonard Wood as commander of the Southwest regiment "because he had won a medal of honor for distinguished gallantry while commanding a detachment of regular troops during the Apache campaigns against Geronimo." President McKinley appointed both men to the regiment and this move was seconded by the Secretary of War "because he felt that their training and experience in the past peculiarly fitted them to do good service with the cowboy regiment."[3]

It is only occasionally hereafter that the name of Leonard Wood is mentioned with the cowboy volunteers. From this time on, Teddy's Rough Riders, Roosevelt's Rough Riders, Teddy's Terrors, Teddy's Holy Terrors, Roosevelt's Rough 'Uns, Teddy's Gilded Gang, Roosevelt's Wild West, Teddy's Texas Tarantulas, Teddy's Cowboy Contingent, Teddy's Riotous Rounders, Fighting Cowboys, Cowboy Regiment, The Fighting First, Cowboy Cavalry, Cowboy Volunteers, Roosevelt's Regiment, Teddy's Canvasbacks, and Uncle Sam's Brownies are some of the names tagged to the volunteers by the ingenious press.[4]

In commenting on the variety of nicknames, the *Denver Times* remarked: "The alliterative three R's remind us of the ill-fated Rum, Romanism and Rebellion of Burchard, and the later Raines, Roosevelt and Reform of Strong's administration."[5] The *New York Press* commented: "Colonel Wood is lost sight of entirely in the effulgence of Teethadore."[6] However, Teddy was something more than all "teeth and tweed" and, according to *Chicago Inter Ocean,* Lieutenant Colonel Roosevelt did not approve of these glamorous alliterative titles. "Don't call them rough riders," says Theodore Roosevelt, "and don't call them cowboys. Call them mounted riflemen. If any man believes this regiment will go on the hippodrome order he has made a bleeding mistake, particularly when we get in the midst of the fight."[7]

The name Roosevelt was on every tongue. George Burch, chief of the cowboys in Buffalo Bill's Wild Wild West Show, expressed much confidence in Roosevelt as a commander, offered his assistance, and ventured to say that within sixty days he, himself, could recruit two thousand cowboys from the cattle ranches in the Western states. Other members of the troupe were most enthusiastic over the idea of a cowboy regiment and "hoped to be given a chance to fight the Spaniards."[8]

Roosevelt's qualifications to lead the regiment are simply expressed in the words of the *Daily Oklahoma State-Capital* of May 4:

> Ex-Secretary of Navy Roosevelt . . . was himself a cowboy early in his life and is willing to take desperate chances. He does not know the meaning of "fear." It is foreign to his composition. He is not handsome, but as the Dutchman said about his mule, "He's not so much for pretty, but hell for strong."

The following telegram, received at the Capitol in Denver, caused considerable consternation throughout the state:

> WASHINGTON, APRIL 28, 1898
>
> *Alva Adams, Governor,*
> *Denver, Colorado*
> Am requested by General Alger to inform you that change from battery of artillery for your state, to two troops of cavalry has been made, that the cavalry will form part of Second regiment, U. S. Volunteer cavalry, which I am authorized to organize.
>
> MELVIN GRIGSBY[9]

"Who Griggsby [sic] Is," was the *Denver Evening Post's* answer to the concern expressed. No one in the state capital seemed to know Melvin Grigsby! His name did not appear in the United States Army roster, or among the list of officials of the War Department. The *Denver Evening Post,* although it had misspelled the name, supplied the needed information after a twenty-four-hour search.

Melvin Grigsby was from Sioux Falls, South Dakota, and was the law partner of United States Senator Pettigrew of that state. Briefly reviewing Grigsby's early life, the paper states:

At 16 years of age he ran away from home and joined a cavalry troop in the civil war. He distinguished himself on several occasions, having been captured three times by the Confederates, escaping just as many times without a scratch. He was promoted to a lieutenancy for his bravery before the war was over. Ever since the American-Spanish troubles began Griggsby has been in Washington, trying to get authority to organize a regiment of Western cavalry. He gave up a lucrative law practice at Sioux Falls to go to the front.[10]

Grigsby was described as "a daring, dashing fellow, with enough nerve and energy for half a dozen men."[11]

The correspondent seemed more assured of Grigsby's qualifications when he noted that the Colonel had relatives living in Denver![12]

Previous to Grigsby's telegram to Governor Adams, according to the daily *News,* the cowboys of the Centennial State were keenly disappointed that the War Department had failed to call for a regiment of cavalry from that area. In reviewing the situation, the paper pointed out that only twelve troops were being called for in the entire plains country—four from New Mexico, two each from Idaho and Arizona, and one each from Nevada, Oklahoma, Utah, and Wyoming. This comprised one regiment. If North and South Dakota were included in the plains country, another regiment of cavalry could be furnished. Kansas and

Nebraska were not called upon for any cavalry. The *News* deplored the fact that only two regiments of cavalry were requested from the whole trans-Missouri region, which might easily furnish two brigades.[13]

> To put it mildly, our wild riders of the plains are disgusted. They have anxiously awaited the calls to arms. They have selected their best horses and put them in condition, revived their revolver practice and limbered up their lariats —all in preparation for an active campaign against the dons. Their indignation therefore at discovery that only two regiments are wanted may be better imagined than described in detail. But to go to war they will, if not on horseback, then on foot, and if at any time mounted infantry are required, the cow boy will be glad to mount into the saddle and charge with the same reckless courage that he heads off a cattle stampede on the plains, or plunges into a camp of hostile savages.[14]

Time was to prove that the Grigsby telegram of April 28 was premature and that the cowboys of Colorado did not know just where their destination would be, or whether Grigsby would command the Third Volunteer Cavalry Regiment.

On the last day of April, Senator George W. Fox, of Wyoming, received the following letter from Jay L. Torrey, whose name was henceforth to be connected with the Wyoming volunteers:

> WASHINGTON, D.C.,
> Arlington Hotel
> April 26, 1898

The Hon. G. W. Fox, Laramie, Wyoming.:
DEAR SIR—Sound "boots and saddles."
I have just obtained a call for a regiment of frontiersmen who are marksmen and horsemen, but not of necessity

cowboys. They are to be not under 18 or over 45 years of age, physically sound and of good character.

Please inform me at once how many such men, in your judgement, will enlist from your county and gallop with us to the front.

We are to organize under the last proviso of section six of the volunteer army law heretofore sent to you.

I will return home and give attention to the details of the organization, just as soon as it is possible for me to get the necessary orders and papers.

The War department is in a great rush, in view of the vast amount of work which is being done in connection with the organization of the volunteer army, and hence I may be delayed a few days.

Looking forward with pleasure to touching my shoulder to yours, in a very few days, I am, very sincerely and truly yours.

JAY L. TORREY[15]

Colonel Torrey was born at Pittsfield, Illinois, and educated at the University of Missouri, Columbia, and at Washington University, St. Louis. While studying law in St. Louis, he carried newspapers for the *St. Louis Globe Democrat* to earn his way, and "to this fact is attributable the unusual physical development which he enjoys."

In his younger days Torrey had been captain of cadets at the state university, and also served several years in the National Guard where he reached the rank of assistant adjutant general of the Eastern Military District of Missouri.

Upon his graduation in law in 1876, he practiced as a lawyer in St. Louis. Some years later he took over a large cattle business in northern Wyoming and was closely identified with that interest for several years. He took an active part in Wyoming politics as a representative from Fremont County to the legislature; was the author of the Torrey bankruptcy bill, and was in Washington for this purpose when war was declared.[16] Fellow Wyomingites hailed him as a fine leader and had great confidence in his ability. "Those who ride with him will have a chance to make the earth tremble and win glory in some of the grandest cavalry charges of modern times."[17]

All three leaders of the cowboy volunteer cavalry regiments were lawyers and participated in state and national politics and government in varying degrees. When the war broke out, according to their supporters, each was the originator of the idea of the cowboy regiments. This claim is not so pronounced in the case of Theodore Roosevelt, although in his introduction to the history of his Rough Riders, published in *Scribner's Magazine,* he does mention, in relation to his discussions with Leonard Wood, that "Our doubts were resolved when Congress authorized the raising of three cavalry regiments from among the wild riders and riflemen of the Rockies and the Great Plains."[18] It is probably this attitude of Roosevelt that gives the impression that the cowboy volunteers were Rough Riders, and the Rough Riders were Roosevelt's men. The unforeseen turn of events which developed during the short war and the unprecedented publicity accorded the Rough Riders and their vigorous, manly, dashing young leader only serve to give the legend more credence.

Between Torrey and Grigsby, however, intensity mounted in the contest concerning which of the men first suggested the cowboy volunteers for the Spanish-American War.

It is already known that Colonel Alexander O. Brodie, a graduate of West Point, who at that time resided in Arizona, enrolled an entire regiment of cowboys in that territory and made strenuous efforts to have his regiment, which had been organized for two months, accepted at Washington.[19] On April 19, Governor Myron H. McCord, of Arizona, telegraphed President McKinley as follows:

I beg you to remember that Arizona was the first to offer to the government a regiment of cavalry recruited from the cowboys of the Southwest. The regiment can be ready for muster in ten days and will be an honor to the Territory and to the nation. Please give me authority to raise such a regiment outside our quota of volunteers to be called for.[20]

It is interesting to note that on March 8, Jay Torrey telegraphed Governor William A. Richards of Wyoming: "Will the organization of a cavalry regiment of Wyoming cowboys meet with your approval? Please answer." In reply to this message, the Governor answered in the affirmative.[21] Two days later, the *Sun-Leader* of Cheyenne, Wyoming, mentions that Senator Francis E. Warren presented Torrey to President McKinley and to General Miles, the commander of the army. At this meeting Torrey asked for authority to organize twelve troops of cowboys, stressing their bravery, loyalty, hardiness, and horsemanship. General Miles said of the cowboys:

The services of such a regiment would be invaluable to the government. The cowboys are able in a pre-eminent degree to take care of themselves, and always know where they are; why, you cannot lose one of them, no, not even in a blizzard. They are the best horsemen in the world, and do not know what fear is.[22]

Still later that month, the Honorable A. M. Appelget, Sheridan, Wyoming, received a letter from Torrey. Torrey requested him to secure names of men who would become members of the proposed cowboy cavalry and stated that, since it was impossible to call out such a regiment under existing laws, he was having a bill prepared to enable the President to do so. He also hoped to have the bill passed by Congress, then in session. In conclusion to his letter, with a fine patriotic gesture, he agreed to bear all the expenses of organization of the regiment.[23]

The above statement concerning the preparation of a bill to aid in securing a call for the volunteer cowboy is significant. Otto Sues, author of *Grigsby's Cowboys,* maintains that to Colonel Melvin Grigsby "the nation is indebted for the skill and judgement in legislative matters that secured the law providing for the Cowboys, or Rough Riders. . . ."[24]

In a letter written to Sues, Colonel Grigsby gives a brief account of his connection with the law that authorized the Cowboy Volunteers of 1898.

During the month of January, 1898, and the early part of February, and while I was at Pierre, S. D., attending to my duties as attorney general, there was much war talk. Pierre, as you know, is a great center for cattle interests of the West and a place where the cowboys often congregate. It was while watching these cowboys riding their bronchos in the streets of Pierre that the idea first came to me that these rough and bronzed riders of the plains, used to camp life in all kinds of weather, and expert shots with a rifle and revolver, would make gallant soldiers and daring fighters, in case the government should be drawn into war with Spain and need volunteers to be sent to Cuba. I found upon talking with a number of them that such service would be eagerly sought by them in case they were needed.

On March 23d there was no longer any doubt in my mind that war would be declared; and on that day I wired the Secretary of War tendering my services and suggesting that the Western cowboys would make the most effective soldiers in case volunteers should be called for.[25]

Grigsby received an encouraging reply to his telegram, but in the following weeks he saw no opportunity for such an organization unless some measure other than the above-mentioned bill could be secured. Upon his arrival in Washington, he talked to members of both houses of Congress concerning the organization of cowboy cavalry regiments. His idea was popular and, in pursuing his mission, he discovered that earlier Senator Warren, of Wyoming, had, at the request of Colonel Torrey, introduced a separate bill for the organization of one regiment of cowboys.

Meanwhile, the Volunteer Army Bill had been passed in the House and had reached the Senate Committee on Military Affairs, of which Senator Warren was a member. Upon examination of Senator Warren's bill, Grigsby decided it would be easier to amend the Army Bill than to pass a separate bill and, through Senator James H. Kyle, he was able to present his proviso to the Army Bill to Senator Warren for presentation to the committee. This was accomplished at the last moment.

It "provided further, That the President may authorize the Secretary of War to organize companies,

troops, battalions or regiments, possessing special qualifications and regulations, including the appointment
of the officers thereof, as may be prescribed by the
Secretary of War."[26]

The bill passed the Senate and was returned to the
House where the words "not to exceed three thousand men" were added to the proviso, and the bill became a law the same day.[27]

According to Sues, the personality of Colonel Grigsby won him many friends among the lawmakers; and
this, with his spirit of persistence, enabled him to
have the Volunteer Army Bill amended—a prodigious
undertaking when one considers the momentous happenings of the time.[28]

While all three men—Roosevelt, Torrey, and Grigsby—left evidence of their personality and individuality
on the Cowboy Volunteers of 1898, the idea of a cowboy cavalry in case of war was not necessarily that of
any one of them. Certainly Alex O. Brodie anticipated the need. In fact, late in 1895, Governor Albert
W. McIntire of Colorado, expressed his opinion of
Colorado's contribution in the event of war:

> I have an idea which, in case of trouble, will be placed
> into practice and will astonish the world and make the name
> of Colorado known in army literature for some time to come.
> Colorado will have absolutely the best cavalry troop in the
> whole army, barring none. It will be made up of cowboys
> and range men who are accustomed to being in the saddle
> day and night and know no fear.[29]

The Colorado executive then discussed at length the
code of ethics, the riding ability, and the marksmanship of the cowboy. Anticipating the need of leader-

ship, he continued, "Place a couple of troops of this sort under a daredevil leader and the world would be surprised," and with prophetic, although somewhat exaggerated vision, he concluded his comments: "If three companies, for instance, were to be sent out the rivalry between them would make the men perfect demons and absolutely nothing human, except an immense force, could withstand their onslaught."[30]

In addition to the three colonels who eventually led the three volunteer regiments, other men were stirred by patriotism and offered their services. Dave Day, a well-known scout and Indian inspector from Colorado, wanted to organize a company of scouts, all of whom had had valuable experience in the Indian wars. A recommendation to have him appointed a captain was forwarded to the Secretary of War; an official acknowledgment of the same stated that the matter would receive consideration, but nothing further developed.[31]

Also in the Rocky Mountain Empire, William E. Scott (colored), an old soldier who had seen service in the Indian campaigns in Colorado, Idaho, and Wyoming, succumbed to the prevailing war fever and hurried to Cripple Creek, Colorado, to organize a negro troop for Teddy's Terrors.[32]

While the nation's newspapers were daily acclaiming the dangerous, rugged, and wild characteristics of the men from the range who were to constitute the cowboy regiments, it is little wonder that Buffalo Bill (Colonel W. F. Cody) was promoted as a possible leader. The trinity of words "Buffalo Bill, Cowboys, and Indians" was all that was needed to solidify the aura of dashing roughness and daring recklessness which surrounded the volunteers. Even before the regiments were authorized by the War Department, Cody's name was linked with the organization of cowboys and Indians to fight the Spanish.[33]

On April 18, a dispatch from Washington, D.C., reprinted in the *Cheyenne Sun-Leader,* stated that Buffalo Bill's offer to organize a company of cavalry scouts had been accepted by General Miles.

This announcement, along with Cody's appointment as chief of scouts on the staff, was evidently taken seriously, for Cody at once offered four hundred of his horses to be used by the scouts and, in an interview, explained the importance and necessity of such a troop:

My work will be my old role as a scout. It will be necessary to send a body of men ahead of the regular army to discover the whereabouts of the Spanish and to inform the main body. . . . The relation of scouting bands to the army is something like that of the recently purchased auxiliary cruisers to the navy, that is, to discover the enemy; but in addition a most important duty is to discover roads, learn the character of the country to be traversed later by the army, and to report accordingly.[34]

Colonel Cody had many enthusiastic supporters. One of these, Colonel Henry Inman, author of *The Old Santa Fe Trail,* especially emphasized the fact that the Indians both feared and respected Cody and would most certainly be eager to fight under him:

So greatly beloved is Colonel Cody all over the West that thousands would rally around his standard, and he could raise more men than any other man in the United States. . . .

I firmly believe that 3,000 well armed Indian warriors, under
the leadership of such a strategist, diplomat, and statesman
as was Sitting Bull, could soon clear the island of all the
Spanish regulars there, with the help of the cowboys of the
range.[35]

The ardent outbursts, however, apparently were
subdued. The three cowboy regiments were being organized under the colonels three, and, as spring passed
into summer, the beloved and popular Buffalo Bill
toured the country with his famous show. Nevertheless, he was one who "also served"—in keeping with
the momentous events of the day, he featured in his
show a detachment of wounded Cuban veterans, on
furlough due to disabilities, who "were costumed and
equipped with full regular accoutrements and arms
identified with the picturesque insurgents."[36]

NOTES TO CHAPTER II

1. "Regiment of Western Sharpshooters and Cowboy Rough Riders,"
Denver Republican (Denver, Colorado), April 25.

2. "Extra Cavalry Regiments," *Sun* (Baltimore, Maryland), April 27.

3. "Roosevelt Will Go to Cuba," *Chicago Daily Tribune* (Chicago,
Illinois), April 26.

4. "Those Rough Riders," *Denver Times* (Denver, Colorado), May 31.
See "Regiment of Western Sharpshooters and Cowboy Rough Riders,"
Denver Republican (Denver, Colorado), April 25; "Rocky Mountain Regi-
ment Will Be Known as Teddy's Terrors," *Denver Evening Post* (Denver,
Colorado), April 25; "Cowboy Regiment Recruiting," *Denver Republican*
(Denver, Colorado), April 27; "Those Cowboy Volunteers," *Denver Times*
(Denver, Colorado), April 28; "The Fighting First Cavalry," *Denver
Republican* (Denver, Colorado), June 5.

5. "Those Rough Riders," *Denver Times* (Denver, Colorado), May 31.

6. *Ibid.*

7. "Not *'Rough Riders,'*" ibid., "Roosevelt Is Not a Dime Novel Cowboy," *ibid.*, May 27. Concerning the term "Rough Riders," Roosevelt
later wrote: [The First United States Volunteer Cavalry] "was the official
title of the regiment, but for some reason or other the public promptly
christened us the 'Rough Riders.' At first we fought against the use of
the term, but to no purpose; and when finally the Generals of Division
and Brigade began to write in formal communications about our regi-

ment as the 'Rough Riders,' we adopted the term ourselves." Theodore Roosevelt, *The Rough Riders* (New York: Charles Scribner's Sons, 1899), p. 7.

8. "Lieut-Col. Roosevelt at Head of Cowboy Cavalry," *New York World* (New York, New York), April 26.

9. "Part of the Second Regiment, U. S. V. Cavalry," *Denver Evening Post* (Denver, Colorado), April 28.

10. "Who Griggsby Is," *ibid.*, April 30.

11. *Ibid.*

12. *Ibid.*

13. "The Cowboys Lament," *Rocky Mountain News* (Denver, Colorado), April 27.

14. *Ibid.*

15. "Colonel Torrey Is Coming Here," *Denver Republican* (Denver, Colorado), May 1.

16. "Jay Torrey Leads," *Denver Evening Post* (Denver, Colorado), May 4. See *Torrey's Rough Riders, Historical and Biographical Souvenir of the Second United States Volunteer Cavalry* (Jacksonville, Florida: Vance Printing Co., 1898).

17. "Wyoming To Be In," *Cheyenne Sun-Leader* (Cheyenne, Wyoming), May 6.

18. Theodore Roosevelt, "The Rough Riders," *Scribner's Magazine*, XXV (January, 1899), 6.

19. "Western News," *Fort Collins Courier* (Fort Collins, Colorado), March 3; "Denver the Rendezvous," *Rocky Mountain News* (Denver, Colorado), April 24.

20. "Arizona's Cowboy Regiment," *Sun* (Baltimore, Maryland), April 20; "Arizona Troops Were First," *Albuquerque Daily Citizen* (Albuquerque, New Mexico), May 5. "Colonel Torrey claims credit as the originator of the idea of organizing troops consisting of 'frontiersmen, who are marksmen and horsemen,' and secured the legislation pursuant to which three regiments of cavalry of this character have enlisted." "Col. Jay L. Torrey," *Florida Times-Union & Citizen* (Jacksonville, Florida), July 31.

21. "A Cowboy Cavalry Regiment," *Cheyenne Sun-Leader* (Cheyenne, Wyoming), March 9.

22. "Wyoming Cowboys To Have a Chance," *ibid.*, March 10.

23. "Cowboy Cavalry," *ibid.*, March 22.

24. Otto L. Sues, *Grigsby's Cowboys* (Salem, South Dakota: Privately printed, 1900), [Introduction] p. 1.

25. *Ibid.*, pp. 1-2.

26. *Ibid.*, pp. 2-4.

27. *Ibid.*, p. 4.

28. *Ibid.*, p. 7.

29. "Cowboys and Dynamite," *Rocky Mountain News* (Denver, Colorado), December 22, 1895.

30. *Ibid.* In August of 1886, when strained relations existed between the United States and Mexico, Theodore Roosevelt notified the Secretary of War that he was ready to organize and lead a company of cowboys against the prospective enemy. When the strained relations did not

materialize into war, Roosevelt, realizing the triviality of the incident, wrote to the Secretary of War as follows: "I wrote as regards Mexico *qua* cowboy, not *qua* statesman; I know little of the question, . . . If a war had come off, I would surely have had behind me as utterly reckless a set of desperadoes as ever sat in the saddle." Hermann Hagedorn, *Roosevelt in the Bad Lands* (New York: Houghton Mifflin Co., 1930), p. 415.

31. "Dave Day Will Take a Cowboy Regiment to Manila," *Denver Times* (Denver, Colorado), May 21.

32. "Colored Troop of Rough Riders," *Rocky Mountain News* (Denver, Colorado), May 6.

33. "Buffalo Bill's Offer," *Sun* (Baltimore, Maryland), April 18.

34. "Buffalo Bill's Work," *Denver Times* (Denver, Colorado), May 24.

35. "Cowboy and Indian Army," *Chicago Daily Tribune* (Chicago, Illinois), May 31.

36. "Buffalo Bill's Show," *Sun* (Baltimore, Maryland), May 11; "Buffalo Bill's Wild West," *Chicago Daily Tribune* (Chicago, Illinois), July 22.

CHAPTER III

WE ARE COMING!

We are coming, Governor Otero, Yea, we're coming on the run
For we've heard the proclamation, that hostilities have begun,
Between this glorious nation and the monarchy of Spain
On behalf of bleeding Cuba, and our battleship, the Maine.[1]

FROM THE MOMENT the need for volunteers was made public, the men of the New Mexico Territory were enthusiastic and spontaneous in their response. Excitement ran high throughout the nation and every newspaper featured day-by-day developments of the cowboy volunteer regiments. This excitement and interest did not wane during the entire life of the organizations, nor did it subside until many months after they ceased to exist.

The capital in New Mexico was flooded with offers to raise troops and to give service and aid. George

Curry, El Paso, Texas, informed the adjutant general's office: "I will have 50 men at Las Cruces sure on Monday next. Fifteen cowboys come from Pecos valley under C. L. Ballard, deputy United States marshal, who is a brave man and experienced officer, and wish you could appoint him second lieutenant, as he is a valuable man."[2] Mr. A. M. Bergere, a clerk of the First Judicial District Court in Santa Fe, physically disqualified to serve in the volunteers, demonstrated his patriotism to the Governor in a magnanimous offer: "I have on my ranch about 800 good horses and I would be pleased to tender 100 of these through you to the United States government free of charge."[3]

During those last days of April, controversies developed in two newspapers which caused not only a great deal of discussion but also revealed the tenseness of emotions which existed between the communities vying with one another in demonstrations of their loyalty. Albuquerque aspired to be the rendezvous of the troops and when it was rumored that, through the efforts of Governor Otero, Santa Fe had been so named, the *Daily Citizen* questioned bitterly, "What is the matter with Delegate Fergusson?" Evidently, the congressional delegate had been besieged with telegrams from his constituents, requesting him to exert every effort to secure the location of the rendezvous at Albuquerque. In answer to the query of the *Daily Citizen*, the newspaper of the capital remonstrated:

There is no rumor about this. It is an accomplished fact. The best interests of the service and of the territory demand that the rendezvous for the New Mexico volunteers be at the seat of the territorial government and Governor Otero, having presented the matter to the proper authorities in Washington clearly and forcibly, Santa Fe was selected for the purpose named. It was not a question of towns, it was a question of what was best for the country. The Citizen need not pour out the vials of its wrath on Delegate Fergusson's devoted head, the delegate's tow line is not nearly as long or as strong or as powerful as that of the governor's from Santa Fe to Washington. That's all.[4]

To call upon the delegate to Congress who had nothing to do with military affairs was foolhardiness; the Governor alone, as commander-in-chief of the territorial forces, had the authority to make these decisions. The *Santa Fe New Mexican,* in an attempt to settle the matter, issued the following statement in the form of a warning:

It is reported that officers of the National Guard of New Mexico in Albuquerque and probably one or two other places are taking it upon themselves to criticise the acts of their superior officers and of the commander in chief. Such acts are military offenses and liable to punishment by court martial. The law under which officers and enlisted men of the New Mexico National Guard are enlisted or commissioned is amply strong for this purpose and officers should remember that Governor Otero is commander in chief and as such, from a military standpoint, his acts are above criticism or cavil. No foolishness will be allowed or tolerated, and the law and regulations will be rigidly enforced in such cases as come before the notice of the officers. The officers who have so little consideration of military law and conduct that they take the liberty of expressing opinions regarding the actions of superior officers will be taught a lesson.[5]

Early in May, while the examination of recruits was taking place, another controversy developed. During those first exciting days, flushed with faith, patriotism,

and nobility, a highly idealized concept of the type of
men wanted for the volunteer troops appeared in the
New Mexican:

> The four troops of mounted riflemen being organized in
> New Mexico for service in Cuba, will in many respects be
> the most noted volunteer squadron ever enlisted. Every man
> is to be picked with reference to special qualifications. He
> must be a good shot, be able to ride anything in the line of
> horseflesh, a rough and ready fighter, and above all must abso-
> lutely have no understanding of the word fear. The primary
> object of the organization of such a body of soldiers is to
> teach the civilized world that America possesses a class of men
> who, when armed and brought face to face with an enemy,
> never quit fighting until victory or death comes. To belong
> to New Mexico's mounted riflemen as a private is an honor
> which will be looked upon as beyond that of a commissioned
> officer in many another organization of volunteers, and one
> which will place a premium upon the places on the enlist-
> ment roll.[6]

Again the *Daily Citizen* of Albuquerque was involved, but this time with a "rebel" sheet, as the *Citizen*
disparagingly denounced the *Albuquerque Democrat,*
its rival in the city. The discontented faction, smart-
ing under the turn of events, criticized the volunteers
from Albuquerque in the press, calling them "drunken
stiffs," "hobo volunteers," and "tenderfoot cowboys."
This criticism was directed chiefly at the troop being
organized by Captain Max Luna, a scion of one of the
oldest families of the territory.[7] The *Daily Citizen*
proceeded to call the *Democrat* a "copperhead press,"
with "symptoms of disloyalty in every issue," and the
owner was labeled a "kid glove foreign born capitalist"
who had "no sympathy with the United States or friend-

ship for the men who are enlisting to defend the Union."[8]

After recovering from the first shock of this adverse criticism, the editor of the *New Mexican* took the situation in hand and wrote:

As a matter of fact, Captain C. L. Cooper today complimented Captain Luna on the splendid physique of his men and expressed great satisfaction at their deportment. Out of 15 men examined this afternoon 13 were accepted for service and even better results are anticipated from further examinations.

Citizens of Santa Fe are highly indignant over the cowardly course pursued by the Democrat, and the feeling that the perpetrator of such a dastardly outrage merits severe punishment, is general. A man whose patriotism runs so low that he can see nothing commendable in the action of a person who offers to sacrifice his life on the altar of his country's honor and glory, is a yellow cur of the most despicable variety and his contracted brain, if he has such an article, has never experienced a respectable or honorable motive.[9]

As if to reassure the readers that it had not lost all dignity, the *New Mexican* regathered its poise and philosophically commented the following day:

These "hobos" (?) though innured [sic] to hardships and sufferings know the nobility of sympathy. Their hearts ache for oppressed humanity and they stand ready to blot out the wrongs of a maltreated and tyrannized race with their own blood.

Whether born a blacksmith or king, washwoman or queen, true manhood is gauged only by nobility of motives; and true bravery only by valorous deeds.[10]

The criticism of the volunteers by the Albuquerque newspaper as "hobo volunteers" brought several strong, patriotic, sentimental, and threatening protests from the citizens of Santa Fe. There were also comments concerning the physical appearance of the volunteers as "fine specimens of physical manhood," "huskiest specimens of manhood," "great, big strapping young men," and "fine riders, excellent shots."[11]

Theodore Roosevelt, in his book *The Rough Riders,* expressed his opinion: "They were a splendid set of men, these Southwesterners—tall and sinewy, with resolute, weather-beaten faces, and eyes that looked a man straight in the face without flinching. They included in their ranks men of every occupation; but the three types were those of the cow-boy, the hunter, and the mining prospector. . . ."[12]

In order to allay some of the fears expressed by the citizens of Albuquerque concerning the quality of their volunteers as compared to men from other parts of the Southwest, Governor Otero wired Thomas Hughes: "The Albuquerque men are all right, adverse criticism to the contrary. Out of 15 examined 13 have been accepted and mustered in. Your son passed. He will be cared for. . . ."[13]

Several days later, a "loyal" New Mexican sent a telegram to the New York *World* which in no way eased the tense situation.

Roosevelt's cowboy regiment is liable to be a fake. The members of the regiment, so far as New Mexico is concerned, are being recruited in railroad towns. Probably not 10 per cent of the men recruited ever were cowboys in their lives, and I doubt if one-fourth of them ever rode a horse. Lincoln county, New Mexico, of which I am a resident, is one of the chief cattle counties of the Territory, and not the slightest effort has been made to enlist a single cowboy. This statement I stand by, regardless of what may be said by those in authority. A large proportion of the applicants for enlistment are foreigners, while the cowboy element is purely native born.[14]

In opposition to this statement, the newspapers of the Rocky Mountain Empire published long lists of names of alleged cowboys and, also, their place of residence. This enthusiasm persisted during the entire period of recruitment and even long after the troops were on the way to San Antonio, Tampa, and, Cuba. Without any difficulty, replacements for the First U.S. Volunteer Cavalry Regiment were constantly being supplied from the ranges of the territories.

The volunteers were not concerned about the financial matters involved. Many paid their own railway fares to the places of enlistment and bore the greatest portion of their immediate expenses. One volunteer, when questioned about the scant pay he received in exchange for his services, replied, "We did not enlist for money, but to fight for our country."[15]

During the first ten days of the month of May, patriotic songs, sentimental poetry, and lusty cheers appeared in the capital city newspaper in considerable numbers. Appropriate words were written to the tunes of "Good-Bye, My Lover, Good-Bye," and "Marching Through Georgia,"—the latter being popularly known as the "Cuba Libre Song."[16] The various songs of the three regiments constitute a later chapter in this study, hence only a few examples of poetic expression are given here:

> A blare of bugles through the land
> "To horse!" the call; 't is full and clear.

A loosening of hand from hand;
A teardrop's fall; a kiss so dear!
A father's clasp, a mother's prayer,
A rose hid in the knapsack there.[17]

A lusty cheer, more typical of the mood of the men, came from San Antonio, Texas, where the volunteers were in training:

Rah! Rah! Rah!
Ray! Ray! Ray!
We're the cowboy Regiment
From Santa Fe,
Bound for Cuba.[18]

Meanwhile, on May 5, a Washington dispatch relayed the message that Theodore Roosevelt was about to complete his work with the Navy Department and would leave on the following day for San Antonio, Texas, there to assume his duties as lieutenant colonel of the regiment which would assemble in that city before departing for the port of debarkation.[19] When Roosevelt was sworn in, a "select party" which had assembled to join his regiment, was present. Among the thirty-one men were fifteen students from Yale and Harvard, three mounted policemen from New York City, and three members of the United States Cavalry. The group also included three Southerners who had just returned from cowpunching in the West, and the remaining seven were all members of the "dead swell Knickerbocker and Summerset [Somerset] Clubs," the former in New York, the latter in Boston.

"All go in as troopers. All stand upon an equal footing. The cow punchers and the Knickerbockers

ride side by side. The best man is to be advanced.
The inferior man, if there be any, is in the language
of the range, to be 'cinched.' "[20]

Another correspondent wrote:

The members of the party were decidedly unique in appearance. The plainsmen and rough riders wore broad-brimmed
sombreros and were all tall, well-built, athletic fellows, bronzed
from exposure. There were several young Englishmen in the
party, who had preferred this service as more exciting than
ranching. Colonel Roosevelt greeted each man personally,
and the men were unanimous in pronouncing him a "brick."[21]

Before this interesting news reached Santa Fe, the
Arizona contingent of cowboy volunteers, composed
of 7 officers and 179 men, passed through Isleta, New
Mexico, on its way to San Antonio, Texas, the rendezvous of all the troops of the First Volunteer Cavalry.[22]
Upon arrival at the New Mexico station, they sent
the following telegram:

Roosevelt's Troopers, Santa Fe.
ISLETA, N. M., May 6,—Wat 'ell matter with New Mexico.
Come running or will never get to Cuba.
BRODIES ARIZONIANS, 200 STRONG.[23]

Another report from Albuquerque mentions 7 officers and 190 men. "The cars were decorated with
banners and streamers bearing the mottoes, 'Cowboy
Regiment of Arizona,' 'Remember the Maine,' and
others."[24]

Meanwhile, news was filtering back to the capital
of New Mexico about the activities of the other troops
being recruited for the First Volunteer Cavalry Regiment. A dispatch from Guthrie, Oklahoma, stated

that Troop A, Volunteer Cavalry of the United States
Army, had departed for San Antonio and would be
the first group of special riflemen for Roosevelt's regiment to arrive at the rendezvous. "The best of good
humor prevailed among the boys when the train pulled
in after a long wait. The good-byes had been said
early in the evening, but few relatives of the boys
being present when the train left. San Antonio will
be reached tonight."[25]

Ardmore, Oklahoma, reported that, from every part
of the Indian territory, the cowboys were gathering
to enlist in the cowboy mounted rifle regiment. "Ardmore is the stamping grounds for about 300 cowboys,
and every day they are riding in by fours and fives,
and sometimes ten deserters from a big cow ranch
put in their appearance at once at the recruiting station in this city."[26]

The *San Antonio Daily Express*, May 8, gave a detailed account of the arrival:

The nucleus of the First regiment at the Exposition Hall
barracks was first augmented yesterday afternoon at 4:30
o'clock when the two coaches were drawn up to the Fair
Grounds over the San Antonio & Arkansas Pass track and
83 Oklahoma troops were drawn up in front of the train
and the roll was called by a sergeant and they then marched
in a double column to the barracks. Most of the Arizona
men were gathered around the entrance to the barracks and
gave three roaring cheers and a thundering "tiger" for the
Oklahomans as they marched in.[27]

Three days later the same newspaper reported that
one complete squadron of cavalry (four troops) was
at the barracks—three troops from Arizona and one

from Oklahoma. It also commented on the vim and vigor of the cavalrymen, who resorted to various forms of recreation to while away the time.[28]

According to the *Chicago Daily Tribune,* all the men were big, broad-shouldered, and strapping fellows, at home in the saddle and accustomed to the use of firearms. Mounted on the best selected Texas horses, they were, in the opinion of experienced army officers, the best material for soldiers to be found in the world.[29]

"The men have been selected with care," commented the *State-Capital.*

Every one of them is stalwart in stature, strong and hardy in constitution, of rugged character and accustomed to an outdoor frontier life. Everyone of them is a fine horseman and all are familiar with firearms. Many of them have been in service in the Indian campaigns in the West and there is about them a sturdy selfreliance, characteristic of the true Westerner.[30]

When the news of the progress of the Arizona and Oklahoma troops reached the men at Santa Fe, considerable restlessness was evident. To cover the seeming delay of the New Mexican volunteers, the *New Mexican* commented: "When one considers the great distances men have to travel in New Mexico and the time required to communicate with the many places, having no telegraphic connection with the outside world, the recruiting of the four troops of picked men in five days shows great work."[31]

The New Mexico squadron was made up of territorial militia and volunteers who were mustered into military service as the First Volunteer Cavalry. The four companies had for their immediate officers men

of the areas from which they were recruited: Captains
Frederick Muller, Maximiliano Luna, W. H. H. Llew-
ellen, and George Curry commanded the troops E,
F, G, and H, respectively.[32]

The afternoon of departure (May 7) was a typical
Santa Fe holiday. Stores were closed, a long procession of men, women and children—almost five thousand in number—bearing food, trinkets, and mementos,
marched to the station where, amid much cheering,
weeping, and waving, the troops left on two sections
of the long train, one at five-thirty, the other, ten
minutes later.[33]

From Dodge City, Kansas, the day after the de-
partures, came a dispatch from Harman Wynkoop:
"All through Colorado and Kansas enthusiastic crowds
meet the train at the stations. Some of the boys developed their warlike proclivities by sinking schooners
here (beer)."[34] A comment from Oklahoma City said,
"The train stopped but a short time and most of the
men aboard were asleep, and an accurate estimate of
their soldierly qualifications could not be made. They
are not as uniform an appearing body of men as Oklahoma's troops, but they are composed of men that are
good riders and shots and hardened to exposure."[35]

So the New Mexican volunteers were sent on their
way, business went on in the casual manner of *mañana,*
and, as a finale to the long period of organizing the
troops, the *New Mexican* reported: "The pleasant
work of kissing their girls good-bye is over for a time
for the New Mexico volunteers. They are now at
San Antonio, Tex., where it is drill, drill, drill and
no chance to flirt with the girls."[36]

NOTES TO CHAPTER III

1. "We Are Coming, Governor Otero!" *Santa Fe New Mexican* (Santa Fe, New Mexico), April 29.

2. "Governor Otero's Good Work Secures Volunteers Rendezvous for Capital," *ibid.*, April 28.

3. [News Item] *ibid.*, April 29.

4. "Our Mounted Riflemen," *Albuquerque Daily Citizen* (Albuquerque, New Mexico), April 28; [News Item] *Santa Fe New Mexican* (Santa Fe, New Mexico), April 29.

5. [News Item] *Santa Fe New Mexican* (Santa Fe, New Mexico), May 3.

6. "The Kind of Men Wanted," *ibid.*, April 28.

7. [News Item] *Albuquerque Daily Citizen* (Albuquerque, New Mexico), April 30; "Wail of the Democrat," *ibid.*, May 2; [News Item] *Santa Fe New Mexican* (Santa Fe, New Mexico), May 2.

8. [News Item] *Albuquerque Daily Citizen* (Albuquerque, New Mexico), May 2; "Glance at Our Neighbors," *Denver Evening Post* (Denver, Colorado), May 6.

9. [News Item] *Santa Fe New Mexican* (Santa Fe, New Mexico), May 2.

10. *Ibid.*, May 3.

11. *Ibid.*, May 2.

12. Theodore Roosevelt, *The Rough Riders* (cited hereafter as Roosevelt, *Rough Riders*) (New York: Charles Scribner's Sons, 1899), p. 15.

13. [News Item] *Santa Fe New Mexican* (Santa Fe, New Mexico), May 2.

14. Edward J. Murray, "Are the Cowboys a Myth," *Las Vegas Daily Optic* (Las Vegas, New Mexico), May 17.

15. [News Item] *Santa Fe New Mexican* (Santa Fe, New Mexico), May 4.

16. *Ibid.*, May 4, May 6.

17. *Ibid.*, May 5.

18. *Ibid.*, May 10.

19. "Roosevelt Goes to Texas," *Chicago Daily Tribune* (Chicago, Illinois), May 6.

20. "Teddy's Terrors," *Sun* (Baltimore, Maryland), May 6; "Roosevelt and His Riders," *Denver Evening Post* (Denver, Colorado), May 6; "College Men to Join Teddy," *ibid.*, May 4.

21. "Roosevelt Joins the Army," *ibid.*, May 7.

22. [News Item] *Santa Fe New Mexican* (Santa Fe, New Mexico), May 6. See "Arizona's Cowboy Contingent," *Denver Republican* (Denver, Colorado), April 30.

23. [News Item] *Santa Fe New Mexican* (Santa Fe, New Mexico), May 6.

24. *Ibid.*

25. "Cavalry Boys Off," *Daily Oklahoma State-Capital* (Guthrie, Oklahoma), May 6.

26. "Cowboys Have War Fever," *Denver Evening Post* (Denver, Colorado), May 9.

27. "Rough Riders Are in Barracks," *San Antonio Daily Express* (San Antonio, Texas), May 8.

28. "Sunday With the Rough Riders," *ibid.*, May 8, 9.

29. "Roosevelt's Rough Riders," *Chicago Daily Tribune* (Chicago, Illinois), May 8.

30. "Troops in Camps," *Daily Oklahoma State-Capital* (Guthrie, Oklahoma), May 9.

31. [News Item] *Santa Fe New Mexican* (Santa Fe, New Mexico), May 6.

32. Otero, *My Nine Years as Governor,* etc., p. 42.

33. [News Item] *Santa Fe New Mexican* (Santa Fe, New Mexico), May 7.

34. Ibid., May 10.

35. "More Soldiers," *Daily Oklahoman* (Oklahoma City, Oklahoma), May 9.

36. [News Item] *Santa Fe New Mexican* (Santa Fe, New Mexico), May 10.

CHAPTER IV.

RECRUITS AND RENDEZVOUS

WILD EXCITEMENT and enthusiasm spread over the northern plains states when the news concerning the formation of regiments of cowboy cavalry was verified. Several weeks before the declaration of war and the official pronouncement of the establishment of these regiments, the Western newspapers followed avidly the development of the Volunteer Army Bill in Washington; every issue gave a report on up-to-the-minute trends and lauded the Western horseman to the skies. As early as April 1, the *Sun-Leader* of Cheyenne waxed enthusiastic about the plainsman and his horse:

The western cowboy is accustomed nearly every day of his life to ride from 60 to 100 miles a day and does not consider such a ride unusual. The animals ridden are the wild, un-broken cow ponies and the natural and correct inference is that living as he does in the saddle, the western cowboy is more at home therein and has better possession of his wits and muscles when riding than the average man does when walking. The western cowpony will contribute much to our forces in case it is necessary to press him into service. The cow pony of the plains knows no fatigue, needs no grooming, does better without it, and only expects to be turned loose occasionally where there is a little grass, and it is even claimed by some riders that the animals thrive fairly well on old shoes and tin cans.

But to go back to the cowboy. What cavalryman has training more conducive to health, strength, endurance, picket duty and expert rifle manipulation than he? The greatest part of his life is spent in the open air on the plains and in the mountains. In rain, sunshine and blizzard he does picket duty at night and keeps his herd of cattle together. Looking for stray steers, he wanders miles in gulches and mountain heights and in places where man never trod before. You can't lose the western cowboy, who only wants a place to start from. He encounters the fierce animals of the mountains; he spends his leisure moments in shooting heads off of prairie chickens, the bodies of which are buried at a distance of 50-100 yards; he is absolutely fearless. The Texas rangers have another advantage. They have had diversified experience with Mexican greasers and know their nature and customs, which would help them in case of war.[1]

Letters from Wyoming citizens, offering service to the country, continued to pile up on the desk of Governor Richards. Many called in person to volunteer. One hundred citizens of Buffalo, Wyoming, each donated one hundred to five hundred pounds of flour to be sent to the starving Cubans; another patriotic citizen of the same city offered free transportation of twenty thousand pounds to the railroad.[2] As progress on the Volunteer Army Bill was reported, the Westerners let their spirit have free rein in praise of their horsemen. The *Sun-Leader* wrote:

There can be no question as to the accuracy of his marksmanship or his ability to show even the Cossacks of the Don tricks in fancy riding. His value as a scout is almost beyond computation; in all winds and weathers he rides the wild, free range, alike unheeding the March blizzards or the blazing heat of mid-summer. His home is in the saddle and his bed, at least one-half of the time, is the grass grown prairie. He can get along with less "grub" and do more work on short rations than any living thing outside of an army mule.[3]

The same newspaper quotes the comments of General Miles:

The services of men whose lives are spent in the saddle as herdsmen, pioneers, scouts, prospectors, etc., would be exceedingly valuable to the government in time of hostilities. They are accustomed to a life in the saddle, most excellent horsemen, fearless, intelligent, enterprising, accustomed to taking care of themselves in bivouac, skillful in landcraft and as a rule excellent riflemen. Such a force would be a valuable auxiliary to any army.[4]

Colonel C. G. Coutant, a local historian, opposed to needless war but aware that war was impending, said:

I hope Wyoming will take a conspicuous part in this contest. We can furnish some of the ablest and bravest men that ever trod a battlefield. The regiment of cowboy cavalry which Judge J. L. Torrey proposes is an inspiration. Ten or twelve hundred cowboys mounted and armed could lead a charge that would forever remain an incident in the history of modern warfare. . . . They are the best shots to be found in any country—experts everyone of them—and in a charge would sweep every living thing before them, leaving only death and destruction in their path.[5]

Various kinds of rumors swept the state during the days immediately preceding the declaration of war.

Cowpunchers, eager to enlist, stormed the office of Senator Fox; Torrey was in Washington, endeavoring to raise the allotted eight troops of cowboy cavalry from Wyoming to twelve.[6] The state militia authorities, who were not in agreement with the plan, indicated that the quota would be so small that Torrey could not collect a regiment,[7] and many were of the opinion that the cowboy regiment would not be utilized.[8]

A letter from Torrey received by Senator Fox on April 25 contained detailed information concerning the efforts being made to organize the regiment and to secure recognition from the military authorities. The War Department placed the total expenses of preparing the regiment for service at $250,000; $197,000 of this was for transportation and horses; $31,392 for equipment; and $15,000 for subsistence. Colonel Torrey urged the War Department to allot the money in advance of the call for volunteers, but in this he was unsuccessful. Nevertheless, the Volunteer Army Bill, with the added cowboy regiment clause, did assure the recognition of the regiment. Torrey also sent to Fox a copy of an urgent letter to President McKinley in which he stressed the need of prompt action in mustering in the regiment of cowboys as "horsemen and marksmen without peers."[9]

Three days later Senator Fox received a telegram with more pertinent information concerning the Second Volunteer Cavalry Regiment. In it, Torrey indicated that the men would enlist as individuals, at places which he (Torrey) would arrange in the near future; he also urged young men—especially those with-

out families—to enlist, and requested from Fox a conservative estimate of the number who would enlist
from his county.[10]

The requirements to be applied to the Torrey regiment were "strict in the extreme." The intention,
according to the Colonel, was "to make the regiment
of the highest standing in every way, so that only
good men will seek to enlist, while others will feel
out of place in such surroundings."[11] The age limit
was eighteen to forty-five years, and the men had to be
physically sound and of good moral character. Horsemanship, marksmanship, and the qualifications of the
frontiersman were assumed to be necessary adjuncts.
In addition, Torrey stressed uniformity as an essential factor in the regiment. Consequently, a recruit
could not weigh over 165 pounds, and his height had
to be between 5 feet 4 inches and 5 feet 10 inches.
A notable restriction, placed by Torrey upon his prospective men, one that was unique in that it was not
characteristic of other regiments, was the ability to
speak, read, and write English. The volunteer who
could fulfill all these qualifications was allowed to enlist for a term of two years, or for the period of time
necessary to bring a victorious end to war between the
United States and Spain.[12]

After the declaration of war, Colonel Torrey had
spent much time in Washington, making arrangements
with, and securing requisitions from, the War Department, including the sanction of an order to purchase
horses for his regiment. Early in May he was scheduled
to arrive in Wyoming, where Cheyenne was desig-
nated as the rendezvous for the troops to be encamped

at the near-by Fort Russell reservation.[13] Major Percy S. Hoyt, of the Quartermaster's Department, was instructed to join Captain Charles A. Varnum, Seventh Cavalry, in Cheyenne; and, with another cavalry officer, these men constituted a board to purchase horses at Cheyenne and Laramie, Wyoming, and at Denver, Colorado. According to the dispatch from Washington, "the ordinary specifications for cavalry horses will not be observed, but they will purchase horses which have been found most serviceable in the Western country as saddle horses." Approximately one thousand horses were to be purchased and the animals were to be about fifteen hands high, weigh about one thousand pounds, and to be of black, brown, bay, chestnut, and roan colors.[14] Several days later, in order to secure the type of horse required for the Torrey regiment, the board was authorized to purchase horses at $110 per head.[15]

While still in Washington, Colonel Torrey expressed his pleasure with the progress in the formation of the Second Volunteer Cavalry Regiment, which the newspapers were naming as the rival of Teddy's Terrors. Torrey, in his interview, probably unconsciously encouraged this rivalry:

I may not know every man in the regiment, but I have a personal friend in every cowboy camp in the West, and so the nucleus of the regiment will be personally familiar to me. Some idea of the men I am going to command is the fact that I am going to tap Wyoming University and the other large Universities out west. In the winter, you know, the cowboys get what education they can. They are brave, ambitious and splendid fellows all around. Here in the east you think no cowboy is fit for decent company. This is a great error. I do not make any boast of what we will do, but we will have the crack regiment in the service. Every man will be a frontiersman, a marksman, a horseman. All we want is a chance to show what we are made of and I think we will surprise the people of the east.[16]

Torrey's statement concerning students caused a number of men from the University of Wyoming at Laramie to rush to Cheyenne to enlist. They had hoped to be rated as officer material but, since no definite orders had been received, they returned to Laramie to await the arrival of the Colonel.[17]

Colonel Torrey reached Cheyenne on the morning of May 9 and, at his headquarters in the Inter-Ocean Hotel, he proceeded at once to attack the many problems confronting him. One of his first duties concerned troops from Colorado. Earlier, officials of this state had received notice from the War Department that the original plan for one battery of light artillery from Colorado had been canceled and that the state was to be assigned to Torrey for recruiting purposes and would provide one troop, or possibly two, of cavalry.[18] A delegation from Colorado, composed of Major Chase and Lieutenants A. H. Williams and H. B. Kerr, now requested Torrey to take three troops from the neighboring state.[19] However, other Western states were also eager to have their quotas increased, and the final decision on allotments was: Colorado, two troops; Idaho, Nevada, and Utah, one each; Wyoming, seven.[20]

Meanwhile, Melvin Grigsby, Attorney General of South Dakota, had been notified, on April 15, of the authorization of his proposal to recruit a company of cowboys and was advised to make preparations to establish recruiting stations.[21]   Almost immediately, Senators Hansborough from North Dakota, Kyle from South Dakota, Carter from Montana, and Thurston from Nebraska conferred with the War Department to determine the quota of men from each state to constitute the Third Volunteer Cowboy Cavalry Regiment. With daily reports of the progress of the other two regiments constantly being flashed before them, these men were determined to stand by their people; they were convinced that volunteers from their respective states could well meet the necessary qualifications and were firm in their requests. Actually, enthusiasm and patriotism ran wild in the Northwest and each state offered several troops, the total number of which included three times the number required for the regiment. Finally, an agreement was reached, formally written and signed, allotting a total of twelve troops: Nebraska, one; North Dakota, two; Montana, four; South Dakota, five.[22]

Grigsby was named colonel and, on May 2, arrived in Sioux Falls where a large crowd of loyal-spirited citizens and followers demonstrated their support with rousing cheers and stirring band music.[23] With the echo of the hearty welcome still resounding in his ears, Colonel Grigsby went to work at once and, on the first evening, issued several commissions.[24]

The work of recruiting and organizing progressed rapidly and with little difficulty. The men, especially the cowboys, were so eager to volunteer for this great venture, and enthusiasm was so pronounced that Governor Smith, of Montana, had hardly issued the call when the state's quota of four troops was filled.[25]

During the first physical examination of men in Sioux Falls, approximately one in ten was accepted; many applicants discovered they were not physically fit; from 105 men only six were taken—later three of these were sent home. Rupture, varicose veins, and varicocele[26] were the principal objections.[27]

Men in the smaller towns of Nebraska fared better before examining boards than did the recruits in Omaha and Lincoln. One newspaper reported "the cowboys being found to be almost perfect specimens. From these companies the most of the rejections are because the boys are too light."[28]

The cowboys were eager to go to war but they had two concerns—they wanted to use their own saddles and they wanted quick action. Not one of them was particularly hankering to ride "one of the little cavalry scoops on a horse," and all agreed "that they would be all right if they were allowed to rush the fighting when it once started, but the long waits would have a tendency to demoralize them. They would be ready at any time for a quick fight but would not feel easy in waiting under orders."[29]

Within twenty-one days the twelve troops were recruited, officers and noncommissioned officers appointed, and the Third Volunteer Cavalry Regiment organized. Mustering in took place between May 12 and 23. With the convergence of the troops upon Sioux Falls, Colonel Grigsby issued the first of his general orders in which he impressed upon the officers the necessity of maintaining "the dignity, bearing, cour-

tesy and demeanor commensurate with the position
they had been called upon to fill. They should not
only by example discourage drinking, gambling, and
other demoralizing conduct, but should encourage
friendly rivalry in horsemanship and general military
qualities that will make them both good citizens and
efficient soldiers."[30]

After the mustering in, various rumors were current as to the destination. Omaha and San Francisco
were mentioned as possible places of rendezvous; when,
on May 18, orders were received for a general move
two days later to Chickamauga Park, Georgia, the
Third Regiment volunteers were wild with joy—surely,
they were on their way to Cuba![31]

Seemingly, the Second and Third Regiments were
on their way, but both were to be confronted with
unforeseen delays. Torrey, because of his strict qualifications for men and horses, was scouting wildly in
his recruiting territory; Grigsby, upon arriving in
Chickamauga, discovered that much of his equipment
had not been delivered. These events will be discussed in detail in subsequent chapters; meanwhile,
the war is on, and, in San Antonio, Roosevelt is riding
proudly with the First Regiment, preparing to entrain
for Tampa and then to take off for Cuba.

NOTES TO CHAPTER IV

1. "Western Cowboys," *Cheyenne Sun-Leader* (Cheyenne, Wyoming),
April 1.

2. "Buffalo Sends Flour," *ibid.*, April 7.

3. "Cowboys as Cavalrymen," *ibid.*

4. "Approval of the Plan," *ibid.*, April 8.

5. "The Cowboy Cavalry," *ibid.*, April 22.

6. "Cowboys to Muster," *Denver Republican* (Denver, Colorado), April
24.

7. "A Cowboy Regiment," *Cheyenne Sun-Leader* (Cheyenne, Wyoming), April 20.

8. "Will Rendezvous Here," *ibid.*, April 26.

9. "The Wyoming Cowboy Regiment," *Denver Republican* (Denver, Colorado), April 26.

10. *Ibid.*, April 29.

11. "Work of Raising a Cowboy Regiment," *ibid.*, May 1.

12. *Ibid.*

13. "Torrey's Cavalry," *Cheyenne Sun-Leader* (Cheyenne, Wyoming), May 4.

14. "Horses and Equipments of the Torrey Cowboy Regiment," *Denver Republican* (Denver, Colorado), May 6.

15. "Captain Torrey at Cheyenne," *ibid.*, May 10.

16. "Col. Torrey Pleased," *Daily Oklahoma State-Capital* (Guthrie, Oklahoma), May 5.

17. "Couldn't Be Officers," *Cheyenne Sun-Leader* (Cheyenne, Wyoming), May 10.

18. "Cavalry in Place of Artillery," *Denver Republican* (Denver, Colorado), April 30.

19. "Captain Torrey at Cheyenne," *ibid.*, May 10.

20. "Torrey's Rough Riders," *Salt Lake Herald* (Salt Lake City, Utah), May 10.

21. "Cowboy Company Is To Be Formed," *Chicago Daily Tribune* (Chicago, Illinois), April 16.

22. "The Cowboy Regiment," *Bismarck Tribune* (Bismarck, North Dakota), May 5. See "Cowboys," *Yankton Press and Dakotan* (Yankton, South Dakota), April 28; "Grigsby's Cavalry," *ibid.*, April 30; Grigsby's Cavalry," *ibid.*, May 4; "Teddy Will Rival Grig," *Daily Argus-Leader* (Sioux Falls, South Dakota), April 25; "The Smoked Yank On Top," *ibid.*, April 27.

23. "Order Is Changed," *Bismarck Tribune* (Bismarck, North Dakota) April 27; Sues, *Grigsby's Cowboys*, p. 8.

24. *Ibid.*, p. 9.

25. "Montana's Quota of Volunteers," *Rocky Mountain News* (Denver, Colorado), May 2.

26. The original source used the word "varicole," which was probably a typographical error. Varicocele is a varicose enlargement of the veins of the spermatic cord.

27. "Third Regiment," *Daily Argus-Leader* (Sioux Falls, South Dakota), May 9.

28. "Guards Cheer News of Dewey," *Chicago Daily Tribune* (Chicago, Illinois), May 8.

29. "Cowboys Talk of War," *Daily Argus-Leader* (Sioux Falls, South Dakota), April 25.

30. "Third Regiment," *ibid.*, May 13. See "Grigsby's Speech," *Yankton Press and Dakotan* (Yankton, South Dakota), May 10; "Grigsby's Regiment," *ibid.*, May 18; "Grigsby's Cowboys," *ibid.*, May 16.

31. Sues, *Grigsby's Cowboys*, p. 17. See "Grigsby's Cowboys," *Yankton Press and Dakotan* (Yankton, South Dakota), May 16.

CHAPTER V

TEXAS TO TAMPA

LIFE IN SAN ANTONIO for the First Volunteer Cavalry Regiment was indeed different and difficult. The hot, humid weather was most disagreeable; a ferocious and unkind sun scorched the campgrounds day after day, and clouds of dust rose unmercifully from the dry, parched earth. The men of the West, accustomed to the torrid sun and blinding dust on the endless plain and prairie, accepted this discomfort more readily, but the freedom of the open space was sadly lacking in their training quarters. To the volunteers from the Eastern cities, frontier life, desolate surroundings, and the frank, lusty air of their cowboy associates were entirely unfamiliar. All in all, camp life was hard for the most of them.[1]

At first tents were not as yet available, and the

men were housed in the exposition building. The
majority of volunteers in the regiment were men
from the plains—cowboys and miners, at home in the
open and well accustomed to the saddle and rifle.
Such a situation, created by the meeting of East and
West, emphasized by inconvenience and discomfort,
strange quarters, and lack of equipment to keep men
occupied, might well have been an explosive one; yet
the twain, pledged to one cause, resulted in no important clash in personality. "Some wore the broad-
brimmed hat and had the bronzed cheek of the plains,
and others bore the unmistakable stamp of the stu-
dent and club man, but these latter were athletes
and trained sportsmen. All mingled with easy good-
fellowship."[2]

The newspapers on the whole, however, were greatly
concerned about the mixture of dude and cowboy
and, in the unwarranted publicity, the Easterners suffered more because of alleged favoritism and more
rapid promotions in their group.[3]

With tongue in cheek, the *San Antonio Daily Express* commented:

The Texas cowboys who have the pleasure to mess with
this party of New York "high rollers" will have an enjoyable
time, so long as they are in camp in San Antonio. Ninety per
cent of them carry a large wad in their side pockets with
which to play a little game of draw and large bank accounts
behind them. Some of them have their "men" with them to
care for their uniforms and top boots at a salary of $60 a
month, also a cook at $100 a month. None of these human
accessories will be taken outside the country with them and
their fastidious tastes will not keep the young bloods from
fighting.[4]

The harangue against the Easterners continued:

The New York swells, who enlisted in the 1st regiment of U. S. volunteer cavalry, had to leave their valets at home. They are probably nice fellows and all that, but it must be remembered that every man sent by New Mexico as a member of that regiment is just as good as the best New York swell. The chances are that all will fraternize and assimilate when it comes to duty and active service, and that this mixture will prove for the best and will make the regiment one of the finest in the service.[5]

There is some local fear expressed since forty of the New York 400 have gone to San Antonio, Texas, to enlist in the First Regiment of Cavalry, Cowboy Battalion, that the simple manners and customs of the New Mexico cowboy may be contaminated and his morals deteriorated by contact with these New Yorkers.[6]

The Fifth avenue recruits had no drilling and little work to do today. Woodbury Kane was detailed for mess duty and helped to cook supper, but the rest had an easy time. They were rather bored, however, as none of them could secure passes. William Tiffany has been coming into town to eat dinner, but he had to eat three meals at the mess table today. He found the bacon and bread hard to swallow, and was hungry and unhappy when the bugle sounded "lights out," and he had to retire to his harsh gray blanket.[7]

A more serious and a very vexatious problem concerned supplies. For at least two weeks some of the troops had no knives and forks and, thus deprived of exhibiting any form of table etiquette, they applied the old adage of "fingers before forks"—but not without many complaints.[8] Uniforms were issued a week after the men arrived in camp and, although there was "little of the army blue about them," they were cheerfully accepted. The predominance of brown in the tunic, trousers, and leggings, with black shoes, navy blue shirt, and gray field hat caused one observer to dub the troopers as "Teddie's Brownies . . . a husky lot of troopers when drawn up in line on horseback."[9]

The amount of equipment with which each man was supplied was prodigious and backbreaking: a McClelland saddle, bridle, water bridle, halter, saddlebags, surcingle, picket pin and rope, nose bag, currycomb and brush, spurs, canteen, mess pan and tin cup, knife, fork and spoon, poncho, body blanket, horse blanket, one-half shelter tent, service belt, machete and scabbard, Krag-Jörgensen .30-30 carbine and scabbard, .44-caliber single-action Colt revolver and scabbard, and cartridge belt. Sergeant T. P. Ledgwidge of Troop E, who listed the above equipment, commented succinctly: "What else we will carry I cannot say, but it seems we have enough now."[10]

Colonel Roosevelt's announcement that his men would carry carbines and revolvers was enthusiastically received. At that time the Krag-Jörgensen carbine was the most modern weapon and was to be used exclusively by the Rough Riders. In addition to these two firearms, the volunteers were also equipped with the machete, a much easier weapon to handle than the regular cavalry saber. This knifelike weapon would be of great advantage to the troopers in slashing their way through the dense thickets and underbrush of the Cuban tropical forests.[11]

An amusing tale was circulated concerning supplies. Facetious remarks and much banter about spurs and lariats for Teddy's Terrors were cast about. A dis-

patch from Washington stated that Colonel Teddy had
sent repeated requests to the Commissary Department,
the last of which was short and to the point:

" 'Please send us our spurs at once.'

" 'Thought you'd win those in Cuba,' replied the
facetious commissary.

" 'We'll come to Washington and win them if you
don't hustle them out here,' was the colonel's reply."

Lest the Rough Riders should attempt to invade
the national capital, Major Humphries of the Commissary Department assured the Colonel that his spurs
and lariats were on the way.[12]

These were trying days in May. Constant drilling,
adverse living conditions, lack of equipment, restless
men rarin' to go—all contributed to the first realiza-
tion that the adventure had its serious aspects. At
this time the *Santa Fe New Mexican,* under the title
"Spanish Views of the United States," reprinted fantastic bits of news which had appeared in some of
the enemy's newspapers. *El Heraldo de Madrid* published on April 20, 1898:

"News is brought to us that Buffalo Bill, a notorious out-
law and leader of a band of half-breeds, has risen against
the American government, and is burning towns near his
birthplace in New York.

"Word has just been received here that the Indians are
rising against the Yankees in Illinois, Ohio, and other places.
The farmers are petitioning the government to protect them
from the blood thirsty savages, who are burning houses and
killing on every side. Troops are asked for at Colorado, in
the state of Denver, and at St. Louis, in Missipa."

Diario tersely reported:

"The Yankee president, Magginly, committed suicide for
fear the Spanish fleet would capture New York."

Pais, in an account on April 20, probably thought it could explain the above happenings:

"The country is not fit to live in. The climate is execrable. When it is not sleeting and snowing, the heat is almost unbearable. Avalanches are frequent at all times, and these threaten the principal cities. As for the people, besides the few whites engaged in business along the eastern coast, the remainder of the country is one vast plain, covered with Indians, called cowboys, and great herds of roaming cattle."[13]

Not only was the geography of the United States distorted in these reports, but also the physical appearance of our fighting men. A Barcelona newspaper stated:

"The average height among the Americans is 5 feet 2 inches, and they have never produced an athlete. This is due to their living almost entirely upon vegetables, as they ship all their beef out of the country, so eager are they to make money. There is no doubt that one full-grown Spaniard can defeat any three men in America."[14]

Many a trooper would probably have agreed with the Spanish opinion concerning the climate—at least in part—especially during the last week in May. Sunday, May 22, Camp Wood thronged with visitors anxious to see the men called "Rough Riders." Earlier in the morning the entire regiment, in full uniform and mounted, drew up before Colonel Wood's tent to listen to a reading of the Articles of War. It was a most impressive occasion.

The day had started at six o'clock when the men began to ride their bucking broncos to water. Meanwhile the kitchen detail began to fry bacon, and "the camp became more interesting." Religious services were held, and the sight-seers continued to find plenty of interest in the ordinary scenes and incidents of camp life. All day long the sun continued to blaze down upon the encampment, and the temperature reached some astronomical figure. Since there were no drills in the afternoon, the Rough Riders spent the greater part of the day in lounging in their tents, reading and catching up on their sleep.[15]

The following day, under similar conditions, the mounted troopers were drilled for almost an hour under the blazing Texas sun at the near-by Mission of San José. The periods of drill had to be shortened; the scorching glare of the sun might have been endured, but the clouds of dust choked and blinded the best of them. At one drill period, the mercury rose to 100° in the shade.[16] "The men from Arizona and New Mexico have come to the conclusion that 'this soldiering ain't what it's cracked up to be,' and the Oklahomans and the boys from the Indian Territory cordially agree with them. Still there is no complaint. The regiment is ready, and the men are praying for an order from the war department to move."[17]

After one such drill period, one man wrote to his home-town newspaper that "the dust blows as hard here as it does in Santa Fe in March," and that "keeping clean is our greatest trouble, except, perhaps, the mosquitoes, which are very thick. Some of us look as though we had small pox from mosquito bites. One man slept with his feet outside of the blankets and they bit him so hard that he can scarcely walk."[18]

By this time the regiment had secured about nine hundred horses and two hundred pack mules. As a

part of their daily routine, the volunteers had to practice putting packs on the mules and there was "lots
of kicking on the part of the mules and lots of fun
and swearing on the part of the boys."[19] The sudden
demand for horses skyrocketed the prices, and "horses
that could not be sold two years ago for $20 per head
are now bringing $80 and $90 apiece."[20]

But all was not work and misery at the camp in
San Antonio. On occasion the "boys" had an opportunity to indulge in lighter activities. One evening
the mayor of San Antonio, accompanied by a band
and a large number of citizens, visited the barracks
and serenaded the "cowpunchers" with "familiar airs
of home." When the "notes of 'Sobre las Olas' died
away, there were many sad hearts among the New
Mexican boys."[21]

On another evening the troopers heard that the
young men were giving a dance at a beer garden
located just beyond the camp. Armed with hole-in-the-
fence passes, the men proceeded to crash the "baile."
Since the fairer sex of the San Antonio elite cast no
admiring glances their way, the boys returned to camp
via the fence.[22]

A dispatch from San Antonio gives a clue to the
amusing activities of the troopers:

For the last few nights the guard house has been doing
a rushing business. It has been filled to overflowing with
the heroic volunteers who have received "hole-in-the-fence"
passes. Last night there were three young men in leggings
who had "spotted the reptile variously" during the evening,
and were returning singing, with great tenderness, "Take
back what you promised me," and looking, with aching head
and rheumy eyes, afar into the future. They had just reached

the hole in the fence when dark forms heaved up in front of them, behind them, all around them, and simultaneously commanded the young men to halt. Then they were marched with great tact down to the guard house where they lingered, shivering and repentant, until early in the morning. They are now older and wiser soldiers.[23]

Two boys from Texas went out one evening and shot up a saloon with such finesse that there wasn't a whole piece of glass left in the place. Upon their return to camp, they carried two of the largest pieces of mirror for their personal use. According to the account, the police were afraid to arrest them.[24]

Probably the greatest disturbance created by the Rough Riders, judging from the far-reaching repercussions, is one of which they were perfectly innocent. During a concert in San Antonio, given for the benefit of the volunteers, the men were requested to shoot their revolvers upon a given signal, in order to promote the success of one particular rendition, "The Cavalry Charge." This they readily agreed to do. Unfortunately, due to an inferior electrical plant, the lights went out, but the musicians nobly completed the program. The following evening "a dirty little 'rat' sheet came out and under a 'blackface,' scare head told how 800 rough riders had punctured a concert." Two thousand shots caused women and children to stampede and scream; "the ungentlemenly cowboys" cut the electric wire and then robbed the tills of the neighboring saloons.[25] Naturally, the press spread the story over the country like prairie fire. The *Daily Oklahoman* proudly said: "It is beginning to dawn on the public that the rough riders, while comprised in part of society youths and men from all walks of life, who are both gentlemen and material for gallant soldiers, . . . also include as hard a lot of cowboys and Indian half-breeds as the western territories could furnish."[26]

The amusement created at home by letters and newspaper observations from camp concerning the reported stupidity of the enemy, the trials and discomforts, as well as the more hilarious activities of the volunteers, was cut short when the regiment received marching orders.[27] For weeks there had been various rumors as to the destination. New Orleans and Galveston were mentioned, but did not appear as likely prospects. Finally the report came that Tampa, Florida, was to be the point of embarkation[28] and, on the morning of May 29, the volunteers entrained for that city. Reports from San Antonio revealed that "the men received three days' cooked rations and a liberal supply of hardtack. All are sunburned and in high spirits and have been impatient to get away."[29] A later report indicated a delay in getting the men aboard, and, as a result, their dinner was postponed for several hours. "About half past 2 o'clock a corporal with two privates passed down the line of cars with a big box filled with sandwiches made of hardtack with a thin slice of corned beef between. This comprised the dinner of the men, but they ate it uncomplainingly."[30] Thus, the Rough Riders experienced the first of many discomforts on the long trip to Florida, but their fighting spirit did not wane—they were made of stern stuff and theirs was a mighty cause:

This is democracy as Washington, Jefferson and the other fathers of the republic dreamed of and gave their best thought and best blood to establish and this is the democracy for which the highest and the lowliest, the rich and poor, the young and the old, are ready to fight side by side and if need be mingle their blood in one common stream of patriotic sacrifice.[31]

Tampa is a one-horse town with a huge hotel, a few fair stores, saloons, etc., and a population made up of natives, Cubans, renegade Spaniards, one-lung northerners, coons and tramps. The principal products are fleas, scorpions, centipedes, pickaninnies, and rattlesnakes. The hotel gives special rates to officers at one dollar a meal. A drink of whisky is "two-bits."[32]

What a dismal reception center for Teddy's Terrors when they arrived there, 1087 strong, on June 3![33] The five-day trip from San Antonio to the Florida camp had been strenuous, chiefly because of poor railroad transportation.[34] More depressing than the physical aspects of Tampa, and more demoralizing than the hard trip and inefficiency of the railroads, was the foreboding note of pessimism which lurked under the headline "Condition of American Troops." During the "Rocking-Chair Period" in Tampa, as it was named by Richard Harding Davis, when the United States military leaders were gathering for the eventual expedition to Cuba, some unfortunate facts came to light. The ineffectiveness of the camps, both for the regulars and the volunteers, had been criticized by American and visiting European military observers. "It is asserted that the men are totally unprepared for a campaign in the tropics by reason of their equipments. The uniforms furnished are not adapted to

tropical heat and dampness, transportation facilities
for camp supplies are inadequate, and altogether forces
assembled to invade Cuba are in bad shape."[35]

Matters were made worse when it was rumored
that the regiment would be split up into battalions
and would go to Cuba on foot.[36] "Roosevelt's Rough
Riders, who cut such a dash down here at first, have
all been dismounted, and now they are called 'Wood's
Weary Walkers.' "[37]

When the citizens of Tampa, having read reports
of the concert episode in San Antonio, learned that
the volunteers were to be paid while in the city, they
implored the paymaster to defer the payment until
the men had departed. "They were afraid of us,"
wrote one trooper. "How absurd! They seem to think
the boys are a set of hyenas, cut throats, murderers
and horse thieves and that they have no regard for
human lives or public property."[38]

Until July 1, the men received no pay. However,
soon another rumor stated that the paymaster had rejected the petition of the Tampa citizens and would
pay the boys immediately.[39] The same trooper wrote:

We have not been paid our small respective mites since
we entered the service, and it has put many of the boys, who
absolutely need cash for necessary articles, in a very embar-
rassing condition.

Many boys have been sick, caused by change of diet, climate,
etc., and could not be properly cared for in the hospital (for
the surgeon has only a limited supply of pills). . . . The delay has been very aggravating, and it seems as though something could be done, by the proper authorities, to have the
boys paid. We are promised to be paid on the 2d or 3d of
next month; we'll then get two months pay at once. Although
none of us entered for the paltry wages which are given we

will, nevertheless, appreciate the government's 'chink' when is it handed over to us.[40]

NOTES TO CHAPTER V

1. "Hard Work for Rough Riders," *San Antonio Daily Express* (San Antonio, Texas) , May 20.

2. "Roosevelt's Cowboys," *Santa Fe New Mexican* (Santa Fe, New Mexico) , May 11.

3. Edward Marshall, *The Story of the Rough Riders* (cited hereafter as Marshall, *Rough Riders*) (New York: G. W. Dillingham Co., 1899) , p. 43.

4. "Fastidious Rough Riders," *San Antonio Daily Express* (San Antonio, Texas) , May 11.

5. [News Item] *ibid.*, May 12; "Dudes Are All Right, Curled Darlings of Society Join Teddy's Terrors," *Denver Evening Post* (Denver, Colorado) , May 11.

6. [News Item] *Las Vegas Daily Optic* (Las Vegas, New Mexico) , May 16.

7. "Recruits to Rough Riders," *Chicago Daily Tribune* (Chicago, Illinois) , May 18.

8. "Rough Riders Have a Battery," *San Antonio Daily Express* (San Antonio, Texas) , May 19.

9. [News Item] *Santa Fe New Mexican* (Santa Fe, New Mexico) , May 17.

10. "The 'Fighting First' Cavalry," *Denver Republican* (Denver, Colorado) , June 5.

11. "Roosevelt's Cowboys," *Santa Fe New Mexican* (Santa Fe, New Mexico) , May 11; "Machetes for Rough Riders," *Chicago Daily Tribune* (Chicago, Illinois) , May 21.

12. "They Want Their Spurs," *San Antonio Daily Express* (San Antonio, Texas) , May 19.

13. "Spanish Views of the United States," *Santa Fe New Mexican* (Santa Fe, New Mexico) , May 16. See [News Item] *Yankton Press and Dakotan* (Yankton, South Dakota) , July 9.

14. [News Item] *Yankton Press and Dakotan* (Yankton, South Dakota) , July 9.

15. "Visit Rough Riders Camp," *Chicago Daily Tribune* (Chicago, Illinois) , May 23.

16. "Riders Are Ready," *ibid.*, May 24; "Soldiering Ain't What It Is Cracked Up to Be," *Denver Evening Post* (Denver, Colorado) , May 25.

17. *Ibid.*

18. [News Item] *Santa Fe New Mexican* (Santa Fe, New Mexico) , May 25.

19. *Ibid.*, May 24. See Theodore Roosevelt, "The Rough Riders," *Scribner's Magazine,* XXV (January, 1899) , 19.

20. [News Item] *Santa Fe New Mexican* (Santa Fe, New Mexico) , May 19. See "Cowboys Hunt Tall Timbers," *Denver Times* (Denver, Colorado) , June 17; "Reminded Cowboys of Old Times," *Rocky Mountain News* (Denver, Colorado) , June 18.

21. [News Item] *Santa Fe New Mexican* (Santa Fe, New Mexico), May 19.

22. *Ibid.*

23. *Ibid.*

24. *Ibid.,* May 25.

25. "News from the Front," *ibid.,* June 13; "Rough Riders Still Drilling," *San Antonio Daily Express* (San Antonio, Texas), May 26; "'Teddy's Terrors' Cut Up High Jinks at San Antonio," *Chicago Daily Tribune* (Chicago, Illinois), May 27.

26. "It Wasn't Our Boys," *Daily Oklahoma State-Capital* (Guthrie, Oklahoma), May 31.

27. [News Item] *Santa Fe New Mexican* (Santa Fe, New Mexico), May 28.

28. "Rough Riders Are All Ready," *Chicago Daily Tribune* (Chicago, Illinois), May 26.

29. "Rough Riders March Today," *ibid.,* May 29.

30. "On the Way to Tampa," *ibid.,* May 30.

31. "Teddy's Bold Warriors," *San Antonio Daily Express* (San Antonio, Texas), May 11.

32. "Distinguishing Features of Tampa," *Denver Evening Post* (Denver, Colorado), May 21.

33. [News Item] *Santa Fe New Mexican* (Santa Fe, New Mexico), June 3.

34. *Ibid.,* June 11. See Theodore Roosevelt, "The Rough Riders," *Scribner's Magazine,* XXV (February, 1899), 136-38; Marshall, *Rough Riders,* pp. 49-51.

35. "Condition of American Troops," *Santa Fe New Mexican* (Santa Fe, New Mexico), June 7.

36. "Want To Be in the Fighting," *Chicago Daily Tribune* (Chicago, Illinois), June 3.

37. "Wood's Weary Walkers," *Sun* (Baltimore, Maryland), June 11.

38. "News from Front," *Santa Fe New Mexican* (Santa Fe, New Mexico), June 13. See "Cowboys at Tampa," *Denver Times* (Denver, Colorado), June 3; "Busy Days at Tampa, Florida," *Denver Republican* (Denver, Colorado), June 12.

39. "News from Front," *Santa Fe New Mexican* (Santa Fe, New Mexico), July 5.

40. *Ibid.*

CHAPTER VI

ROUNDUP IN WYOMING

DURING THE first two weeks of May, confusion reigned in Cheyenne where the Second Volunteer Cavalry Regiment was being organized. Reports and rumors, many of them inaccurate, spread wildly throughout the northern plains and mountain states from which the troops were being recruited. The name of Colonel Jay L. Torrey stood out boldly in every dispatch—one might easily wonder how, in those days of no fast-speeding cars and superhighways, not to mention airplanes, one man could be engaged in so many activities! Work proceeded very systematically under a large secretarial staff at his headquarters; awaiting the arrival of tents and camp equipment, the troops were housed in the barracks of Fort D. A. Russell.

In order to secure the full quota of horses, a board,

appointed for that purpose, moved in rapid succession from Laramie to Denver and was scheduled to travel to other Wyoming towns and also into Utah and Idaho. As was mentioned previously, Colonel Torrey had issued strict qualifications which proved to be a drawback, and the casual observer might have been inclined to think, "horses, horses everywhere, but not a one fit for Torrey!" "This question of obtaining the best horses available in the West by purchase proves to be a vexatious one and finally becomes a stumbling block and point of criticism of Colonel Torrey who insisted that the mounts and equipment of the regiment equal that of any cavalry organization in the world."[1]

Qualifications for the recruits were likewise strict. "The adventurous spirits" were "all to be frontiersmen, horsemen and marksmen"; yet, all were not to be cowboys, for among the recruits were "lawyers, physicians, prospectors, mining men, mining engineers, herdsmen, and preachers." They "all are distinctively Western men with sunburned faces, and the spirit of independence and ability to take care of themselves that is peculiar to life in the West." Special note was made that "the Western character omitted from the ranks of this regiment is the long-haired type of bad man who is a coward at heart and has no place in a regiment of men who will fight in the open."[2]

Colonel Torrey planned a careful schedule of procedure, beginning with the departure of the recruits from their recruiting stations and concluding with their arrival at Cheyenne. This program precluded that equipment and supplies had already been shipped and would be in Cheyenne on May 15. According to the schedule, on the following Monday one troop each from Carson City, Nevada, and Salt Lake City, Utah, would reach the Wyoming capital; on Tuesday detachments from Newcastle, Sundance, Buffalo, Sheridan, Big Horn, Wyoming, and Salmon City, Idaho, would make their appearance. Detachments from several more Wyoming towns would arrive on Wednesday, May 18—Douglas, Casper, Lander, Embar, Wheatland, Iron Mountain, Laramie, Rawlins, Rock Springs, Green River, Evanston and Kemmerer; and the two troops from Denver, Colorado, scheduled for Thursday, would complete the regiment.

Concerning the appointment of officers for the regiment, Torrey officially stated:

The secretary of war will appoint our officers. As soon as our organization is perfected, I, of course, will make a recommendation to him as to who the officers shall be. I have a great confidence in the judgement of the men who are to pull the triggers, and shall not make any recommendation for a troop officer unless the members of such troops, by at least a majority vote, agree upon the man for the place, unless in some very improbable contingency.[3]

Reports from Fort Russell indicated that the troop movements had been accomplished according to schedule except for the two from Denver. Captain William G. Wheeler, the senior officer of the Colorado Cavalry, after consultation with Colonel Torrey, decided to hold the Colorado troops at their present camp.[4]

Organization now proceeded rapidly and, apparently, without difficulty. Praise was showered upon Colonel Torrey; he was hailed as "a master in the

details of organization," and displayed "excellent judgement in counseling his officers and men."[5]

By noon of May 21, 692 men had successfully passed
the medical examination—only 38 were rejected. This
large percentage of physically fit men was due to
the fact that all the troops mustered into service in
Cheyenne had already been examined and passed by
local physicians. It is interesting to note that the
average height of the men accepted was 5 feet 6 inches
and the average weight 145 pounds.[6]

Newspaper records of the time reveal other interesting activities and events. The Reverend Henry G.
Golden, pastor of the First Presbyterian Church at
Laramie, offered his services as chaplain. A graduate
of the Union Theological Seminary of New York City
and chaplain of the Senate of Wyoming, he was well
qualified for the position. He was an excellent horseman and very popular throughout the state; his application received serious consideration and was verified
shortly before the troops left Cheyenne.[7]

Colonel E. V. Sumner, commander of the Military
Department for Missouri and Colorado, was one of
the distinguished visitors at Fort Russell and expressed
great satisfaction over the rapid progress in organization. Earlier it had been rumored that the Torrey
cavalry would be shipped to the Philippines, and, in
anticipation of that journey, one trooper asked the
visitor whether the beef on the islands would equal
Wyoming's. When the Colonel informed him that
goat meat would probably supplement their diet, a
former roundup cook mumbled, "If we don't get beef,
it'll be because there's no steers there. We ain't the

ducks to miss a beefsteak when it's in the country."[8]

Naturally, rivalry among towns was obvious. It was reported that "certain parties" at Casper were hindering enlistments in the Torrey regiment, and particularly in Company F, because the officer selected to head the recruiting board was from a town of another county. The *Cheyenne Sun-Leader,* hoped the rumor was untrue and reported: "It would be very unfortunate if the loyalty of Casper Citizens is such that they can't defend their country's honor, simply because a rival town happened to be the first to respond to the call for the nation's defense."[9]

The scenes of activity around Fort Russell and the neighboring city, Cheyenne, were very interesting. Every company had a barbershop and, in a short time, the troopers who were skilled with mug, brush, and razor were pressed into service—also their ingenuity in equipment, for a cracker box, cushioned with bean sacks, served very well as a barber chair.[10] Once the boys had been established in the regime of camp life, they declared they were "having a picnic." True, life was dull without war, but their eyes sparkled at the mention of killing Spaniards. One husky recruit commented, "It's pretty smooth to put government grub under your belt three times a day, sleep in a nice tent, not too cool nor yet too warm, just enough exercise to make you sleep good and a little wad of dough at the end of each month."[11]

A very elegant two-seated rig, ordered by Colonel Torrey for the use of members of the press, made an impressive sight. It completed a daily trip to the fort and, promptly at twelve noon, delivered members of the press for lunch with Torrey. "The perfect military aspect is in the air at Fort Russell," quipped the *Rocky Mountain News*.[12]

James Gill, a clerk in the Quartermaster's Department at army headquarters in Denver, paid a visit to Fort Russell and commented upon his return:

The men are a fine looking set of fellows, but they know very little about the life of the soldier. The majority of the men have never before been in a military camp and have little idea of the duties before them. A few national guard men in the regiment are doing what they can to bring order out of chaos, and are making as good success as could be expected.[13]

During the next week, the *News,* suspecting that life was not what it seemed at Fort Russell and probably also resenting the fact that the Colorado troops had not yet been called to Cheyenne, opened fire on the Wyoming regiment and particularly its leader, Colonel Torrey:

A surprise is in store for the Colorado cavalrymen at Cheyenne. When they reach Fort Russell all their military ideas of hard drills and discipline will vanish. Instead they will enter a community of good intentions, but lack of system —a community where the commanding officer addressed his men as "Patriot Smith," and received an equally peculiar salutation in reply, but not a sign of a salute. Instead of arduous drills and rigid daily routine of camp life the troopers will go among those to whom the word discipline is foreign. Further, the clean, bright uniforms of the Denver men will make them somewhat conspicuous in contrast with the overalls and buckskin suits of the men assembled under the standard of Colonel Jay L. Torrey. It will be a revelation in military matters that will not serve otherwise than to make the boys glad that they had good officers to put them through their sprouts before the sound of alarm passed through the land.

Colonel Torrey is a man of men. He is a lovable person. His friends are as steel. He inspires affection, not confidence. Men will follow his leadership through love and trust to fate rather than discretion or judgment. There is more to praise; more to command in the private than in the fellow who wears the decorations of Colonel Torrey, and he lives up to it. He almost worships a patriot. His affection must be reciprocated, and this is the secret bond which holds together men who do not imagine the rigors of military precision.

It is a camp of patriotism and mettle rather than discipline and uniform. There is all of the former and none of the latter. The only uniforms in camp are worn by a few officers who held positions in militia organizations which have been attached to the regiment, notably those from Nevada. It must be said that the men from this state and Idaho are practically the only ones who have any knowledge of drilling. Few of the others ever saw a soldier. Their uniforms are the dress of toil. There are some who seem to have been cowboys and look as though they are able to ride anything that runs or jumps. Others are best told in the story of a patriot, who said that the rolling mills at Laramie and switching yards at Rock Springs were shut down because the "cowboys" had all gone to the war.

But at present they are diamonds in the rough. Think of it! Last week an officer was drilling a squad and he gave a command that did not accord with the tactics of one of the patriots. "That's not right," was the complaint from the ranks. "It is," came from the officer. "You're a —— —— liar, it should be fours right." "That's so; excuse me," and drill went on as usual.

How long it will require to get the regiment in shape is a matter of conjecture. It may be a week or it might require a month, but sooner or later the name of Torrey's Terrors

will be written on the pages of American history in ink that
will never fade.[14]

This lengthy and biting comment by the *News* ends
on the above prophetic note—a note which carries im-
plications of both success and failure. As if to ease
the blow of this sarcastic denunciation and revelation,
the same issue of the *News* printed a soothing and ex-
planatory editorial:

Great patriotic interest and pride have been felt by the
people of the state in the crack cavalry regiment being organized by Colonel Torrey. If given an opportunity all feel
that it will immortalize the courage, the manhood and the
patriotism of that distinctive type of western civilization, "the
cowboy," and reflect glory on "the baby state." Anything
which, even apparently, mars the perfecting of the programme
is felt by all. Criticisms of friends is [sic] often great kind-
nesses.[15]

This "criticisms of friends" did not escape the notice
of the Wyomingites. The *Cheyenne Sun-Leader*, act-
ing as spokesman for the state, responded:

It is true, as the sensational, unpatriotic and evidently
"sore" Denver News sarcastically remarks, that the regiment
is composed of cowboys off the range. Col. Torrey should be
proud of this fact, as are citizens of the state of Wyoming.
We are proud that our hardy and brave citizens of the country decided to enlist in their country's defense and glory in
the reflection and assurance of all who have observed them
in the process of organization that they will be the principal
feature of the United States army, that, if called into service,
the enemy will know of their presence and Torrey's regiment
will go down in history with Napoleon's Scotch guards, even
if it is true, as a shallow minded writer on the News remarks,
that "they wear overalls and jumpers." How much more
honest, natural and patriotic is it to fly to the defense of
your country with the garb of the ranch, overalls and jumpers,

which clothes a fond heart that beats at this time only that the blood it impels through the veins of true Americans may be shed in defense of the country's honor, than to belong to the high collar, stiff bosomed, creased pants, long haired, dissipated and cowardly class, whose function is to ridicule, "shoot off their mouth" and finally, as in the last war, after exhausting every means to escape fighting for their country, are drafted and then, in many cases, desert.

This is the only class of human being that, in view of Torrey's husky, skillful and brave riders, dare for a minute to offer an uncomplimentary criticism on account of their dress. The gentlemanly and refined conduct of the cowboys in the city and at Fort Russell is worthy of mention at this time, having been generally remarked by scores of citizens and showing that the brave western lads come from homes of purity and refinement not to be excelled in any city and from parents whose habits of frugality and honesty have been absorbed by the sons, now enlisted as soldiers and patriots.[16]

After these outbursts, nothing further developed from the tense situation which appears to have resulted from Colonel Torrey's failure to call the Colorado troops to Cheyenne. During the time between Gill's statement concerning the chaos he had observed at Fort Russell and the blast by the *News*, the newspapers of Denver bemoaned the fate of the Colorado Cavalry:

The two troops of cavalry at Camp Adams are still waiting for orders. The men are restless and anxious for some change from the monotony of their daily exercises, but it is understood that Col. Torrey will not give orders for the two Colorado troops to join his encampment at Cheyenne until the regiment is about ready to move, having been informed that the Colorado men are thoroughly drilled and equipped and will need no preliminary training before being sent into the field. He is devoting all his energies now to licking the raw cowboy riders into steady disciplined cavalrymen. When they shall have acquired something of the art of war, he will send for the Colorado boys.[17]

The same newspaper, relying on information from a private source in Cheyenne, revealed that Colonel Torrey was having difficulty in the procurement of enough recruits in Wyoming to fill the seven troops allotted to the state: "At that time the citizens of that state were much chagrined because they were not allowed to furnish a full regiment of 12 companies of rough and ready fighters and shooters." Colonel Torrey had hundreds of applications for enlistments from men who wanted to join the regiment, but he did not receive the applications from the men that he first intended should compose his regiment. "Up to date he has between 250 and 300 men according to his liking, and has yet an equal number to find on the ranges of that state." Another difficulty confronted Torrey—the lack of suitable horses, which continued to be a harassing problem throughout the entire period of recruiting and training.[18]

In reporting similar difficulties, the *News* only added fuel to the conflagration:

There are said to be about 800 men now at Cheyenne who have come to join Torrey's regiment. Not one has yet been mustered into the United States service, although about 300 members have passed the physical examination and are ready for it. No equipment has been issued of the two or three car loads now on the track at Cheyenne. The chief difficulty and cause of delay seems to be the inability to procure suitable horses. . . . Colonel Torrey is quite popular with his men. Upon his arrival at Cheyenne he said he wanted men who had square chins and didn't look down their noses; that the regiment would go to Cuba, and his

men must make up their minds to stand up and receive
Spanish lead. This little speech possessed so much earnest-
ness that some of the recruits who were faint-hearted failed
to put in appearance at subsequent drills.[19]

When these various reports reached Colonel Torrey,
he pronounced them as wholly inaccurate. Concerning the moving of the two Colorado troops to Fort
Russell, he said:

We are occupying Fort Russell with 10 troops and all
the barracks are filled. Capt. Wheeler, senior captain of the
Colorado troops, called when we first came here and reported
his men well situated and comfortable and being drilled
and accustomed to camp life. They are provided with Colorado equipments, which if brought away would have to be
bought. It is not desirable to do this, in view of the fact
that equipments for the entire regiment will be sent here
by the War department. Our horses are coming in and
when collected will establish this country as the market for
the cavalry horse for the world.

Four troops have been mustered in. Four more will be
mustered in to-morrow or Tuesday [May 24] and two more
the following day, and these, with the two Colorado troops,
will constitute the regiment. The Colorado troops will be
brought just as soon as they can be comfortably cared for.

Uniforms, underclothing and blankets for the entire regiment are here. Horse equipments, guns and revolvers have
been shipped and are expected in a few days. Every detail
of the organization is proceeding systematically and orderly.

Our men are of a splendid class. None have been in the
guard house. Our men go into the city daily and are noticeable by their good conduct. We have men enough here and
on the way to fill our organization to its maximum strength.[20]

Speculation was rife as to the final destination of
the Colorado Cavalry troops. According to the *Rocky
Mountain News,* evidence existed which pointed to-

ward service in the Philippines. It was reported that
Colonel Torrey preferred those islands to that of Cuba;
and, from all appearances, the First Volunteer Cavalry
Regiment, stationed at San Antonio, Texas, would
be the likely choice for the Cuban invasion. The
fact that the Third Volunteer Cavalry under Grigsby
had already moved in part to the South, also bolstered
Torrey's chances of moving to the Pacific theater of
war.[21] The *News* also informed its readers, through
tips received from the national capital, that it was by
no means definite that the Colorado troops would join
those at Cheyenne:

  Strenuous efforts are being put forth to retain the troops
as a portion of a regiment of cavalry to be organized in this
state. Strong influence is being brought to bear in Washington and if present plans prevail, Colorado will send out a
complete regiment of cavalry. It is understood that Governor
Adams is in favor of this plan. The result of the application
in Washington is being awaited with great interest in many
quarters.[22]

This hopeful speculation crumbled the following day
when the same paper revealed that there would be no
separate cavalry regiment for Colorado in the second
call for troops and that Troops A and B were ordered
to Cheyenne.[23]

  With pleasant memories of a bountiful farewell
feast on the eve of departure, at 6:30 A.M., on Memorial Day, May 30, the Colorado men struck the
tents at Camp Adams and, at nine o'clock, fell into
the march to the Union Depot.[24] Upon arrival, the
baggage was dispatched, and many of the men sat
around and entertained friends who had come to see

them off. Others amused themselves with target practice on tin cans, until they were warned that the carbine was an extremely dangerous weapon at any range
under eighteen hundred yards![25] One sergeant, of
Troop A, stood next to the coach which would carry
him to Fort Russell and announced that he was ready
to kiss all pretty girls good-by who would present themselves. "In rapid succession he had six takes and then
there was a lull for a time."[26] Finally, a very kissable-
appearing young lady stepped up. She was wearing
a yellow shirt waist, the vivid color of which was still
quite noticeable in spite of several yards of red, white,
and blue ribbons draped over her shoulders and bosom.
The gallant trooper took one look and exclaimed, "My
dear, I would like to kiss you, but I'm sorry to say
that I am not color blind. Yellow waists don't jibe
with a Yankee's feelings."[27]

The *Denver Republican* paid a glowing tribute in
its farewell to the troopers:

> They were approved the finest body of men that ever left
> the state on such an expedition. They were the darlings of
> the public and the heroes of the war experts. They will
> infuse life and vigor in the Torrey Regiment of Cavalry, of
> which they will be a part. They will go a great way towards
> making the Torrey regiment as formidable as the more widely
> advertised Roosevelt rough riders.
>
> They are young men, hardy and lusty, who have had ex-
> periences with horses and know how to ride and shoot.[28]

The trip to Cheyenne was made without incident.
At Brighton, many Denver people met the train, their
presence being explained by the fact that the annual
Memorial Day road race took place on the Brighton

road. The Platteville station platform was crowded
with people who cheered the boys on their way; over
two hundred met the troopers at Greeley where the
reception given them "attained the proportions of
an ovation. Among the spectators was Lord Ogilvey
[Oglivy], who was the center of an admiring group."[29]
It was in Greeley that the troopers discovered the
effects of the button craze which was in vogue. As the
unsuspecting boys leaned from the windows or stood
on the platform, innocent-looking maidens armed
with scissors relieved them of their brass buttons as
souvenirs.

"The chief employment between Denver and Cheyenne was eating, and such eating there was. By cater-
ing to his stomach the departing soldier might forget
his heart."[30]

The Colorado troops arrived in Cheyenne at four
o'clock that afternoon. Because it was Memorial Day,
the entire regiment was ordered out to assist the Grand
Army veterans in a service at the Fort Russell cemetery. Over nine hundred strong and in full uniform,
the troops were an impressive sight. Old army officers
who witnessed this turnout were most complimentary.
One observer commented: "Thus far the troopers have
behaved admirably, and not a man is in the guard
house, while in town they are gentlemanly, and they
have created none of the scenes as have Roosevelt's
men in Texas."[31]

The following day and for many days thereafter,
the Fort Russell barracks resounded with the lusty
and hardy battle yell of the Colorado troopers:

Dewey, Dewey, here we be,
Torrey's troopers, don't you see?
Hot, cold, wet, dry,
Get there Eli
Who?
Torrey's troopers, live or die.[32]

NOTES TO CHAPTER VI

1. "Ready to Start for Manila," *Denver Republican* (Denver, Colorado), May 12. See "Captain Torrey at Cheyenne," *ibid.*, May 10; "Cavalry Horses Wanted," *Cheyenne Sun-Leader* (Cheyenne, Wyoming), May 7, 12.

2. "Torrey and Band," *Denver Evening Post* (Denver, Colorado), May 16.

3. "The Torrey Recruits," *Denver Republican* (Denver, Colorado), May 14; "Cowboy Regiment," *Cheyenne Sun-Leader* (Cheyenne, Wyoming), May 14.

4. "Torrey's Cowboy Cavalry," *Denver Republican* (Denver, Colorado), May 13.

5. "News from Fort Russell," *Rocky Mountain News* (Denver, Colorado), May 22.

6. *Ibid.*

7. "Chaplain for Torrey's Men," *Cheyenne Sun-Leader* (Cheyenne, Wyoming), May 11; "Mr. Golden a Candidate," *ibid.*, May 20; "Laramie's Loss, but Torrey's Gain," *Rocky Mountain News* (Denver, Colorado), June 17.

8. "A Distinguished Visitor," *Cheyenne Sun-Leader* (Cheyenne, Wyoming), May 20; "With Torrey's Rough Riders," *ibid.*, May 21.

9. "The Torrey Regiment," *ibid.*, May 13.

10. "Will Arrive Monday," *ibid.*, May 12.

11. *Ibid.*

12. "Experts from Ranges," *Rocky Mountain News* (Denver, Colorado), May 21.

13. "Chaos in Cavalry Ranks," *ibid.*

14. "Breaking in Recruits for Torrey's Rough Riders," *ibid.*, May 29.

15. "Wyoming Department," *ibid.*

16. "Our Husky Cowboys," *Cheyenne Sun-Leader* (Cheyenne, Wyoming), May 31; "The Roast By the News," *ibid.*

17. "The Cavalry May Not Go Soon," *Denver Republican* (Denver, Colorado), May 20.

18. "Torrey's Job Not Too Easy," *ibid.*, May 21.

19. "Daily Drills at Camp Adams," *Rocky Mountain News* (Denver, Colorado), May 22.

20. "Eight Troops Mustered," *Cheyenne Sun-Leader* (Cheyenne, Wyoming), May 23; "All Going Well with Torrey," *Denver Republican* (Denver, Colorado), May 23.

21. "Cavalry Ordered to Cheyenne," *Rocky Mountain News* (Denver, Colorado), May 27.

22. "Troops A and B May Remain," *ibid.*, May 28.

23. "No Cavalry Called For," *ibid.*, May 29.

24. "Troopers Leave At 10:30," *ibid.*, May 30. See "Dined at Camps," *Denver Times* (Denver, Colorado), May 29; "Royal Feast to the Cavalry Boys," *Denver Republican* (Denver, Colorado), May 30.

25. "Gone to Join Torrey," *Denver Times* (Denver, Colorado), May 30.

26. *Ibid.*

27. *Ibid.*

28. "Tender Farewell to the Troopers," *Denver Republican* (Denver, Colorado), May 31.

29. "Tenting at Ft. Russell," *Rocky Mountain News* (Denver, Colorado), June 1; "Denver Cavalry at Greeley," *ibid.*, May 31. Lyulph G. S. Ogilvy joined Colonel Torrey's regiment and became a corporal in Troop A. Three months later, Trooper Carl Linderfelt, at home on furlough, made the following comment: "Ogilvie [sic]? He was the crackajack of the bunch! I have never heard a complaint pass his lips and if there is anything to do he does it. They made him a corporal because he worked so hard and was such a faithful man. He is eternally whistling 'Tommy Atkins,' and puffing his pipe around camp." "Torrey's Men," *Denver Evening Post* (Denver, Colorado), September 10.

30. *Ibid.*

31. "Rough Riders Mustered In," *Salt Lake Herald* (Salt Lake City, Utah), May 31.

32. "The Colorado Troopers," *Denver Republican* (Denver, Colorado), June 1.

CHAPTER VII

THE HUNT FOR HORSES

"Take him away, he's off color."

"Captain, I have half-a-dozen horses outside here that I would like to have you look at."

"Bring them in here if you have horses to sell and will take $100 each for them for that is our limit."

"Take the saddle off that bay if you want us to look at him. Give us room, gentlemen. We can't examine horses in such a crowd, and there's a horse coming on a dead run down the lane."

A roan is led in. "Now gentlemen, don't let us waste any time. The government wants perfectly sound bay, brown, black or chestnut horses, of the proper style, and we have only one more hour to spend with you for we must be in Laramie to-morrow morning. Bring in that bay. No good, he's limping now. We're not buying horses for a horse hospital."[1]

Such was the scene of business at Goulding's Corral on Denver's Fifteenth Street while Captain Varnum

of the Seventh Cavalry, Lieutenant Stockle, Major
Hoyt, and A. A. Holcomb, veterinary surgeon for the
state of Wyoming—all members of the horse-hunting
board—were inspecting the fleet-footed steeds for Torrey's regiment. Over a hundred horses stood within
the inner circle for closer scrutiny; and outside, the
street was lined for blocks on both sides. On this particular day, some two hundred were examined; of
these, only forty-two were accepted, including seven-
teen which the local board had already approved.[2]

Earlier in the week the same board had spent an
entire day at the Cheyenne stockyards for the same
purpose. Constantly conscious of Colonel Torrey's
adamant statement concerning the type of horse he
desired, these men "let legions thunder past" and
selected only two out of eighty.[3] The colonel had
abandoned all hopes of acquiring the necessary number in Colorado and Wyoming and informed Colonel
Sumner, military commander in Colorado, that his
scouts would go to Montana. Of the 1,100 horses required for the regiment, only 175 had been secured
by the third week in May.[4] At the same time it was
estimated that the governmental expenses for pay and
subsistence in Torrey's regiment mounted to one thousand dollars per day.[5]

As the search for horses continued, the daily progress was reported at Fort Russell where the troops
continued to drill on foot and, no doubt, at the end of
each long, weary day silently thought, "My kingdom
for a horse!" Finally, a note of cheer spread through
the barracks. A carload of accepted horses was on its
way from Sheridan and Newcastle, Wyoming, and a

reliable source stated that more would follow rapidly.
As yet, the standards for qualification were not lowered.[6] Colonel Torrey, in fine spirit, brought some of
his own favorite and well-bred horses from his ranch
for inspection, among them "Antelope, the most beautiful and best bottomed steed ever seen in the Wind
River region. Colonel Torrey expects to ride the
animal himself."[7]

By June 2, four hundred horses were at the fort
and were segregated according to color. Each troop
was to be mounted on horses of a distinctive color.[8]
Sheridan proved to be the paradise for horses. Early
in June it was announced that 228 horses were located
in that region and had been secured for the sum of
$18,590.[9] Also, the work of breaking and training the
animals would begin at once, in the hope that the entire quota of mounts would be secured in the next
few days.[10]

Many of the horses offered for purchase by local
ranchers simply were not adaptable for cavalry use.
The average cowboy in those days knew very little
about the requirements of such a horse. On the round-
up, he usually has a string of ten to twenty horses and
rides them recklessly, without much care or attention.
Consequently, in his mind a gentle horse is one that
cannot buck him off, as was demonstrated by a cowboy recruit who offered his horse to the purchasing
board:

" 'Is he gentle and without vicious habits?' he was
asked.

" 'Yes, plumb gentle,' was the reply.

" 'Well, get on him and ride,' he was instructed.

"He got on him and for ten minutes there was a scene of high bucking and furious pitching which would make a wild West show tame in comparison.

" 'Rejected,' said the horse board.

" 'What for?' queried the cowboy. 'He didn't throw me. I call him a plumb gentle hoss.' "[11]

On June 8 the various troops of the Torrey regiment drew lots for the selection of horses. The black horses were drawn by Captain Charles H. MacNutt, Troop A, of Leadville, and Captain John Q. Cannon, Troop I, of Salt Lake City; the chestnut-colored fell to Captain William G. Wheeler, Troop B, of Denver, and Captain William L. Cox, Troop M, of Nevada. Captain George R. Shanton, Troop C; Captain William H. Norfolk, Troop D; Captain Henry H. Austin, Troop A; Captain Willis F. Hoadley, Troop F; Captain John B. Manardi, Troop G; Captain Louis G. Davis, Troop H; Captain Morgan M. Maghee, Troop K; and Captain Robert Calverley, Troop L, drew the bays.[12]

On the same day the organization of the pack train service was completed, comprising three pack trains of fifty mules each. This was composed of thirty-nine skilled packers, almost all of whom had had experience in the army pack trains in Indian campaigns. To facilitate the organization, the packers were sent to St. Louis to secure the animals and equipment and were to join the regiment later.[13]

Very good news to Torrey's headquarters was the announcement that John W. Springer, of Denver, president of the National Live Stock Association, had sold to the United States government 250 horses from

his Montana ranch. They were to be shipped directly
to Fort Russell and trained for service. Negotiations
for this big deal had been going on for some time,
and the closing thereof had been delayed because of
the financial aspect involved. It was rumored that the
horses cost the government from $100 to $125 each.[14]

But the quest was not yet ended. In mid-June,
when it was rumored that the troops might be moved,
there were not enough horses to mount the troops.
This lack of mounts was the main reason for the delay in moving the cavalry to the front. The horse-
purchasing board planned another trip to the Denver
stockyards to seek at least two hundred horses of the
size and quality needed for the cavalry service and
informed Manager George L. Goulding of their intentions:

"There will be no difficulty," said Mr. Goulding, . . .
"in furnishing all the horses needed. There are many
good horses on the ranches in the vicinity of Denver
that will meet the requirements. There are a good
many available horses in the city that will probably
be offered for sale to the purchasing board."[15]

As late as June 17, a week before departure, the
quota was still three hundred short.[16] By this time the
jaunts of the horse hunters were as numerous as the
burrs in a mustang's tail and caused one wag to comment, "Experts confidentially prophesy that at the first
mounted drill it would require half of the regiment
to pick up the other half after the horses are through
with their antics."[17] One trooper by name of Bert
Harris, Troop M, was injured severely when thrown
from a horse which he was riding without saddle or

bridle. The man was considered an expert rider and the accident was attributed to carelessness.[18]

On June 13 orders were received by the commander of the Second Volunteer Cavalry Regiment to move, with the horses, from Fort Russell to Jacksonville, Florida, as soon as possible. At once there were numerous speculations as to the final destination—the immediate conclusion was that the regiment would join the army of occupation for Puerto Rico.[19] "One cowboy trooper unearthed a map of the West Indies far down beneath the more often consulted maps of the East Indies. When his eyes lighted upon the small spot representing Porto Rico he exclaimed, 'Why that place is not large enough to get my horse on.'"[20]

The move was scheduled to take place in a week and, during that period of grace, the search for horses frantically continued. Even the day before departure Torrey requested an additional allowance for mounts. Then came the bitterest news—the proverbial straw that broke the camel's back: "It is intimated, moreover, that when the regiment is sent to the front, presumably to Cuba, almost all of its horses will be left in this country, in which event an increase in the number would be an unnecessary expense to the government."[21]

During the long weeks of the equestrian quest, other military regulations were carried out at Fort Russell. The troops were outfitted with the regulation cavalry uniform, and the Krag-Jörgensen carbines and Colt revolvers were ready for issue.[22] The medical board continued to examine applicants for enlistment and to vaccinate those accepted. "Colonel Torrey was the

894th man examined, he was accepted. The colonel is forty-four years of age, about five feet nine inches high, weighs 235 pounds and shows chest measurement of forty-eight inches. He is the biggest man in the regiment."[23]

As the doughboy in World War I, and the G.I. in World War II, the cowboy volunteer looked for amusement. Fortunately, the Lemmen Brothers' circus came to town and Torrey's men attended in great numbers. During one of the evening performances, after the show was well underway, a typical Wyoming high wind came up and necessitated an abrupt conclusion of the show. Naturally, a number of the troopers were much disappointed and especially provoked over the idea of paying money for nothing. In soldierly fashion, after grumbling and arguing, they sought out the manager and, for a time, trouble was brewing. In their agitative mood, the men proceeded to stop a team of circus horses. At this moment, the sheriff appeared on the scene; in a flash, the boys quietly decided there was no legal basis for attaching the show's property and dispersed as rapidly as, but more subdued than, they had gathered. Actually, there had been only one casualty at the circus. Upon leaving the collapsing tent, Lieutenant Jack Ivey, Troop D, from Sheridan, was struck on the head by a tent pole ripped loose by the squall. At first it appeared that the accident was fatal, but a physician who was summoned revived the trooper. The fiery outbreak of temper was really due, not to this accident, but rather the manager's refusal to refund the admission fee.[24]

The first pay for Torrey's men came on June 9.

As is customary, an armed guard was sent to Cheyenne to escort Major A. H. Jackson, United States Army Paymaster, and his treasurer to the post with a payroll of over $20,000 to be distributed. The men lined up by troops, and the companies took their turn in alphabetical order. A few years earlier, Congress had passed a law which added 20 per cent to a soldier's pay in time of war; translated in terms of the War of 1898, a private in the army received $15.60 per month.[25]

Then, as now, payday in the army was an occasion for celebration. The only casualty on this momentous one was Charles Kilburg, one of Torrey's Terrors, who became intoxicated at Hynd's saloon, carved up another trooper, and was arrested. During the following week he was given a preliminary hearing before Justice Lee and was bound over to the district court "on the charge of assault with intent to do bodily injury." Having been discharged from the regiment for his action, Kilburg, in default of bail, was sent to the county jail. Ike Hartzell, the victim, who lost a part of his nose in the fracas, slowly recovered from his serious wounds in the military hospital.[26]

But every day was not payday. The regular day of the troopers, while in training, was a long and full one. It began at 6:40 A.M. with stable drill; 7:00, breakfast; 8:30 to 9:30, squad drill; 9:30 to 10:30, noncommissioned officers' school; 10:30 to 11:30, troop drill; 12:00 noon, lunch; 1:00 to 2:00 P.M., sergeants' drill, conducted by Colonel Torrey; 2:00 to 3:00, troop drill; 4:00 to 5:00, troop drill; 5:00, stable drill. Civilian interest in the training program of the troop-

ers mounted daily, especially when the news came
that the regiment would be moved at any moment.
The date of departure for Jacksonville, Florida, was
set for June 22, and, at once, the newspapers began
to encourage special weekend excursions to the Wyoming capital. The *Denver Times* advertised a special
excursion rate of three dollars a round trip on the
Union Pacific Railroad for Sunday, June 18, with
appropriate headlines: "To Visit Torrey's Riders,"
and "Going To See the Cavalry."[27]

Rumors spread fast and thick concerning departure
and final destination. It was reported that Colonel
Torrey, having a choice between the Philippines, with
unmounted troops, and Puerto Rico with horses, chose
the latter.[28] Another reporter said:

. . . If the Terrors had been consulted as to their preference
of destination, the vote would have been overwhelmingly in
favor of the Philippine Islands. Ever since their enlistment
the men have been anticipating the pleasure of a sea trip
just half around the world to the mystic Orient, and co-
operation with the heroic Dewey. Nevertheless, as the government has need apparently for all three of its specially
authorized cavalry regiments nearer home, with true soldierly
resignation all eyes are now turned in the opposite direction
and preparations to meet the enemy in the Atlantic islands
are carried on cheerfully.[29]

Finally, as the day of departure drew near, the
railroads were requested to submit bids for the transportation of the regiment from Cheyenne to Jacksonville. The Union Pacific was awarded the contract,
the terms including 47 officers, 780 horses, and over
40,000 pounds of baggage.[30]

The last Sunday before the troops left, large dele-

gations of friends from neighboring cities and states
visited the fort, and, on June 21, a big demonstration
was staged in honor of Torrey's cavalry. The mounted
regiment paraded through the streets of Cheyenne.
Colonel Torrey presented the straps to each officer
in designation of his grade; and he, in turn, received
the insignia of the rank of colonel from Major Thomas
Wilhelm, U.S.A. Fittingly, the demonstration concluded with a few words from Colonel Torrey, who
said in part:

A certain class of misguided people expect to see us reach
the East with long hair and riding spotted horses. They
will be surprised to see one of the finest regiments that any
army can boast. We are going across the entire country and
then to Porto Rico. On the journey, don't let one incident
occur of which you will be ashamed. Be gentlemen and
patriots. I have confidence in every man and want you to
justify it.[31]

NOTES TO CHAPTER VII

1. "Buying Horses for the Army," *Denver Republican* (Denver, Colorado) , May 13.

2. *Ibid.* See "Horses and Equipment of the Torrey Regiment," *Denver
Republican* (Denver, Colorado) , May 6.

3. "Two Out of 78," *Cheyenne Sun-Leader* (Cheyenne, Wyoming) ,
May 10.

4. "Horses Chiefly in Demand Now," *Denver Republican* (Denver,
Colorado) , May 24. See "Montana Chargers," *Denver Evening Post*
(Denver, Colorado) , June 7.

5. "Horses for the Cavalry," *Rocky Mountain News* (Denver, Colorado) , May 25.

6. "Military Matters in Wyoming," *Denver Republican* (Denver, Colorado) , May 25.

7. "Cowboys Are Drilling on Foot," *Rocky Mountain News* (Denver,
Colorado) , May 26.

8. "Cowboys Now Soldiers," *ibid.,* June 2.

9. "Buying Cavalry Horses," *Denver Republican* (Denver, Colorado) ,
June 5.

10. "Troops Pass Through Cheyenne," *ibid.,* June 7.

11. "Torrey and Band," *Denver Evening Post* (Denver, Colorado), May 16.

12. "Torrey Cavalry Horses," *Denver Republican* (Denver, Colorado), June 9.

13. *Ibid.*

14. "Cavalry Horses for Torrey," *ibid.*, June 8; "Money for the Rough Riders," *Rocky Mountain News* (Denver, Colorado), June 10. See "Montana Chargers," *Denver Evening Post* (Denver, Colorado), June 7.

15. "Horses for Torrey's Men," *Denver Times* (Denver, Colorado), June 15.

16. "Coming for Cavalry Horses," *Rocky Mountain News* (Denver, Colorado), June 17. See "Scarred Horses Barred," *Chicago Daily Tribune* (Chicago, Illinois), June 13.

17. "Life in Torrey's Regiment," *Cheyenne Sun-Leader* (Cheyenne, Wyoming), June 11.

18. "Torrey Trooper Injured," *Denver Republican* (Denver, Colorado), June 15.

19. "Terrors Off for Florida," *Rocky Mountain News* (Denver, Colorado), June 14.

20. "Porto Rico Preparations," *ibid.*, June 15; "Torrey's Regiment," *Cheyenne Sun-Leader* (Cheyenne, Wyoming), June 15.

21. "Horses for Uncle Sam," *ibid.*, June 21; "Horses For Torrey's Command," *Denver Republican* (Denver, Colorado), June 22.

22. "Torrey's Regiment Is Complete," *ibid.*, May 31.

23. "Shedding Their 'Chaps,'" *Rocky Mountain News* (Denver, Colorado), May 30.

24. "Cowboys Were Mad," *Cheyenne Sun-Leader* (Cheyenne, Wyoming), May 24; "Rough Rider Seriously Injured," *Rocky Mountain News* (Denver, Colorado), May 24.

25. "Rough Riders Paid," *Salt Lake Herald* (Salt Lake City, Utah), June 10; "Breaking Their Unruly Steeds," *Rocky Mountain News* (Denver, Colorado), June 10; "Torrey Regiment Paid," *Denver Republican* (Denver, Colorado), June 10.

26. "Algers Waiting Orders to Move," *Rocky Mountain News* (Denver, Colorado), June 16.

27. [News Item] *ibid.*, June 17.

28. "Torrey's Rough Riders," *Cheyenne Sun-Leader* (Cheyenne, Wyoming), June 15.

29. "Porto Rico Preparation," *Rocky Mountain News* (Denver, Colorado), June 15.

30. "Transporting Torrey's Riders," *Denver Republican* (Denver, Colorado), June 19.

31. "Torrey's Prize Regiment," *Cheyenne Sun-Leader* (Cheyenne, Wyoming), June 21; "The Torrey Cavalry on Parade," *Denver Republican* (Denver, Colorado), June 22.

CHAPTER VIII

GRIGSBY MOVES SOUTHWARD

UP NORTH, in Sioux Falls, May 20 dawned dark and dreary. It was the day of departure for the Third Volunteer Cavalry Regiment, but nature's drab garb did not dampen the spirits of the volunteers who were eager to move southward and closer to the scene of fighting. The citizens, too, shared the enthusiasm; they, too, were anxious for their men to have an opportunity to take part in the actual combat. To express their gratitude to Colonel Grigsby and the regiment, the loyal citizenry of Sioux Falls had arranged a farewell banquet the evening previous, with the usual toasts, speeches, and humorous anecdotes.[1]

Long before the eventful day arrived, the troops wondered and speculated as to where they were going. One rumor said Omaha would be the rendezvous,

another said San Francisco; and then gossip spread
that the regiment would remain in South Dakota until
fully equipped. Day by day the war fever mounted;
the troops grew more restless and fervently hoped for
the official notice. When, on May 18, definite orders
were received from General Bacon, commander of the
Department of Dakota, a wave of relief swept through
mind and heart of soldier and civilian. All rumors
had been wrong, for the destination was Chickamauga,
Georgia—the first steppingstone, they hoped, to Cuba.[2]

Sioux Falls was astir with soldiers and citizens, everyone eager to lend assistance and to prevent further
delay. Since the entire regiment had not assembled
in that city, the move to Chickamauga was scheduled
to take place from several points. Headquarters and
Stewart's squadron, consisting of Troops B and E,
mustered in at Sioux Falls, entrained May 20, and
were scheduled for arrival May 23. Troops A, C,
and D, French's squadron, departed from Fort Meade,
South Dakota, May 23, and arrived May 27. Captain
Culver, commander of Troop K, from Lincoln, Nebraska, took leave of that city May 20 and reached the
southern destination May 23. The four Montana
troops, I from Fort Keogh, M from Billings, F from
Missoula, and L from Butte, left their respective recruiting centers between May 24 and 26, arriving in
Chickamauga between May 28 and 30; while Troops
G and H left Fargo, North Dakota, on May 25 and
reached the rendezvous four days later.[3]

Chicago was the first lap of the journey for Troops
B and E, departing from Sioux Falls at 9:30 A.M.

Anticipating the arrival of the "cowboys," a correspondent of the *Chicago Daily Tribune* wrote:

. . . These men are all rough riders from the cattle ranges
of the West and include many prominent Indian fighters,
scouts, and chiefs of vigilance committees. Every man is a
fighter and some of them have seen service in the British
army in South Africa.
    The Third claims to be the only regiment made up wholly
of genuine cowboys, as they assert that the First and Second
are composed largely of Eastern club men.[4]

    This claim, whether made by the Grigsby regiment
or by an enthusiastic reporter, is interesting but somewhat exaggerated. A check of the occupations of the
men who composed the Third Volunteer Regiment
reveals every kind of skill and profession—a list of
some eighty individual occupations, far too long and
of so little importance that it is not necessary to give
it space. However, it does reveal certain facts. The
five leading occupations represented were: cowboy,
miner, stockman, farmer, and clerk. In the First Squadron, made of Troops A, C, D, and K, known as the
Black Hills Squadron, the cowboy led in all troops
except A. In the Second Squadron, the Inter-Dakota,
composed of Troops B, E, G, and H, the cowboy pre-
dominated; there is no record of the occupations of
the men in Troop F of the Third Squadron,[5] but
the Montana Squadron, Troops L, M, and I, again
had a preponderance of range riders. Of a total of
1,011 men in the entire regiment, there were 359
cowboys; miners formed the next highest occupational
group with a total of 77 members.[6] In Troops E, G,
H, L, and I, the cowboy by far outnumbered the other

occupations.[7] Thus, cowboys made up a third of the regiment, but this cannot justify the statement that the organization was composed "wholly of genuine cowboys." Records do not show, unfortunately, how many men might have been cowboys at some earlier date, which was often the case in the West.

Newspapers reported daily on the journey southward. Already, on the second day, large crowds of people greeted the 186 men of Troops B and E at the Chicago station. In their excitement and enthusiasm, the mobs pressed so close to the moving train, composed of five coaches and eight stock cars, that the locomotive was forced to slow up to allow the ardent patriots to exchange greetings with the soldiers. Curiosity may have lured them out to see these men of the West who "were dressed in regulation cowboy costume, broad sombreros, etc., with long pistols strapped to their sides." After this first display of enthusiasm, the train proceeded to the stockyards where the tired men and stock were unloaded for a rest from the weariness and strain of travel and allowed to make camp before proceeding on to Chickamauga the following day.[8]

For several days dispatches from Chicago, reporting on the arrival of the various troops of the Grigsby regiment, were reprinted in the newspapers of the Rocky Mountain Empire. At the same time the arrival was featured in the *Times* of Chattanooga—with mixed feelings and provoking comments:

The men are all cowboys and crackshots with a six-shooter. They are right off of the ranches and hail from Deadwood, Lead City, Bellefourche and Sturgis, South Dakota. The

arrival of these plainsmen and "bronco-busters" was made
known by themselves in a studied concatenation of yells and
war whoops. The men made no objection to sleeping on
the grass last night being accustomed to this mode of life
in South Dakota.[9]

One reporter was swept away by enthusiasm, and
probably a great deal of imagination, as he gazed upon Troops F and L from Helena, Montana: "They
are about the wildest looking set of men in the entire volunteer army, many of them wearing their hair
about a foot long. All are well armed, although only
a small portion of the squadron is uniformed. Their
horses are genuine bronchos, deep-chested, long wind-
ed and fleet of foot."[10] As if to combat the exagger-
ation and increasing publicity, Adjutant Otto L. Sues
informed an interviewer: "There is nothing ferocious
about our men," he added, "they are all eager to
learn, and in my opinion we have men here who are
competent to surpass Buffalo Bill's rough riders. Our
regiment contains choice material. It includes five
lawyers and three newspaper men."[11]

On the following day Colonel Grigsby added fuel
to the flames of preconceived impressions of the cowboy regiment:

The boys are ready, willing and anxious to fight. We have
not received our equipments yet, but we will soon begin to
drill and, although none of the men know anything about
military tactics, I hope to have them in first class condition
in a very short time. The boys enlisted in the army for the
purpose of fighting, and if we get a chance at the Spaniards
we will show you what a western cowboy can do. What we
need is guns, horses and clothing; we already have the marksmanship and horsemanship. If we had our equipment now

we could do good fighting without any drilling, but I do not think it is prudent to put a body of men in a battle under ninety days training. Some of the boys of the regiment have already experienced some terrible fighting with the Indians, and when they do go into battle they know what it means.[12]

The cowboys of the regiment were fine material for the press; the sensational pictures, representing the daring men of the plains with a couple of six-shooters and fierce bowie knives, are comparable to the commercialized cowboy of today—the hero of the Western thriller, Hopalong Cassidy or the Lone Ranger, dashing across the movie and television screens.

Otto L. Sues was an eyewitness to the scenes depicted and in his book, *Grigsby's Cowboys,* comments on the reaction of the public:

People who had never been outside of their native burg, and who judged the cowboys entirely by what they had read in yellow-covered literature, came out of curiosity to see the men who picked their teeth with a bowie knife and snuffed candles with the bullet from a six-shooter. Others, who had more knowledge of the world and considerable more sense, came also; but the latter came to pay the tribute American citizens always consider due the patriot. The yellow covers were greatly surprised to find that "Grigsby's boys" were orderly, well-behaved, gentlemanly and intelligent; that even the "long-haired pards" who were with the regiment were as well up on current topics and gentlemanly behavior as the best of the spectators. In short, they soon found that the regiment was no spectacular, grand stand aggregation; no "Wild West" on wheels, but composed of intelligent, sensible cowboys, miners and other Western men, who were in the army for business, and that business any duty the Government might call upon them to perform.[13]

In continuing his tirade, Sues says that, due to the

unfavorable publicity which preceded the regiment to Chattanooga, many of the citizens of that city remained in their homes and barred their doors. Chattanooga newspapers, however, reported no such incidents, but rather commented on the fine type of men, their good behavior, and their friendly attitude. The *Times,* under a bold headline, "COL. GRIGSBY's BRAVE COW-BOYS," was thoroughly impressed: "The improved cow-boy is a new factor in modern warfare, and to see him in cavalry maneuver one could not but be impressed with the idea that he will be as potential as he is peculiar, as effective as he is daring."[14] The skill in riding and roping also won admiration:

The cowboys have had a chance to demonstrate their rough riding. A number of mules have escaped from Gen. Wylie [Wiley] and he sent for the cowboys to capture them. Maj. French, Lieut. Cussick and a detail of several men responded and in a very short time they had all the mules lassoed except one and the boys will make another effort to capture him. They fully demonstrated that they were cowboys of the "real stuff."[15]

The incident that really "sold" the *Times* on the regiment was one concerning the fair sex. Anyone who knows a real honest-to-goodness cowboy is constantly aware of his (the cowboy's) respect for women, for it is one of his virtues and strictly written in the code of the West. About a month after the arrival at Chickamauga, the cowboys had an opportunity to demonstrate. One day several Salvation Army women who worked about the camp were walking along in the park when they were accosted and rudely insulted by a group of infantrymen. The cowboys in the camp near by soon learned of the incident, became quite indignant,

. . . and in a few minutes a crowd of the cowboys went to [the spot] where the soldiers were congregated and without waiting for an explanation they seized the toughs who had offered the insult, and it is stated that the position at that time was anything but enviable. To use street vernacular, "What the cowboys did for the insolent men was enough." The rough riders certainly handled the soldiers very roughly. They then escorted the ladies to the train to see that no further insult was offered. Everywhere the incident has become known the action of the cowboys has been loudly applauded.[16]

After reading such a variety of comments on the cowboy soldier, the newspaper public in those days could assign him to the position of either saint or sinner. However, as time passed, the "reckless, swash buckling, dare-devil riders of the Western plains" won the admiration of all. "Although Col. Melvin Grigsby's cowboys come from the far west and are considered by some people to be rough, they have shown themselves to be gentlemanly and chivalrous on all occasions."[17]

NOTES TO CHAPTER VIII

1. "Grigsby To Be Banqueted," *Daily Argus-Leader* (Sioux Falls, South Dakota), May 19; "Tribute To Grigsby," *ibid.*, May 20.

2. Sues, *Grigsby's Cowboys*, pp. 17, 20; "Grigsby's Cowboys," *Yankton Press and Dakotan* (Yankton, South Dakota), May 16.

3. Sues, *Grigsby's Cowboys*, pp. 17, 20.

4. "Leader of Cowboy Cavalry," *Chicago Daily Tribune* (Chicago, Illinois), May 14.

5. According to Sues, information concerning the occupations of the men of Troop F was not available. Sues, *Grigsby's Cowboys*, p. 299.

6. This does not include the unknown quantity of Troop F.

7. Sues, *Grigsby's Cowboys*, pp. 151, 166, 180-81, 200, 232, 247-48, 265-66, 281, 299, 316, 332, 349.

8. "Our Grig Gets There," *Daily Argus-Leader* (Sioux Falls, South Dakota), May 21; "Grigsby's Cowboys Reach Chicago," *Denver Times* (Denver, Colorado), May 21; "Colonel Grigsby's Cowboy Cavalry," *Denver Evening Post* (Denver, Colorado), May 21.

9. "Troops A, C, and D, Third Volunteer Cavalry," *Chattanooga Times* (Chattanooga, Tennessee), May 27; "Arrived at Destination," *Daily Argus-Leader* (Sioux Falls, South Dakota), May 23; "Grigsby's Troopers," *ibid.*, May 25.

10. "Arrivals Yesterday," *Chattanooga Times* (Chattanooga, Tennessee), May 31.

11. "Col. Grigsby's Cowboys," *ibid.*, May 27.

12. "Grigsby's Cowboys," *ibid.*, May 28.

13. Sues, *Grigsby's Cowboys*, p. 12.

14. "Col. Grigsby's Brave Cowboys," *Chattanooga Times* (Chattanooga, Tennessee), June 3.

15. "Col. Grigsby's Cavalry," *ibid.*, June 12.

16. "Col. Grigsby's Cowboys," *ibid.*, June 20; "Grigsby's Gallant Cowboys," *Denver Evening Post* (Denver, Colorado), June 26; "Grig's Cowboy Camp," *Daily Argus-Leader* (Sioux Falls, South Dakota), June 22; "Compliments for Grigsby's Men," *Yankton Press and Dakotan* (Yankton, South Dakota), August 10.

17. "Grigsby's Gallant Cowboys," *Denver Evening Post* (Denver, Colorado), June 26.

CHAPTER IX

TORREY'S TRAGEDY

THE FAME OF the Rough Riders had gone abroad with Roosevelt and the First Volunteer Cavalry Regiment. Meanwhile, the Second and Third were moving southward, eagerly anticipating the day when they, too, would cover themselves with glory.

In Cheyenne, still short of horses, Colonel Torrey made final arrangements for the departure of his regiment from Fort Russell on June 22. The route of the caravan on the Union Pacific Railroad went via Omaha and Burlington to St. Louis; then a transfer to the Illinois Central and on to Kansas City. From this point the troops continued their long trip on the Missouri and Birmingham and, for the last lap to their destination in Jacksonville, Florida, via the Central Georgia and Plant Systems.

It was to be a long trip, but the troopers looked forward to it with a fine, adventurous spirit. Not only the thought that they would soon get a crack at the Spaniards kept their enthusiasm at high pitch, but also the opportunity of seeing, as they traveled east and south, much of the glorious country to which they had offered their service. "It is the best possible time . . . to see the beauty of the rustling corn, the fields and fields of waving grain ripening for the mowing, and then travel down through the sunny Southland where the cotton plants are just beginning to put forth their snow white blossoms."[1]

Lieutenant Robert C. Gracey, with a detail of thirty-four men, was to remain at Fort Russell to round up more horses; the others busied themselves in gathering together their belongings for the long trek. On the train, sleeping accommodations were assigned — two men in each lower berth and one in the upper; the officers had quarters in first-class sleepers attached to each section. The good women of Cheyenne, who had showered food and attention on the men during the weeks at the fort, again came to the rescue and prepared a bountiful lunch; in fact, the quantity of food which appeared was sufficient for the entire trip to Jacksonville. The weighty, well-packed boxes, however, did not prevent the troopers from pulling a stunt, characteristic not only of soldiers but of any group of men bound for adventure, and "they got away with a carload of watermelons, bag and baggage, and left the shipper and Chief Clerk Anderson of the Union Pacific to squabble over whose loss it was."[2]

On the first day of the trip, curiosity was at a peak.

The men inspected the cars and accommodations.
Harry B. Tedrow informed the folks back home that

the coaches . . . consist of tourist sleepers of various styles
and construction, and the men find them very comfortable.
It is a satisfaction to be able to convert the seats into bunks
at will and lie down. Some of the bunks are a little crowded.
This happens where two men of large dimensions occupy
the same bunk. The men carry their blankets with them
and also their saddle bags and nose bags for feeding horses.
The saddle bags are used as valises and they make good ones.[3]

Torrey's Terrors were pursued with bad luck from
the start, and tragedy rode with them all the way,
almost, it seems, concurrent with the foreboding signs
that swept through the nation. Newspapers were bannered with black, lurid headlines, anticipating the invasion of Cuba, and everywhere, through the various
states, patriotic citizens displayed their warmhearted
interest in the volunteers of the Second Regiment,
who were destined to be the victims of the delay and
disaster that had been conspicuously absent from the
First and Third.

In Nebraska and Missouri, people knew the approxi-
mate hour of the arrival of the four sections and enthusiastic receptions awaited the troopers; from St.
Louis on, it was a question of hit or miss, but interest and concern did not wane, in spite of long hours
of waiting. Large banners distinctly marked the cars
carrying the war-bound soldiers, and "off comes every
hat and up goes every handkerchief and apron as
soon as they are read, . . . at Columbus, Nebraska,
two patriotic women ran the full length of the train

to give Colonel Torrey a dish of ice cream before it melted."[4]

The first accident occurred the first night out. The platform of one of the coaches was badly crushed; no injuries resulted, but the car was left at Omaha. Also several men became ill, not seriously, and, in all probability, due to an overeager attack on the culinary triumphs contained in the boxes from the ladies in Cheyenne.[5]

The trooper, writing almost a day-by-day account, reported on everything and everybody, including the porters, and continued: "Everywhere the troopers were greeted enthusiastically and with cheers as in contrast, according to the porters when they accompanied the Tennessee volunteers to San Francisco. They had much to say of the inhospitality of the coast towns."[6]

Also, he did not forget the horses. They were holding up quite well, had been fed properly along the way, and unloaded and exercised in South Omaha. If anything there were too few horses to a car—twenty; the cars were large and this allowed too much room for bumping, swaying and jamming. Colonel Torrey personally supervised the care of the horses at the first stop.[7]

In Missouri the reception "passed beyond the point of ovation and became a triumphal progress" and "certainly surpassed anything that could be expected outside of a reception to a presidential candidate or the welcome they will give the soldier boys upon their return." Every city and town, every farmhouse displayed the national colors, and "out in the fields the toilers mounted their plows or fences and waved their

hats until the train was out of sight." The troopers'
arms were sore from acknowledging waving hats and
aprons.[8]

Thomas W. O'Donnell, Troop B, enthusiastically
wrote to a friend:

Our passage through Missouri was more like a triumphal
march of a retiring victor than the weary journey of an unknown soldier to the front. At every town and hamlet it
appeared as if the entire population turned out en masse to
greet and cheer us onward; not by mere words alone, for
they did not forget a soldier sometimes eats and drinks (but
d—n little in the army though) and accordingly they came and
stormed us with appetizing lunches and refreshing drinks,
completely capturing us.[9]

Had there been radio broadcasts at that time, the
reporter of the St. Joseph *Herald* would have had
several occasions to announce, "We interrupt this program to bring you . . ." for the press kept on the trail
of the Terrors whose "movements . . . have been quite
as puzzling during the past two days as those of the
Cadiz fleet." It also reported the exact whereabouts
of the four Burlington trains from Omaha, the various
stops for coffee, lunch, and the condition of the horses.[10]

A second accident occurred on June 24. The engine
of the second train section, moving into the Union
Station at St. Joseph, jumped the track, plowed through
the earth for a distance of thirty feet, and then toppled
over. The engineer died at the throttle; the fireman
was seriously scalded and little hope was held for his
recovery; the cars carrying the precious mounts were
derailed but, much to Torrey's relief, not a horse

was hurt.[11] As a result the welcome for the traveling
troopers was all the more enthusiastic.

There were a great many women there . . . and made the
acquaintance of the mountaineers without useless ceremony,
swapped hat pins for troop and regimental insignia and all
but persuaded the rough riders to abandon the invasion of
Porto Rico and lay siege to the city of St. Joseph, or at least
carry off a lot of fair prisoners of war.[12]

One hundred and twenty gallons of hot coffee disappeared like dry grass in a prairie fire among the
"typical cowboys . . . with a nobility of soul that is born
of a life on the mountain and plain, and of constant
communion with nature in her grandest form."[13] Previously, in the towns of Hamburg and Craig, "women
met the coaches with baskets of cherries."[14]

The accident did not cause too much delay. The
train, scheduled to reach St. Louis that same evening,
arrived in the early morning hours, yet "6,000 people
waited at the union depot until midnight to give
Torrey's men a welcome."[15]

The above-mentioned Trooper O'Donnell wrote:
"Our short stay was a continuous round of pleasure
in that city, owing in no small degree to the breweries,
who turned over their establishments for the time being to 'Torrey's Terrors,' and strange to relate, for
once the boys did not abuse their prerogative."[16]

In St. Louis the horses were again fed, exercised,
and reloaded; then the train slowly increased its speed
and moved on smoothly. The troopers, joyful over
the reports that the remainder of the trip would
progress more rapidly, settled back in their seats or

drifted out to the platform to catch a last glimpse of the ever-changing sights before the entrance into the tunnel at East St. Louis. But bad luck was still traveling with Torrey's men. As the train approached the tunnel, Archie A. Sackett failed to leave the platform with his companions, became suffocated by the smoke, and, unconscious, fell from the platform. The press gave a gruesome report of the accident—"the body was badly mangled and his head was cut off."[17]

On they moved; through the night they traversed Illinois and Kentucky, but the people "had strong lungs and cheered the passing train until midnight."[18] The troopers woke up in Tennessee, and at once the Negro became a source of curiosity to the men from the West. All along the way, black woolly heads appeared at the doors and windows of the cabins; in a short time, the cowboys learned the "you-all" of the Southerner and shouted as they passed, "Hello, Rastus . . . Hike dar Snowball, what you all doin'?"[19] Negroes of every size, sex, and shade crowded to the stations, all barefooted, women and girls in gaudy cotton dresses, bright-eyed and wide-grinning pickaninnies in briefer costume. "A coal black negro was seated on a load of melons being pulled along by a sleepy mule. The train stopped and instantaneously a grand charge took place upon the wagon. The negro held up his hands helplessly and his only defense was repeated warnings to get back on the train, for it was going right out."[20]

Nearer and nearer the train sped toward its destination. With numerous delays and three accidents already, the troopers fervently hoped that now the remaining one fourth of the long distance would be covered rapidly. But tragedy in its worst form was still to visit the Wyoming contingent. Some of the troopers, however, had a sinister feeling and actually expected more bad luck. Albert Bristol concluded a letter written to his father after the wreck at St. Joseph and the unfortunate death of the soldier in East St. Louis with "That makes two accidents we have had, and now we expect another."[21]

On the afternoon of June 27, the *Sun-Leader* of Cheyenne appeared with a stark, unforgettable head-line—"FIVE TROOPERS KILLED." The accident occurred on the afternoon of June 26 at Tupelo, Mississippi, when the second section of the train moved into the station where the first section had already come to a full stop. A reporter for the regiment, traveling in the last car, which was considered headquarters, gave a detailed account from the moment he heard someone yell to jump.

I looked out of the window and saw a man waving a flag frantically, but there was no appearance of slowing down on the part of the coming train. . . . There was a deafening crash and the engine almost disappeared under the head-quarters car. Col. Torrey was in the last room . . . but had a miraculous escape. He was carried out about 300 feet among a pile of breaking wood and glass. Fortunately the smashing timbers closed only around his feet, leaving his head clear. Finally he was thrown out and escaped with only a few scratches on his head. His feet were crushed, but not seriously. . . . He is, as he says himself, on his back, but still in command.[22]

Fatalities were most serious in the center coach of the first section, which was completely telescoped. The occupants, all members of Troop C from Laramie,

Wyoming, suffered severe cuts and bruises from the crash of falling timbers, window glass, and broken car seats.[23]

Reports on the wreck continued to flood the press and offered more detailed information. The first section of the train had stopped for water at 3:40 P.M.; then a whistle was blown as a signal to start moving, and suddenly the second section rounded a sharp curve and ploughed into the halted train. Considering the serious nature of the wreck, it was almost miraculous that only five deaths and fifteen serious casualties resulted. It was miraculous, too, that the men in the headquarters car escaped alive.[24] The blame for the accident was attributed to gross carelessness on the part of the engineer of the second section, who disappeared from the scene—no doubt fearing the wild cowboys who threatened to lynch him if he could be found. "Some say he was intoxicated. The fact remains that the throttle of the engine was wide open and the air brakes were not used."[25]

The people of Tupelo, both white and colored, turned out in full force to offer aid to the stricken soldiers, and "many touching scenes occurred. In two cases men who were taken out with broken limbs and possibly more injuries, begged their comrades to put them down and run to help others who were more in need of assistance than they."[26] Every bucket in the town appeared with water to soothe the dry, parched lips of the wounded; both water and milk were passed to those still immovably pinned in the demolished cars. Vacant buildings were quickly transformed into emergency wards, and a great number of women immediately volunteered for nursing service and took care of the casualties.[27]

The headquarters train reached Birmingham on the morning of June 27. Colonel Torrey still suffered from his bruises but expected to be able to move in about ten days. En route, due to the excitement, confusion, and delay, rations were not distributed regularly, and several times the Terrors suffered terrific hunger pangs. Upon their arrival in Birmingham, a welcome feast awaited them; the sight of the long tables laden with food soon dispersed the blues and gloom, and, amid rousing cheers, "the boys did justice to a substantial dinner."[28] The horses showed evidence of the long days of heat and delay and were given expert attention while the boys feasted. Also, from Birmingham, dispatches went West reporting the death of Henry S. Mapes, Troop C, at Tupelo and the almost hopeless condition of Charles Guemmer, Troop L. All other casualties were doing well.[29] Before leaving Birmingham, Colonel Torrey, still hopeful of pushing off to Cuba soon, commented on the men in his charge: "They are no long-haired hoodlums and wild Westerners of the Nick Carter type. Our men are intelligent, clean-cut, educated, well-drilled and experienced, and we mean business."[30]

At last, after six days and nights of travel through eleven states, plus three accidents, the Second Regiment, the men from the rarefied Rocky Mountain atmosphere arrived in Jacksonville where, at Panama Park, they went into camp at sea level and only a few miles from the coast itself. The camp was conveniently located near an old deserted winter resort on an inlet from the St. John's River where "a pier runs out into the water, and an old toboggan slide is there, and altogether it is a much appreciated luxury and one of which the travel-worn Westerners took advantage as soon as their tents were pitched."[31]

Here, in oppressive heat, Torrey's Terrors settled down to rest up, but their minds were still on war. The horses were well situated in a shady pine grove on sandy ground; drilling took place in the early morning and again in late afternoon; "taps" were sounded at nine o'clock and reveille at 3:30 A.M. The fame of the Westerners had preceded them, and they were held in much higher esteem than a Mississippi regiment which was also encamped in Panama Park. A good example of the reputation that goes before was soon to be observed at a negro revival which was in full blast. The Mississippians had molested it on several occasions, and the Negroes added "to their prayers an entreaty that the cowboys would soon arrive, relying upon them for protection, and sang a loud hosanna last night when they appeared."[32]

NOTES TO CHAPTER IX

1. "With the Rough Riders," *Rocky Mountain News* (Denver, Colorado) , July 8.

2. "In Good Trim to Fight," *ibid.*, June 24.

3. "Torrey's Men En Route," *ibid.*, June 26.

4. *Ibid.*

5. *Ibid.*

6. *Ibid.*

7. *Ibid.*

8. "With the Rough Riders," *ibid.*, July 8.

9. "Torrey's Terrors in Camp at Panama Park," *Denver Evening Post* (Denver, Colorado) , July 19.

10. "Torrey's Rough Riders," *Herald* (St. Joseph, Missouri) , June 24.

11. "Torrey's Train Wrecked," *Denver Republican* (Denver, Colorado), June 25.

12. "Torrey's Noble Riders," *Cheyenne Sun-Leader* (Cheyenne, Wyoming), June 28.

13. *Ibid.*

14. *Ibid.*

15. "With the Rough Riders," *Rocky Mountain News* (Denver, Colorado), July 8.

16. "Torrey's Terrors in Camp at Panama Park," *Denver Evening Post* (Denver, Colorado), July 19.

17. "Troopers in Wreck," *Sun* (Baltimore, Maryland), June 27; "One of Torrey's Riders Killed," *Rocky Mountain News* (Denver, Colorado), June 26. "Roll of Deceased Patriots," an annotated list by Colonel Torrey, found in his personal signed copy of *Torrey's Rough Riders, Historical and Biographical Souvenir of the Second United States Volunteer Cavalry* (Jacksonville, Florida: Vance Printing Co., 1898).

18. "With the Rough Riders," *Rocky Mountain News* (Denver, Colorado), July 8.

19. *Ibid.*

20. *Ibid.*

21. "Torrey Cavalry Expected Trouble," *Denver Republican* (Denver, Colorado), June 30.

22. "Torrey Cavalry Meets Disaster," *ibid.*, June 27; "Torrey's Men in a Wreck," *Florida Times-Union & Citizen* (Jacksonville, Florida), June 27.

23. "Torrey Cavalry Meets Disaster," *Denver Republican* (Denver, Colorado), June 27.

24. "Five Troopers Killed," *Cheyenne Sun-Leader* (Cheyenne, Wyoming), June 27.

25. "Torrey's Rough Riders in a Fatal Collision," *Rocky Mountain News* (Denver, Colorado), June 27; "Troopers in a Wreck," *Chicago Daily Tribune* (Chicago, Illinois), June 27.

26. "With the Rough Riders," *Rocky Mountain News* (Denver, Colorado), July 8.

27. "Torrey's Rough Riders in a Fatal Collision," *ibid.*, June 27.

28. "Torrey at Birmingham," *Cheyenne Sun-Leader* (Cheyenne, Wyoming), June 28; "From Torrey's Regiment," *ibid.*; "Torrey's Men's Bad Luck," *Rocky Mountain News* (Denver, Colorado), June 28.

29. "One More Torrey Man Dead," *ibid.*, June 28; "Torrey at Birmingham," *Cheyenne Sun-Leader* (Cheyenne, Wyoming), June 28.

30. "Torrey's Troopers Here," *Florida Times-Union & Citizen* (Jacksonville, Florida), June 29.

31. "With the Rough Riders," *Rocky Mountain News* (Denver, Colorado), July 8.

32. *Ibid.*

CHAPTER X

GOD BLESS THE LADIES!

WHEN THE CALL to arms came about a half century ago, woman's place was still in the home and she was, for the most part, content with her tasks of "today we wash, tomorrow we bake." However, there were some who, like Joan of Arc, deserted their flocks, left others to sew and spin, and made haste to offer their services. In 1898 the military department of our government gave no thought to such terms as WAAC, WAVE, and WASP; nevertheless, women in the West were accustomed to hardship; they, too, "rode in the saddle" and, when cowboys galloped off to volunteer, some of the more daring petticoats mounted their ponies and took to the patriotic trail.

In Chadron, Nebraska, enthusiastic women under the leadership of Miss "Girlie" Adams organized a complete cavalry of one hundred, every member of which was "a crack shot and excellent horsewoman,"[1] and notified the governor (Holcomb) that they were prepared to fight. The leader, however, was quite modest in respect to publicity, and the photographer of the *Denver Evening Post* soon discovered that he was not "shooting" a Hollywood star, for the patriotic miss consented to pose only after a prolonged entreaty and vowed that she "preferred making a record in action before being heralded as a fighter."[2]

Women in Colorado rallied to the cause earlier. In Denver, Mrs. Shute of the State Horticultural Society informed the governor that two hundred women were ready to form a cavalry.[3]

The news that a female brigade would, in all probability, not be a reality did not dim the ardor of some members of the fair sex. If they could not serve, their horses could. Blanche McHenry, a cowgirl attached to a Wild West Show in Denver, gave her finest horse to a fellow cowboy performer who decided to give up thrilling wild rides to join the Rough Riders on the trail to Cuba.[4]

So the female volunteers trotted home and joined their hearth-bound sisters whose spirits had been stirred to do their share in a more gentle manner. Volunteer Aid Societies sprung into being; the various women's organizations offered their services and looked about for things to do. One of the first projects in the several states and territories concerned flags for the respective troops. In this respect Western women were not to be outdone by Betsy Ross of Revolutionary fame. Members of the Women's Relief Corps in Phoe-

nix rummaged in trunks and scrap bags to provide a
regimental flag for the Rough Riders. Women and
children in New Mexico raised over two hundred dollars for a flag for the First Volunteer Cavalry; however, the troops entrained for San Antonio before the
colors arrived and the banner was presented later. Harman H. Wynkoop, a member of the volunteers (still
living at the present time in Santa Fe, New Mexico),
expressed the sentiments of the troopers in a letter to
the *Santa Fe New Mexican:* "Yes, the flag arrived. I
cannot say anything as to the beauty it presents to the
eye—words cannot express it. It is not only the ex-
quisite workmanship and the material it contains, but
it carries a message from our homes, a message from
our government; one breathes of love, the other of stern
command."[5]

In Wyoming, where Colonel Torrey was busily
rounding up men and mounts, the ladies also made
arrangements for a flag for the Wyoming volunteers.
Women from the five states represented in Torrey's
regiment (Colorado, Idaho, Nebraska, Utah, Wyoming) took part in the project, and the flag was presented with fitting ceremonies on Governors' Day,
with the governors of the five states in attendance,
Governor Adams of Colorado making the presentation.[6]

The nimble fingers did not rest. During the month
of May, Mrs. L. Bradford Prince, State Regent of the
Daughters of the American Revolution in New Mexico,
assisted members of the Colorado chapter in making
one hundred abdominal protectors for the Colorado
volunteers who had arrived in San Francisco, bound
for the Philippines. Mrs. Prince was most enthusiastic

over the project and immediately sent a sample and instructions to her sister members in New Mexico. The protectors were

. . . made double, of soft all-wool flannel, a half yard long and about ten inches wide. . . . They are stitched together once, then turned over and stitched again; two and a quarter yards of tape is then sewed flatly across the top to fasten it around the body. White flannel is not used for obvious reasons, nor red, because it irritates the skin.[7]

These protectors were supposed to be an excellent preventative against tropical diseases and, in due time, reached the troops in Tampa, Florida. The distribution of them caused great hilarity among Teddy's cowboys because the surgeon had neglected to give information concerning the use of the peculiarly fashioned piece of wool. Harman Wynkoop informed the folks back home in a letter of appreciation:

. . . Many had different ideas as to the use of the belt. It was near supper time when the bandages were given out, and so many of the belts adorned the breasts of innocent soldiers, bib fashion, during the meal. Many others thought it was a new uniform, especially adapted to Cuban climate. This was very appropriate, for we need to be covered with something more than glory. . . .[8]

The craze for making protectors spread to Wyoming, and what was good for Roosevelt's Riders was considered a necessity for Torrey's Terrors. To help cover the cost of Laramie's quota of one hundred, Frank W. Eggleston, druggist, proclaimed "Soda Day" and pledged one day's receipts from his soda fountain.[9] A similar day was sponsored by the Palace and Capital pharmacies in Cheyenne. The ladies used every means possible to entice one and all into the drug-stores, where attractive young women, with their best "come-on" look, sat and chatted with the consumers of the day's concoction. The druggists were not at all concerned about the vast yardage of flannel that was being supplied as a result of the sudden thirst for sodas, for they well knew that later they would recoup their financial losses by prescribing remedies for queasy stomachs.[10]

Prior to the abdominal protector project, Wyoming women had busied their fingers in making pocket needle cases for the volunteers who were soon to leave Fort Russell. In letters to representative women in each city and town in Wyoming, Mrs. H. B. Hender-son launched the campaign for one thousand cases and supplied instructions:

. . . light weight linen canvas is a suitable material, with the fastening of ribbon or colored tape. Please furnish each case with two dozen pins, three coarse needles, one dozen assorted underwear and shirt buttons, and wind the bobbins with cotton thread, number 12, black and white, about 10 yards of each.

In conclusion, Mrs. Henderson exhorted her sisters of the needle with these words:

War never had a holier cause; husbands, fathers and brothers go to protect our country's honor with the sacrifice of their lives if need be in this great struggle for humanity's sake. . . .[11]

Needless to say, the full quota of needle cases was turned out in the time specified, each one graced with the visiting card of the maker. As a fitting climax for the project and for the presentation, Ladies' Day at Fort Russell was proclaimed. As an added attraction, the ladies made it a Cake Day also and agreed "to supply the troopers with cakes, pies and other delicacies not embraced in the mess cuisine of the company cooks."[12] All the favorite family-treasured recipies and appropriate sentiments went into the makings of "the mother's cake, the sister's cake, the grandma's cake, the old maid's cake, and in fact all kinds of cake. . . ."[13] Of the quality one can be assured, and the quantity was evidenced by the two big wagonloads of cake that proceeded to the fort, along with many carriage loads of ladies and over a thousand needle cases. The program of procedure had been arranged to the last detail. Ladies and cakes, respectively, were escorted and carried to the various barracks; then followed a tour of inspection and the return to headquarters where Mrs. Henderson, in behalf of the patriotic women, presented the cases. Her address, long and effusive, concluded with a scriptural passage:

We know that our country's honor is in safe keeping and that its brave defenders are in the hollow of God's hand. "His truth shall be thy shield and buckler. Thou shalt not be afraid for the terror by night; nor for the arrow that flieth by day; nor for the pestilence that walketh in darkness. A thousand shall fall at thy side, but it shall not come nigh thee."[14]

The needle cases were probably more appreciated than the abdominal protectors; at least, the volunteers could make no mistake as to the use thereof! That there was a definite need for such sewing kits is evidenced in a letter from Captain W. H. H. Llewellen in Cuba to Governor Otero (New Mexico Territory) in which he asked that packages with stout thread, needles, shaving soap, and scissors—along with smoking tobacco—be sent to the boys.[15]

Everywhere women and children showered departing groups with mementos and trinkets; in some towns en route small girls tossed flowers, but always food— good food—for the boys was uppermost in the minds of the women who were left behind. The members of the Volunteer Aid Society in Denver, already on the third day of its existence, prepared a feast for the two troops of the Colorado Cavalry about to leave Denver to join Colonel Torrey in Wyoming. The menu for this banquet, served at the camp, would certainly make the mouth of any departing male water.

First Course	Second Course
Roast Chicken, Mashed Potatoes	Assorted Cakes
Baked Beans	Bananas, Oranges
Buttered Biscuits	Assorted Fruits
Eggs Served Boiled	Ice Cream
Pickles of All Varieties	Cigars[16]
Coffee	

There were "Bon Voyage" gifts, too! An amusing sight at the departure was millionaire Captain William Cooke Daniels as he struggled through the crowd with a box of oranges—the gift of Mrs. Nathaniel P. Hill.[17]

The fond mothers, wives, sisters, and sweethearts —then, as now—were keenly aware of the fact that the food in store for the men of their hearts was not going to be exactly "like mother used to make." In Wyoming, when the troops at Fort Russell were about to entrain for Florida, the women prepared a train lunch "consisting of every kind of cooked edible, confection and fruit—in fact, everything the market afforded, not known to be included in the regulation rations."[18]

This deluge of food which was showered upon the soldiers, here, there, and everywhere, eventually warped the enthusiasm of some of the newspapermen and caused comment:

The Baltimore American asks the Government to issue a list of those things it would be best to send to our sailors and soldiers. When did mothers and wives and sweethearts take such advice? Let the Government alone—it has enough to do—and let the poor fellows continue to get sick on cake and pickles; they will be reminded of home any how.[19]

But in the War of 1898 there were women who were not left behind. A bill had been introduced in the Senate which provided for matrons to be sent with the volunteer army—"women to mend and wash clothing and to see to the sanitary conditions of the men" —but it did not materialize.[20] However, the nurses and members of the Red Cross received great praise from the soldiers, both during the war and after. The feeling of the men toward these noble women is aptly expressed in the words of a negro soldier: "Boys, I am not a Catholic, but on every pay day, so long as I remain in the United States Army, and I hope to die in it, I shall give a dollar to the first nun I see."[21]

NOTES TO CHAPTER X

1. "Cavalry Composed of Women," *Chicago Daily Tribune* (Chicago, Illinois), April 19.

2. "Miss 'Girlie' Adams, Woman Cavalry Leader," *Denver Evening Post* (Denver, Colorado), April 28.

3. "Female Cavalry Troops," *Cheyenne Sun-Leader* (Cheyenne, Wyoming), March 15.

4. "The Girls They Left Behind Them," *Denver Republican* (Denver, Colorado), May 15.

5. [News Item] *Santa Fe New Mexican* (Santa Fe, New Mexico), July 5.

6. "Gala Day at Fort Russell," *Cheyenne Sun-Leader* (Cheyenne, Wyoming), June 3.

7. [News Item] *Santa Fe New Mexican* (Santa Fe, New Mexico), May 31.

8. *Ibid.*, July 5.

9. "Making Abdominal Protectors," *Denver Republican* (Denver, Colorado), June 7. Mrs. E. Deane Hunton, Laramie, Wyoming, the daughter of Frank W. Eggleston, made available to the author her scrapbook of photographs, as well as a vivid account of this patriotic and amusing occasion.

10. "Patriotic Women," *Cheyenne Sun-Leader* (Cheyenne, Wyoming), June 18.

11. "For the Soldier Boys," *Denver Republican* (Denver, Colorado), May 11.

12. "Ladies Will Visit Fort Russell," *ibid.*, June 1.

13. "Cake Day at Fort Russell," *Cheyenne Sun-Leader* (Cheyenne, Wyoming), June 2.

14. "Ladies Day at Fort Russell," *Denver Republican* (Denver, Colorado), June 4.

15. [News Item] *Santa Fe New Mexican* (Santa Fe, New Mexico), July 22.

16. "Dined at Camp," *Denver Times* (Denver, Colorado), May 30.

17. "Gone To Join Torrey," *ibid.*

18. "Toward Cuba and Glory," *Rocky Mountain News* (Denver, Colorado), June 23.

19. "Summary of the News," *Florida Times-Union & Citizen* (Jacksonville, Florida), June 28.

20. "Matrons To Be Sent with Volunteer Army," *Denver Evening Post* (Denver, Colorado), June 3.

21. "The Other Heroes," *Santa Fe New Mexican* (Santa Fe, New Mexico), September 7.

Courtesy Historical Society of New Mexico, Santa Fe, New Mexico

COWBOYS BECOME ROUGH RIDERS

Standing in front of the Palace of the Governors, Santa Fe, New Mexico, recruits for the First United States Volunteer Cavalry are sworn in by Captain Charles L. Cooper, U.S.A. *Identified figures in foreground:* (1) Major Henry B. Hersey, (2) Governor Miguel A. Otero, (3) Captain Charles L. Cooper, U.S.A., and (4) Dr. James A. Massie, Assistant Surgeon.

PLATE II

Courtesy Historical Society of New Mexico, Santa Fe, New Mexico

OFF TO SAN ANTONIO

The Rough Riders entrain May 7, 1898, at Santa Fe for San Antonio, Texas. *Identified figures:* (1) First Lieutenant Sherrard Coleman. (2) Captain Frederick Muller. (3) Major Henry B. Hersey and (4) Second Lieutenant W. E. Griffin.

PLATE III

Courtesy Rex Morrison, Rex Studio, Las Vegas, New Mexico

REMEMBERING THE MAINE

Recruits from northeastern New Mexico—Raton, Springer, Clayton, and Las Vegas—join the Rough Rider cavalcade at the depot in Las Vegas, New Mexico, while saddened relatives and patriotic citizens gather for a last farewell.

PLATE IV

Courtesy Harman H. Wynkoop, Santa Fe, New Mexico

BRASS AT EASE

Left to right: Lieutenant Colonel Theodore Roosevelt, Colonel Leonard Wood, and Major Alexander O. Brodie, May 12, 1898, at San Antonio, Texas.

PLATE V

Courtesy Wyoming State Historical Department, Cheyenne, Wyoming

COLONEL JAY L. TORREY AND STAFF, SECOND UNITED STATES VOLUNTEER CAVALRY

Left to right: Major Mortimer Jesurun, Lieutenant Colonel John Q. Cannon, Colonel Jay L. Torrey, Major James Harbord, Major William G. Wheeler, and Major Robert Calverley. At Fort D. A. Russell, Cheyenne, Wyoming.

PLATE VI

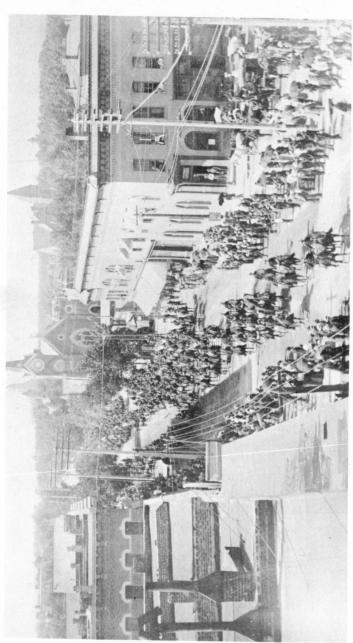

Courtesy Wyoming State Historical Department, Cheyenne, Wyoming

FAREWELL, CHEYENNE, FAREWELL

The last parade of the Second United States Volunteer Cavalry, "Torrey's Rocky Mountain Riders," in Cheyenne, Wyoming, before their departure for Jacksonville, Florida.

PLATE VII

Courtesy Mrs. E. Deane Hunton, Laramie, Wyoming

FRANK W. EGGLESTON PHARMACY, LARAMIE, WYOMING, 1898

The proprietor, Frank W. Eggleston, leans against a counter display of lotions and toilet water; to the left stands the soda fountain of the "Soda Day" fame.

PLATE VIII

Courtesy Sioux K. Grigsby, Sioux Falls, South Dakota

AT CAMP GEORGE H. THOMAS, CHICKAMAUGA, GEORGIA

Seated, left to right: Chaplain Galon S. Clevinger, Colonel Melvin Grigsby, and Lieutenant Colonel Charles F. Lloyd. *Standing, left to right:* Adjutant Otto L. Sues; Major Robert W. Stewart; Major James H. Monteath; Lieutenant Roy A. Wilson, Assistant Surgeon; Captain Ralph W. Parliman, Quartermaster; Major Leigh H. French; and Major H. Gurdon Fish, Regimental Surgeon.

PLATE IX

Courtesy Sioux K. Grigsby, Sioux Falls, South Dakota

HORSE CORRAL, CAMP GEORGE H. THOMAS, CHICKAMAUGA, GEORGIA

The Western horses suffered severely in the heat of the South and sought relief under the protective oaks and pines. Horse funerals were not an uncommon event during the summer months.

PLATE X

Courtesy Rex Morrison, Rex Studio, Las Vegas, New Mexico

ROUGH RIDERS ON PARADE. FIRST REUNION OF ROUGH RIDERS, LAS VEGAS, NEW MEXICO, 1899

The enthusiasm of the Rough Riders survived the mustering out of the regiment. Every volunteer who could ride, walk, or crawl reached Las Vegas in 1899 to honor the illustrious leader and pay homage to a glorious past.

PLATE XI

Courtesy New Mexico Highlands University, Las Vegas, New Mexico

INTERESTED SPECTATORS, FIRST REUNION OF ROUGH RIDERS, LAS VEGAS, NEW MEXICO, 1899

The Indians, in colorful regalia, vied with the world-renowned regiment in an effort to draw the attention of observers

PLATE XII

Courtesy New Mexico Highlands University, Las Vegas, New Mexico

GOVERNOR THEODORE ROOSEVELT AT THE FIRST REUNION OF THE ROUGH RIDERS, LAS VEGAS, NEW MEXICO, 1899

"The parade started and ended at the fair grounds, where Frank Springer made a speech, presenting Governor Roosevelt with a gold medal and the cowboys gave several exhibitions of riding, racing, and lariat throwing. . . ."—*from* Miguel Antonio Otero, *My Nine Years As Governor of the Territory of New Mexico, 1897-1906* (Albuquerque: University of New Mexico Press, 1940), p. 63.

PLATE XIII

CHAPTER XI

SING THEIR PRAISES TO THE SKY

ONCE WAR was evident, after the declaration and during the months of organization, entraining, fighting, waiting, and mustering out, enthusiastic veterans, volunteers, citizens, and journalists hailed the ensuing events in appropriate song and verse. Stirring words, adapted to old and familiar melodies, heroic odes, and rollicking rhymes were as numerous as Solomon's "thousand and five."

A goodly portion of these poetic efforts concerns Teddy's Rough Riders; but Torrey's men and their supporters were not to be outdone; they, too, rallied to the cause and let their spirits soar in fitting song. Grigsby's troops, too, had their marching airs, one of which, no doubt because of its rhythm and sentiment, the Wyoming volunteers duly appropriated with acknowledged apology. Troops from individual states, such as Colorado and Nebraska, also had their poets and poetic supporters. And, as always, poetic pens dipped into the fountain of the heart, and sentimental words flowed in farewells to sweethearts, a final toast to fair women and glowing wine.

From Oklahoma came a lofty ode, filled with inspiration and patriotism:

ON TO CUBA![1]

On to Cuba, on to Cuba!
   Sound the war note high and shrill,
Rescue from the vulture tyrant
   City, village, plain and hill.
As ye rush against the trocha,
   As ye charge across the plain,
Smite to earth the Spanish coyote;
   Slay! in vengeance for the Maine.

On to Cuba, on to Cuba!
   Valiant Gomez waits your aid,
Save from foul disgrace and famine
   Prisoned mother, wife and maid.
Burst like lightning on the traitors,
   Mow their ranks like ripened grain;
Think upon our slaughtered brothers—
   Martyred heroes of the Maine.

On to Cuba, on to Cuba!
   Drive the warship, point the gun,
Flash the sword, ring out the bugle,
   Wait not till the set of sun;
Bear Old Glory o'er the waters
   Let him gleam from mount and plain,
Succor dying concentrados,
   Wreck our vengeance for the Maine.

Back from Cuba, back from Cuba!
   Proudly march—her people free—

Weyler's scalp a gory token,
  Weyler's scalp a glory token,
Then Columbia grand, victorious
  Through your valor, toil and pain
Shall with those enshrine your mem'ries
  Those who died upon the Maine.

When reports were abroad in New Mexico to the effect that some of the people in the territory were sympathetic toward Spain, Governor Otero participated in a mass meeting which had been called by prominent citizens to refute the disparaging rumors. The Governor was assured of the full support of the people in his charge, and Sam Cary Meek, a loyal veteran of the Civil War, dedicated the following poem to him:

WE ARE COMING, GOVERNOR OTERO![2]

We are coming, Governor Otero, Yea, we're coming on the run
For we've heard the proclamation, that hostilities have begun,
Between this glorious nation and the monarchy of Spain
On behalf of bleeding Cuba, and our battleship, the Maine.

Likewise our noble seamen, who perished in the waves
Of old Havana's harbor; and found their watery graves.
So we're coming, Governor Otero, ten thousand men, or more
Of New Mexico's patriotic sons; to sail for Cuba's shore.

To help chastise a nation of murderers serene
Of women and of children, though governed by a queen.
Lost to every sense of charity, who neither virgins fair
Escape their brutish passions; will God his vengeance spare?

Let patriots from the east and west, and, from the north and
        south,
Make them dance to deadly music, from our cannon's mouth,
And give the Cubans liberty; baptized in patriots' blood,
To bequeath to their posterity; a birthright born of God.

The mounted riflemen of New Mexico composed words to be sung to the tune of an old "stand-by," and on their way to San Antonio the volunteers "serenaded" the various stations they passed en route:

GOOD-BYE, MY LOVER, GOOD-BYE[3]

We cowboy lads are starting out,
   Good-bye, my lover, good-bye.
Just listen to our yell and shout,
   Good-bye, my lover, good-bye.

CHORUS:
   Bye baby, by-low,
   Bye baby, by-low,
   Bye baby, by-low,
   Good-bye, my lover, good-bye.

We left our good, old, happy home,
   Good-bye, my lover, good-bye.
And now we're bound for San Antone,
   Good-bye, my lover, good-bye.

Captain Max is the very man,
   Good-bye, my lover, good-bye.
To lead this brave and western gang,
   Good-bye, my lover, good-bye.

Dewey fixed them on the water,
   Good-bye, my lover, good-bye.
But we will give them something hotter,
   Good-bye, my lover, good-bye.

The martial melody of "Marching Through Georgia" was heard throughout the barracks in the "Cuba Libre Song":[4]

Come on, boys, and all join hands,
   And proudly we will sing,

Just to let the people know,
   That we're the proper thing;
We're among the terrors
   That first to Cuba go,
To face the dirty Spaniards
   Under Blanco.

CHORUS:
   Hurrah! Hurrah!
      Now shout and let all see
   That we are bound that
      Cuba shall be free.
   Shout and raise your voices, boys,
      And raise them once again,
   While we go forward
      To Cuba.

Then with Sergeant Sherman
   Our boys will bravely stand;
And under Captain Luna
   We will fight that dirty band,
Get your guns and saber, boys,
   And ready we will be,
To fight for the Cubans
   And our flag, boys.

The men of the West among the volunteers had been somewhat skeptical concerning the Eastern dudes who were to join their ranks. The fun-loving cowboys, always ready to play a joke on the tenderfoot, made plans accordingly. The dudes, however, proved to be good sports—the "college terrors" went through thick and thin, both in training and in battle, as the following two selections show:

TEDDY'S COLLEGE TERRORS[5]

The laffin' we indulged in when we heerd that them galoots
Of college dudes was comin' shuck the spurs plum off our boots,

Fur it seemed a cranky idee that the Eastern tenderfeet
Could affiliate with cowboys after bein' so elite.
Used to of'n tell each other, with a quite expressive wink,
That we wouldn't do a thing to them, we didn't scurcely think,
An' we passed some resolutions with unanimous accord
Thankin' Teddy fur the fun an' the amusement they'd afford.

Used to work our 'magination fur the picters it would draw
Of the riotous perceedin's when we'd yank the kids to taw,
Of their ridin' pitchin' bronchos, glasses flyin' in the air
An' their eyes a poppin' out'ards with an agitated stare.
Used to think we heerd their panties pattin' on the saddle seat
As the bronchos pounded dinges in the pampas with their feet,
An' we thought we soon'd send 'em back towards the Eastern
    star
In a crippled-up condition incompatible with war.

We was somewhat disappointed, I'll acknowledge, fur to see
Sich a husky lot o' fellers as the dandies proved to be,
An' the free an' easy manner in their bearin' that they had
Sort o' started the impression that they mightn't be so bad.
There was absence of eye-glasses, an' of center parted hair,
An' in social conversation they was expert on the swear,
An' the way they hit the grub-pile sort o' led us to reflect
That our previous impressions mightn't prove so damn correct.

But we shorely looked fur trouble of a quite amusin' kind
When it came to broncho bustin', an' the present undersigned
Done a lot o' chaffy talkin' how we'd see some rattlin' fun
When the buckin' exercises had successfully begun.
We'd selected of a critter that was noted fur his skill
In a treatin' ol'-time riders to an unexpected spill,
An' when one o' Teddy's chickens hit the saddle we all thought
That our mortuary record'ed be started on the spot.

I'm a jidge o' pitchin' hosses, an' admit quite candidly
That the action o' that broncho was a wild surprise to me!
Pitched the polish off the saddle, pitched the hair plum off his
    back,
An' at every wild gyration we could hear his muscles crack!

But that Eastern college feller only smiled an' held his seat
Like a cussed porous plaster till that broncho gave up beat.
An' we switched to the opinion, jidgin' by that sample cuss,
That ol' Teddy's college terrors might be good enough for us.

THE DUDES BEFORE SANTIAGO[6]

They scoffed when we lined up with Teddy,
    They said we were dudes and all that;
They imagined that "Cholly" and "Fweddie"
    Would faint at the drop of a hat!
But let them look there in the ditches,
    Blood-stained by the swells in the van,
And know that a chap may have riches
    And still be a man!

They said that we'd wilt under fire,
    And run if the foeman said, "Boo!"
But a fellow may have a rich sire
    And still be a patriot, too!
Look there where we met twice our number,
    Where the lifeblood of dudes drenched the earth!
The swells who be in their last slumber
    Prove what we are worth!

They laughed when we said we were going,
    They scoffed when we answered the call;
We might do at tennis and rowing,
    But as warriors!—Oh, no—not at all!
Ah, let them look there in the ditches
    Blood-stained by the dudes in the van,
And learn that a chap may have riches
    And still be a man!

The battle at El Caney was vividly portrayed by
John Paul Bocock:

ROUGH RIDERS AT EL CANEY[7]

It was on July the first,
    In the year of '98.

When the shells began to burst
    And the air to palpitate
With the blood and heat and Santiago stenches,
    That a four-eyed man in buff,
With a smile, 't was good to see
    Yelled: "You riders in the rough,
Will you climb that hill with me
    And drive those bloody Dagoes from their trenches?"

Then all the rough riders said, "Yes, sir, we will;
    With the greatest of pleasure we'll charge up that hill;
Wherever there's scrapping, we're bound to be there;
    You lead, and we'll wallop those Spaniards for fair!"

Then the shells began to rain,
    And the Mausers shot to kill,
But the men thought of the Maine
    And they went on up the hill,
A-singing of the "Star Spangled Banner,"
    And they laughed, and shot, and swore
They would climb that hill behind him,
    If they had to swim in gore
And go halves with hell to find him—
    Our Teddy rode in such a handsome manner.

Just then, biff! a bullet knocked over his horse
But Teddy jumped off him, right side up, of course.
And he brandished his sword and went on up that hill,
With a yell that the Spaniards are shaking at still.

O, we swarmed along the crest
    Of the hill of El Caney;
And our bravest and our best
    Shed their blood that fearful day,
But they drove the flying Spaniards all before them.
    And they didn't care a cuss
For a bullet more or less
    And they didn't make a fuss
When they fell and died there, yes—
    With the Star Spangled Banner flying o'er them!

A complete account of Teddy's men, from beginning to end, appeared in a long ballad and also in a roundelay which was sung to the tune of "Irish Fusiliers." The words for the latter were composed by Private Edwin Emerson, Jr., Troop K.

THE BALLAD OF "TEDDY'S TERRORS"[8]

There wus a lovely regiment, whose men was strong and stout,
For some they had diplomas and fer some wus warrants out,
Wood, he wus their Colonel bold, an' Teddy wus his mate;
And they called 'em "Teddy's Lamkins," fer their gentleness
    was great.

Now a good ole man named Shafter says to Teddy and to
    Wood:
"There's a joint called Santiago where we ain't well under-
    stood,
So take yer lamblike regiment, and if you are polite,
I think yer gentle little wags'll set the matter right."

So, when Teddy's boys got movin' and the sun wus on the fry,
And the atmosphere was coaxin' 'em ter lay right down an' die,
Some gents from Santiago who wus mad 'cause they was there,
Lay down behind some bushes ter put bullets through their
    hair.

Now, Teddy's happy Sunday school wus on its way,
A-seekin' in its peaceful style some Dagos fer to slay;
And the gents from Santiago, with aversion in their heart,
Wus hidin' at the crossroads fer to blow 'em all apart.

There's a Spanish comic paper that has give us sundry digs—
A-callin' of us cowards an' dishonest Yankee pigs;
An' I guess these folks had read it, an' had thought 't would be
    immense
Jest to paralyze them lamkins they wus runnin' up agains'.

So, when our boys had pretty near arrived where they wus at,
An' the time it was propitious fer to start that there combat,

They let 'er fly, a-thinkin' they would make a dreadful tear,
An' then rubber-necked ter see if any Yankee wus still there.

Now you can well imagine wot a dreadful start they had
To see 'em still a-standin' there and lookin' bold an' bad;
Fer when this gentle regiment had heard the bullets fly,
They had a vi'lent hankerin' ter make them Spaniards die.

So Teddy, he came runnin' with his glasses on his nose,
An' when the Spanish saw his Teeth you may believe they
    froze;
An' Wood wus there long with 'im, with his cheese knife in
    his hand,
While at their heels came yellin' all that peaceful, gentle band.

They fought them bloody Spaniards at their own familiar
    game,
An' the gents from Santiago didn't like it quite the same—
Fer you plug yer next-door neighbor with a rifle ball or two,
An' he don't feel so robustious as when he's a pluggin' you.

So when the shells wus hoppin', while the breech-blocks clicked
    an' smoked,
An' the powder wouldn't blow away until a feller choked,
That regiment of Yankee pigs wus gunnin' through the bush
An' raisin' merry hell with that there Santiago push.

Then Teddy seen 'em runnin' and he give a monstrous bawl,
An' grabbed a red-hot rifle when a guy had let it fall,
An' fixin' of his spectacles more firmly on his face,
He started to assassinate 'em all around the place.

So, through the scrubby underbrush from bay'n't plant ter tree,
Where the thorns would rip a feller's pants a-shockin' sight
    ter see—
He led his boys a-dancin' on, a-shoutin' left and right,
An' not missin' many Spanish knobs that shoved 'emselves in
    sight.

An' when them Santiago gents wus finished to their cost,
Then Teddy's boys they took a look an' found that they wus
    lost;

An' as their crewel enemies wus freed from earthly pain,
They all sat down to wait fer friends ter lead 'em back again.

That's the tale of Teddy's Terrors an' the valiant deed they
  done;
But all tales, they should have morals, so o' course this tale
  has one.
So paste this idea in yer cage, wotever else you do,
Fer perhaps you'll thank me fer it yet before yer game is
  through;

The soldier boy that wears the blue is gentle-like an' meek.
But I doubt he'll mind the Bible if you soak him on the cheek;
An' should you git him riled a bit, you want ter have a care,
Fer if he ever starts ter fight he'll finish—Gawd knows where!

ROUGH RIDERS' ROUNDELAY[9]

Rough Riders were we from the West,
  Gallant gentlemen the rest,
  Of volunteers the best.
Rallied to the flag at Roosevelt's behest
  To carve our way to glory.

When the Spanish skills and shrapnel burst,
  Our losses were the worst—
  The chaplain even cursed.
"Charge!" cried Col. Roosevelt, and charged the First
  To carve our way to glory.

Our rapid fire tore the Spanish line to bits,
  And scared them into fits;
  Their leaders lost their wits;
Up the hill we went and stormed their rifle pits
  To carve our way to glory.

Intrenched within the pits long we lay,
  By night as well as day,
  Sore at the delay;
In our rear the yellow fever raged at Siboney
  To cheat us out of glory.

When no bloody Spaniards are left to run,
  Cuba will be won,
  Our duty will be done;
Dead and living, every single one
  Has carved his way to glory.

Meanwhile, Torrey's men in Wyoming, also with boots and horses, fitted themselves with appropriate song. "Marching Through Georgia" was also a favorite here:

AS WE GO RIDING WITH TORREY[10]

Now up and cinch your saddle, boys,
  And buckle on your gun,
And when you touch the stirrups
  Let your horse be on the run;
For they tell us down in Cuba
  That we boys will have some fun,
  While we go riding with Torrey.

CHORUS:
  Hurrah! Hurrah! The chorus we will swell.
  Hurrah! Hurrah! It's the cowboys' turn to yell;
  There's a gun for every puncher,
  And we know our leader well,
  While we go riding with Torrey.

Uncle Sam will make a round-up
  On the range across the bay—
He wants a thousand "reps" to go
  With Torrey, so they say,
To handle U.S. irons
  In a systematic way,
  While we go riding with Torrey.

Now, when it comes to riding, boys,
  Our bronchos are the best;
They'll find Wyoming cowboys
  Are all equal to the test;

It's cartridges and guns we want
   And we will do the rest,
   While we go riding with Torrey.

So, boys, we'll make a round-up
   Of the Dons who fired the Maine;
We'll burn the U.S. brand so deep
   'T will not be held by Spain;
And on Wyoming's soil we'll meet
   At the home ranch once again,
   While we go riding with Torrey.

When a banner was presented to Torrey's troops at Fort Russell, the gratitude of the volunteers was fittingly expressed in a song sung to the tune of "Rally Round the Flag, Boys":

FLAG OF THE TORREY MEN[11]

O the banner of the Torrey men,
   We'll wave it at the front,
   Shouting the war cry of the border.
Its folds shall be upborne
   In the battle's fiercest brunt,
   Shouting the war cry of the border.

CHORUS:
   Flag of the Torrey men,
   Above us let it wave;
   In battle we will carry it,
   Heroically and brave;
   'Neath the banner of the Torrey men
   We'll ride to victory,
   Shouting the war cry of the border.

We'll charge the Spanish foemen
   Wherever they will fight,
   Shouting the war cry of the border.
Those saffron rag defenders

> We'll strike with all our might
> Shouting the war cry of the border.
>
> We have a bold commander,
>   A brave and fearless man,
>   Shouting the war cry of the border.
> Destined to be of the border land
>   The Philip Sheridan,
>   Shouting the war cry of the border.
>
> And when the cause of freedom
>   Triumphant shall have been,
>   Shouting the war cry of the border.
> Untarnished we will bring back
>   The flag of Torrey's men,
>   Shouting the war cry of the border.
>
> Proud veterans of the future,
>   Of three score years and more,
>   Shouting the war cry of the border.
> Shall tell their children how
>   The flag of Torrey's men they bore,
>   Shouting the war cry of the border.

The news that there were not enough horses for the volunteers was distressing to the cowboys. In language not befitting a Sunday school they expressed their views on the matter and were heartily in accord with the Frenchman who said *sans cheval, pas de cowboy;*[12] however, they had volunteered and were ready to do it on foot:

ROUGH RIDERS AFOOT[13]

Teddy's lambs and Torrey's angels, roughest riders on the
    earth,
Play the rattlin' game of wildness up on G fur all it's worth,
Snicker in the face of hardship, snap their fingers at ol' care,
Sit astraddle of their bronchos with a devil-reckless air.

Trained to danger on the ranges, fightin' rustlers well as reds,
Heaven's dome the roof above 'em, nature's prairie grass their
    beds,
Nasty rough-an'-tumble riders on their horses strong an' fleet,
An' they're provin' that they're ditto when a-fightin' on their
    feet.

Never hold no prayer meetin's in their bivouacs at night,
Never do no Bible readin' by the campfire's ruddy light,
An' the language they uncouple from their talkers as a rule
Wouldn't fit in the perceedin's of a Christian Sunday School.
But in patriotic ginger an' in loyalty they stand
In the Uncle Sam procession mighty close behind the band,
An' they're provin' when they haven't got no bronchos fur a
    seat
That they ain't no peaceful cherubs when a scrappin' on their
    feet.

Then hurrah fur Teddy's terrors an' fur Torrey's tigers, too,
Fur the wildest aggregation that's a wearin' of the blue,
Fur the cowboys of the prairie an' the riders of the slope,
Fur the reckless, darin' heroes of the saddle an' the rope!
They have rallied to the colors, an' they'll play a lively hand
In a markin' up the Spaniards with the Yankee Doodle band,
An', although they're short of horses, don't you hesitate to put
Every dollar you're possessin' on the fight they'll make afoot.

The hardships en route to Florida and the disappointment on the part of Torrey's men have been
discussed in a previous chapter. The poetic expression of those same feelings is conveyed in the following selections:

TORREY'S TIGERS[14]

In Panama Park, with its forest of pines,
Where the ground is all covered with bushes and vines;
Where the fierce, burning heat of the tropical sun
Beats down on the head of the innocent one;

Where shoulder-stripes, non-coms, privates, and all,
Must suffer the heat of the fiery old Sol;
There are camped Torrey's Tigers, the pride of the West,
Who are never found wanting when put to the test;
Men who never look back with a tear or a sigh,
But will go into battle to conquer or die.
There are men from the round-up on Wyoming's plains,
Who are ever at home with their hand on the reins,
Utah and Idaho each a troop send,
While far off Nevada comes in at the end.
From rocky Colorado come Troops A and B,
And the skirmish they make it's a caution to see.
They are troops to a finish in all kinds of weather,
And under our leader we'll all fight together.
We have left homes and friends just to join in the fight,
And no one denies that our boys are all right.
For behind Colonel Torrey, so brave and so grand,
Though against all the world, there we'll take up our stand,
And the most gallant colonel that ever drew breath
Will lead us to victory or lead us to death.
With him as our leader we'll never know fail,
And we'll make Cuba warm when we once strike the trail.
We'll remember the boys that went down on the Maine,
Freedom for Cuba and death to old Spain;
And boys, if ever we do march home again,
Let us march home as victors, and show we are men.
We'll remember our leader and give him three cheers
That will shake the whole earth, and deafen Spain's ears.
Then we will know that our troubles are past,
We've fought and we've won, and are happy at last.

TORREY BOYS' LAMENT[15]

When your Uncle Sam called out,
"I want some men,"
We quit all of our positions to go and fight for him;
He sent us down to Jacksonville, but no fighting we have
         seen;
And now the war is over we want to come home again.

CHORUS:
Then it's home, boys, home, it's home you ought to be;
Home, boys, home, in our own country.
For the plains are always healthy, the climate is first rate
In our dear old native country, in old Wyoming state.

Down in this hot country, someone is always ill,
They take you to the doctor and he gives you a quinine pill;
It will either kill or cure you, they don't give a damn;
The doctor has done his duty, you belong to Uncle Sam.

Then it's home, boys, home, it's home you ought to be;
Home, boys, home, in our own country.
Where we never took quinine to make our old head shake,
And we never had a fever in our old Wyoming state.

And now our dear old Col. Torrey,
I think you have heard of him;
A better man than Torrey the country never saw,
And to have him lead us through the war we thought was
    real fine,
But doing garrison duty was never in our line.

Then it's home, boys, home, it's home you ought to be;
Home boys, home, in our own country.
For the plains are always healthy, the climate is first rate,
In our dear old native country, in old Wyoming state.

The rivalry among states to send volunteers was
obvious. Colorado's men were "rarin' to go" and com-
peted with their neighbors to the north:

THE COWBOY VOLUNTEERS[16]

It was told us on the round-up an' discussed in camp at night
That the cowboys of Wyoming were preparin' fur the fight.
That a regiment of riders of the rough-an'-ready brand
At the openin' of trouble would be there to take a hand.
Texas Tom made the suggestion that he wa'n't the sort of cuss
Fur to see the Northern riders jumpin' in ahead of us,

An' he thought it was our duty fur to make a little noise
That'd show the fightin' temper of the Colorado boys.

So we organized a meetin' in the campfire's cheery light,
An' I want to tell you, pardner, that it was a purty sight.
Fur to see the earnest faces of the cowboys payin' heed
While ol' Texas was oratin' on the manner to proceed.
There was forty in the party, every one a nervy chap,
An' when Tex pulled out his pencil an' his brandin' tally book
Every cussed man enlisted but the Mexicano cook.

The election of a captain was the next in order, and
Broncho Jack of Arizony nominated Billy Bland,
Sayin' he was in the army in the Yankee-Rebel muss,
An' his military trainin' ort to come in play with us.
Billy bellered in a second, an' indignantly declined,
Said the officers in battle had to keep away behind
A-directin' of the movements, an' he wa'n't the sort of chap
That'd be away off yonder when the rest was in a scrap.

Every rider on the round-up then was named fur the command,
But there wa'n't a cuss among us'd agree to play the hand,
Each decliner emphasizin' the remark almighty clear
That 't was fightin' he was after, not a sneakin' in the rear.
So we write to Gov'ner Adams fur to send at our expense
A commander out from Denver who had had experience
Fur to do our hidin' fur us when the Dons begun to shoot,
An' we'll surely hit the saddle when we hear the bugle toot.

Before the Colorado troops left Denver to join ranks
with those in Cheyenne, Fred G. Shaffer of the *Times*
editorial staff composed a battle song—another one to
the tune of "Marching Through Georgia." Throughout the state the words were known and sung in schools
and churches:

COLORADO'S BATTLE SONG[17]

We're soldiers from the Silver State
    Centennial boys are we—

We're children of Old Glory
    From a mile above the sea
And all the Sons of Cuba's star
    Forever shall be free
        As we go marching to Cuba!

CHORUS:
    Hurrah! Hurrah! We won't forget the
        Maine!
    Goodbye! Goodbye! Old yellow rag of
        Spain!
    Let us swell the chorus from the mountain
        and the plain
        As we go marching to Cuba!

We'll bear the starry banner
    From the land of Columbine
And plant her on the battlements
    Across the Spanish line
So Cuba's Star may brighter glow—
    Forever may she shine
        As we go marching to Cuba!

Let every son of freedom's cause
    Sing Cuba's glad refrain!
Let subjects of Old Glory
    Sing it o'er and o'er again!
We'll bear our flag to victory
    And bury Spanish reign
        While we go marching to Cuba!

Over in Nebraska, Private Norris was hailed as poet laureate of Company M:

WE ARE THE BOYS OF COMPANY M[18]

We are the boys of company M,
    And we are out of sight
We're for Cuban independence,
    Even if we have to fight.

Although some of us are small,
    We only want a chance
To show Grand Island people
    How to make the Spaniards dance.

For inspiring tunes Grigsby's men chose "There
Will Be a Hot Time in the Old Town Tonight," and
"The Battle Cry of Freedom." The former was very
popular—so popular that Torrey's men appropriated
it!

ODE TO GRIGSBY'S COWBOYS[19]

Come along and get you ready
And bring your good old gun
For the cowboys are a comin'
And there's going to be some fun.
They are comin' on their bronchos
And they are comin' mighty quick
And when they meet those Spaniards,
Well—won't they make 'em sick.

1st Chorus:
When they hear
    Those cowboys comin' in
With Grigsby at their head
    Well—won't they give 'em sin;
    Oh, Yes!
They will give them h——l
    And then they'll rub it in,
There'll be a hot time in Cuba that night,
    My Baby!
When they shoot
    Someone feels a pain;
For they never miss
    And they'll not forget the Maine.
With the "Smoked Yank" in the lead,
    They'll lick the whole of Spain
And there'll be a hot time in Cuba
    that night.

They are comin' from the prairies
And they're coming from the hills,
They are going to free Cuba
And give those Spaniards chills,
They will hang old butcher Weyler
High upon a cypress tree,
And they will drive the Spanish army
Way back into the sea.

Their leader is a soldier
Who doesn't know how to fear,
They are fighting for a cause
Which to patriot heart is dear,
For humanity and justice
To set a nation free,
And when they meet the Spaniards
A hot time there will be.

They are not the best at drilling
And on discipline rather weak,
Their clothes are not the finest
For valets they don't keep;
But when it comes to riding,
Shooting, fighting, anything,
They are the finest of the fine,
So everybody sing.

2ND CHORUS:
　When they hear
　　Those cowboys comin' in
　With a whoop and a yell,
　　While the bullets gaily sing;
　　Oh, My!
　To the Spaniards
　　They won't do a thing
　But drive them off Cuba for good,
　　My Baby!
　When the war is over
　　They'll come home again
　Back to Dakota,
　　To the mountains and the plain.

But before they do
    They'll avenge the sunken Maine,
So three cheers for Grig's cowboys
    tonight.

COWBOYS' BATTLE SONG[20]

Bidding wives and girls adieu,
    We will soon come back to you,
Shouted the farewell cry of cowboys;
    When we avenged the Maine,
    Paying tribute to her slain,
Victory will be the cry of the cowboys.
    With our pistols by our side,
    We are ready for a ride,
Shouting the voice of western cowboys.
    We're the kind that never scare,
    Live on crow or hardtack fare;
We're a band of wild and woolly cowboys.

CHORUS:
    The cowboys are coming, Hurrah boys, hurrah;
    The Spaniards are running, Hurrah boys, hurrah!
        'T will be like a hornet's nest,
        From the wild and woolly west,
    When you hear the whooping of the cowboys.

    We have true Dakota grit,
        That will make a Spaniard "git,"
    When he hears the music of the cowboy.
        He will think Old Nick's inside
        When he sees us shoot and ride,
    Chased by a band of western cowboys.
        We have had a cavalry drill,
        Over western plain and hill,
    Shouting the cattle cry of cowboys.
        We will round the Spanish in,
        While this little song we sing;
    Death to the Spaniard by the cowboy.

We will never know retreat,
For we will go in to defeat,
Spanish, Turk or Devil by the wholesale.
All we capture we will brand
With U. S. for Uncle Sam,
Shouting the battle cry of cowboys.
Starving Cubans we will aid,
With our cavalry brigade,
Shouting the battle cry of cowboys.
While Dewey eats a "Philopene,"
We are anxious to begin,
Shooting the Spanish by the cowboy.

Before departing for the fray, the volunteers, too, had their last fling and raised their toast to wine, women, and song:

Throughout the world two things retain
Their chief supremacy o'er man,
Hot wine that steals away the head,
And lovely woman's lips of red.

Then here's to wine, it is divine,
To it my happy song shall freely start,
But womankind is not behind
Who wins the eye of man, and then his heart.

Thus woman wins, for wine 'tis said,
Hath only power to steal away the head,
While woman holds the better part
Who hath the power to steal away the heart.

Then here's to wine, it is divine,
To it my happy songs shall ever climb,
But higher still my song shall swell
To praise fair woman in wandering rhyme.[21]

Once away, after the day's hardships, the soldiers,

even the roughest and toughest of them, turned their thoughts to the girls they left behind:

A ROUGH RIDER'S LAMENT[22]

I am lying in my tent, Sweet Marie,
And my soul with rage is pent-up in G,
   For I know almighty well you have caught
      another fel,
And your thoughts no longer dwell, love, with me.

When we kissed a last good-bye—tearfully—
You but worked a girlish guy off on me.
   O, you sweet, bewitching jade, what a clever
      game you played,
For your tears were ready made, Sweet Marie.

When I donned the soldier blue, Sweet Marie,
Like a picnic woodtick you stuck to me;
   And a smile you used to wear was as full of
      gleaming glare,
As a sunbeam on a tear, Sweet Marie.

How your cunning head you'd lay—lovingly—
On my bosom, while you'd say things to me;
   There you'd rest in loving pose, right beneath
      my very nose,
Swiping buttons from my clothes, Sweet Marie.

To the Cuban isle I go, Sweet Marie,
Where the tropic sun will glow over me;
   And I'll wander through the hills with the
      dusky Cuban belles,
Who are dressed in beads and shells, scantily.

There your face I'll soon forget, Sweet Marie—
I'll be frisky, you can bet, as a flea—
   I'll be giddy, I'll be gay, I will sing the
      hours away—
Ta-ra-ra-ra boom de-ay! Hully gee!

NOTES TO CHAPTER XI

1. "On to Cuba," *Daily Oklahoma State-Capital* (Guthrie, Oklahoma),
May 6.

2. "We Are Coming, Governor Otero!" *Santa Fe New Mexican* (Santa
Fe, New Mexico), April 29.

3. "Good-Bye, My Lover, Good-Bye," *ibid.*, May 4.

4. "Cuba Libre Song," *ibid.*, May 6.

5. "Teddy's College Terrors," *Denver Evening Post* (Denver, Colorado),
May 21; *Cheyenne Sun-Leader* (Cheyenne, Wyoming), May 23.

6. "The Dudes Before Santiago," *Chicago Daily Tribune* (Chicago,
Illinois), July 12.

7. "Rough Riding at El Caney," *ibid.*, July 13.

8. "The Ballad of Teddy's Terrors," *Rocky Mountain News* (Denver,
Colorado), July 20.

9. "Rough Rider's Roundelay," *Las Vegas Daily Optic* (Las Vegas, New
Mexico), August 26.

10. "As We Go Riding with Torrey," *Cheyenne Sun-Leader* (Cheyenne,
Wyoming), May 21.

11. "Flag of the Torrey Men," *ibid.*, June 14.

12. Paul Coze, *Rodeos de cow-boys et les yeux du lasso* (Paris: Société
française et de librairie d'éditions, 1934), p. 35.

13. "Rough Riders Afoot," *Denver Evening Post* (Denver, Colorado),
July 11.

14. "Torrey's Tigers," *Florida Times-Union & Citizen* (Jacksonville,
Florida), July 31.

15. "Torrey Boys' Lament," *Cheyenne Sun-Leader* (Cheyenne, Wyoming), September 12.

16. "The Cowboy Volunteers," *Denver Evening Post* (Denver, Colorado), April 8.

17. "Colorado's Battle Song," *Denver Times* (Denver, Colorado), June 12.

18. "Glance at Our Neighbors," *Denver Evening Post* (Denver, Colorado), April 8.

19. "Ode to Grigsby's Cowboys," *Daily Argus-Leader* (Sioux Falls, South
Dakota), May 14.

20. "Cowboys' Battle Song," *ibid.*, May 24.

21. "They Sang Songs and Then Went Out," *Denver Evening Post*
(Denver, Colorado), May 17.

22. "A Rough Rider's Lament," *Denver Republican* (Denver, Colorado),
August 23.

CHAPTER XII

CUBA LIBRE!

WITH THE ARRIVAL in Tampa, Florida, the days of the First United States Volunteer Cavalry were numbered. Colonel Wood, who had come there June 1 with the first section of 330 men, was eager for quick action and frankly expressed his sentiments in an interview for the *Chicago Daily Tribune:*

We're here for business and if there is to be any fighting we intend to be in it. This regiment has too much at stake to be left behind. . . . The regiment was organized on the basis of its special fitness for fighting. The eyes of the world are upon us, and we do not intend to disappoint our friends. There has been some talk of splitting up our regiment into battalions, but we will insist on fighting as a body. Of course we would not disobey direct orders, but we will resist every effort to split the regiment.

We also want to do our fighting on horseback; that is the way our men have been trained to fight, and that is the way we can do the most execution. There is not a man in the regiment who has not made a name for himself in a quiet way. It is a good body of men, the like of which the world has never furnished before. There are 960 men in the regiment, and we bring 1,000 horses and 200 mules, with 36 pack trains. We are ready this instant. We have no time for camp life or child's play, as our men are as hard as iron. We want action.[1]

The men of the regiment, however, did not share the enthusiasm of Colonel Wood. They had not lost their taste for war, but they were dirty, tired, and hungry after the five-day trip from San Antonio, an arduous one punctuated with unreasonable delays, faulty arrangements, and poor accommodations. In Florida, without due consideration of the hardships they had endured, they were, so to speak, dumped off at Ybor City—several miles from Tampa and the camping grounds. Here the horses, who had likewise suffered, were unloaded and fed; then the whole company, dispirited and with little attempt at troop formation, began the eight-mile trek to the camp site.

The troopers had traveled through the poorest sections of the country, and the sight on reaching Tampa, with its dirty, tumbling shacks and desert wastes, was no more inspiring. The camp, formerly the drill ground for the Sixth Cavalry and located only a short distance behind the Tampa Bay Hotel, was hot, damp, dirty, and infested with insects. According to reliable sources, the troopers were to spend only a few days in the camp before taking off for Cuba; consequently, no effort was made to set up permanent quarters.[2]

After four or five days in these unpleasant surroundings, orders came on the night of June 7 to move on the following morning to the Port of Tampa, the point of embarkation. This order might have caused the low spirits to soar again had not a disheartening report, most unexpected and undreamed of, swept through the ranks. The story was confirmed — the horses, as much a part of these men of the plains as the weapons they carried, were to be left behind, and only eight troops of the entire regiment would proceed now to satisfy their thirst for glory on foreign soil.[3]

Troops C, M, I, and H were detailed to remain in Tampa, and, although these rugged hearts had been hardened by hardships and disappointments on the frontier, the psychological effect of this action was almost disastrous. The fact that they were left behind to care for the deserted horses and mules, to suffer the heat, dirt, disease, and vermin of the camp was serious enough; but, in addition, there was the endless waiting for the call which would rejoin them with their comrades. Several times word came to prepare for the move; but, at the last moment, the orders were countermanded and the long, dreary wait began anew. Here was truly a case of "they also serve who only stand and wait," for these men, too, were heroes and fought a battle, not on enemy soil but a battle against fever and sickness which was greater than that suffered by the Rough Riders in Cuba.[4]

After much delay in leaving camp and many difficulties in finding transportation to the port, the volunteer cavalry finally arrived and boarded the transport—the *Yucatan*. It was crowded and uncomfortable, a situation which became more serious due to an order, received just before sailing time, that the ship be held in port. Consequently, the men remained in harbor almost a week and suffered intense misery in the tropical Florida heat at that time of year.[5]

One Rough Rider, in his reminiscences, complained that they had a bad time from the very first: "The grub was horrible; we had no freshly cooked food for fourteen days. 'Salt horse,' hardtack, one-eighth can of tomatoes, and water coffee constituted a ration. The lack of variety at first made the food disagreeable, then nauseating."[6]

Edward Marshall, in *The Story Of The Rough Riders,* wrote concerning the transport:

. . . the quarters were anything but pleasant. Most of the bunks were in the vessel's hold—and she was a rattle-trap old hulk that had been used in the freight-carrying trade —and they were badly built of rough and unplaned lumber. The work of the contractors who had put the berths up, proved to be so inefficient that many of them fell down when the men piled into them the first night. After that those particular Rough Riders were without beds. At the best, the bunks were so close together that the men could move about between them only with the very greatest difficulty, and when they crawled into them at night they found them so narrow that turning over ordinarily meant splinters in their skins.[7]

Finally, on the evening of June 13, the expedition set sail for Cuba, and the tension and discomfort of the cramped men was somewhat relieved. The transports traveled at the rate of about five to seven knots, and frequently there were long periods during which the ships did not move at all. The delay was due chiefly to the fact that several of the ships pulled scows or lighters which would later move the troops ashore. The speed of the slowest ships set the pace for the whole invasion fleet.[8]

On June 20 the expedition neared the coast of Cuba, remained off Santiago for two days, then landed at Daiquiri "after a heavy bombardment of the coast by several of our men-of-war."[9]

On June 25 and 26 the newspapers of the nation blazed front pages with the ominous news that the American forces had met the enemy in bloody battle. In the Rocky Mountain Empire, the home of the Rough Riders, stark and shocking headlines met the eye:

FIRST BAPTISM OF BLOOD ON CUBAN SOIL. NEW MEXICO VOLUNTEERS IN BATTLE — ENEMY, AL-THOUGH IN STRONG FORCE, COMPELLED TO RE-TIRE — AMERICAN LOSS 60 OFFICERS AND MEN — LIST OF DEAD AND WOUNDED.[10]

TEDDY'S TERRORS DECIMATED BY DON'S FIRE[11]

INTO DEATH'S JAWS MARCHED THE TERRORS[12]

The First United States Volunteer Cavalry met the enemy in battle on June 24, and, according to the dispatches received in Santa Fe, bore the brunt of the fight.

Col. Wood's men, with an advance guard well out in front, and two Cuban guides before them, but apparently with no flanks, went squarely into the trap set for them by the Spaniards and only the unfaltering courage of the men in the face of a fire that would even make a veteran quail, prevented what might easily have been a disaster. . . .

"There must have been nearly 1,500 of us," said Lieut.

Col. Roosevelt . . . when discussing the fight. "They held
the ridges with rifle pits and machine guns and had a body
of men in ambush in the thick of the jungle at the sides
of the road over which we were advancing. Our advance
forward struck the men in ambush and drove them out. . . .

"The Spanish firing was accurate, so accurate, indeed, that
it surprises me; and their firing was fearfully heavy.

"I want to say a word for our own men," continued Lieut.
Col. Roosevelt. "Every officer and man did his duty up to
the handle. Not a man flinched."[13]

As the days passed, more detailed and personal accounts of the landing, march, and the battle at Las
Guasimas reached home. Lieutenant Sherrard Coleman, Troop E, in a letter from the field of action, recounted the first phase of the march:

We left Baiquiri [Daiquiri] at 4 P.M., and by 8:30, by
forced marching reached Juragua, 12 miles distant over a
narrow trail through the Cuban jungle. The temperature
was simply burning and about 20 per cent of the regiment
fell by the wayside from exhaustion, as we had to carry
whatever we wanted on our backs, and three days' rations.[14]

The dismounted plainsmen, unused to marching,
suffered severely under the scorching sun and the torrential tropical rains which plagued their advance to
the front. At intervals they halted to rest—so weary
were the men that they threw themselves to the ground
without removing their packs; sometimes into the fever-
breeding mud and rotting vegetation; at other times,
to the steaming jungle floor alive with insect life. In
camp the first night, stripped of their clothing wet
from sweat and rain, they gathered like strange, white
savages around the campfires to dry their bodies and
garments.[15]

The next morning, June 24, reveille sounded at three o'clock and, two hours later, the Rough Riders were on the march to climb the foothills of the mountains which lay across their path. As they pushed forward, they took a trail which gradually narrowed to a path, winding its way into the tangled interior of the fetid Cuban jungle. This, the third day in Cuba, found them marching Indian fashion in single file at about a four-mile gait. The men now began to discard their rations and blanket rolls—the load proved too great even for these sturdy backs, under adverse conditions.[16]

On this path the advance guard were fired on from ambush—they had pushed into the enemy's fortified position and were caught in the cross fire of Mauser rifles and batteries of rapid-fire guns. The situation became even more serious and terrifying because the Spaniards used smokeless powder, and the troopers could not locate the enemy position. For a time they feared they were victims of the fire from their own men.[17] One officer ran forward, shouting, "For God's sake stop! You are killing your own men! You are supporting the firing line." The troopers were horror-struck, and a groan swept the ranks.[18]

Lieutenant Coleman gave a vivid picture of those first moments of fear and confusion.

. . . We were raked by a terrible fire and held our men under excellent control by making them lie down flat on the ground, and well did they stand firm.

It was terrible. The bushes were cut to pieces, but we had only one man wounded, . . . and none killed. We captured several Spaniards, who said they did not understand the Americans, since they did not retreat from the heavy fire, but "kept on coming."[19]

Information from several reports indicated that about nine hundred Americans were pitted against the superior numbers of four thousand Spaniards. While the main forces of the invading army were behind this advance group, they never reached the scene of battle until it was over. The fight lasted about two and a half hours, and almost all Rough Riders were hit, either on their person or on their clothing —hats, leggings, canteens, knapsacks, and, blanket rolls all displayed gaping holes. The losses in this engagement were nine killed, thirty-three wounded, and nine missing.[20]

Lieutenant Coleman concluded his letter with a note of sadness and concern:

We are now burying the dead. Poor boys; the tears will come as taps is sounded, but such is the fortune of war. It is a wonder we were not all cut to pieces. It was a complete ambuscade and the Cubans all disappeared at the first shot. Lieutenant Will Griffin will probably reach us today with rations. We have nothing left. All of us are well except that we are tired. Everything I have on, even at this hour, is soaking wet, nothing but sweat, sweat, until you think it will never stop.[21]

Immediately following the fight, the wounded were cared for in a small field hospital on the edge of the battlefield, under a large mango tree whose spreading and protective branches were the only covering for the wounded and dying. During the first twenty-four hours following the battle, the doctors worked feverishly to relieve the suffering; men were detailed to bury the dead as rapidly as possible in order to prevent mutilation by the loathsome land crabs and vultures which infested the island.[22]

Meanwhile, the troopers set up a makeshift camp about two miles from the battlefield to supply a shelter for the men and especially replacements for the blankets which had been discarded during the march. The lack of suitable quarters became more apparent as the rainy season advanced upon the encamped troopers. What tents there were offered little protection against the recurring, violent electrical and tropical rainstorms. Pitched in a hollow, where the torrential downpour formed a small lake, the tents soon became sodden masses of canvas in a mire of mud and putrefying vegetation—a perfect culture for the tropical fevers which were soon to appear among the troopers. Added to these discomforts was the dangerous location of the camp, which was within two thousand yards of the Spanish trenches.[23]

Not only did the men suffer from the lack of protection, the climate, the scourge of fever and vermin, but the commissary service was wretched. Tons of food and supplies still remained on the transports in the bay. The logistical branch of the invading army broke down and retarded the movement of supplies and rations to such an extent that the men were reduced to one third of their normal rations which consisted of bacon, hardtack, and coffee without sugar. This not only taxed the physical endurance and strength of the men, but also lowered their morale. More devastating, however, and probably the severest test to which they were put, was the absolute lack of tobacco, a trial which aggravated the serious situation to major proportions.[24]

Under such cheerless and disheartening conditions the troopers lived for several days before they received orders to move toward Santiago. They had passed though their first baptism of fire, buried their dead, cared for their wounded, and suffered unbelievable discomforts; yet, without a murmur, they took to the narrow, muddy trail which led through dank jungles and sapped their strength with every step. On the last day of June they advanced to El Poso, not far from the Aguadores River.[25]

When sickness overtook General Wheeler and General Young, the cavalry division was placed under the command of General Sumner. Under this change, Colonel Wood became a brigadier general and assumed the command of Young's brigade; Lieutenant Colonel Roosevelt was promoted to a colonelcy and, of course, took command of the First United States Volunteer Cavalry.[26]

On the morning of July 1, the Rough Riders were stationed in the yard of the farmhouse at El Poso, about a hundred yards from an American battery which had drawn up ahead of them to shell San Juan. It was indeed a precarious position, for the heavy pall of black smoke, hovering over a battery after each firing, furnished an excellent target for the gunners of the enemy.[27]

The men were at breakfast when the first American shell made a direct hit among the Spanish. This cheering sight brought the troopers to their feet with lusty shouts and yells of joy. Their rejoicing had not yet subsided when they heard the enemy's answer—a missile of metal screaming as it hurtled through the air— then the terrific explosion in their midst. The horror of this catastrophic happening sent them temporarily to flight and cover; but, before they could find protection, two of their members were dead and seven were badly mangled. A second battle for the Rough Riders had begun.[28]

After recovering from the shock of being under heavy fire, the troopers regrouped for orders to move. During this morning they had watched many regiments move forward and, two hours after their nerve-shattering experience, they were ordered to follow the advancing regiments. Once again they took to the narrow, muddy trail through a maze of underbrush. An hour later they were within the zone of Spanish fire —unaware of the enemy weapons on either flank—an easy and helpless prey to sharpshooters and guerrillas. Due to one of the many military blunders which seemed to characterize the Cuban campaign, they were caught in the enemy fire as they crossed a stream in an open area. Colonel Roosevelt tried to extricate his men, but the constant fire held many waist deep in the stream. Finally, they shifted to the right of the trail to a near-by wood where they remained, still under Spanish fire, awaiting further orders to advance.[29]

Action did not come until midday; in fact, the order for advance never did come. Several regiments lay between the Rough Riders and the objective, San Juan. The Ninth Regiment, consisting of colored troops, was directly in the troopers' path, and the obviously serious situation became almost hopeless when the leadership of the campaign at top levels disintegrated, and decisions had to be made by the immediate commanders of the regiments. Since orders to move the Ninth Regiment forward were not forthcoming, Roosevelt realized that the enemy position had to be taken in order to prevent disaster for the invading forces. Moving his men to the rear of the Ninth Regiment, he demanded passage for his troops through the stalled ranks. As he and his men advanced, they were soon followed by the men of the Ninth and two companies of the Seventy-First of New York.[30]

An interesting incident which supposedly took place between a member of the Ninth Regiment and one of Roosevelt's Rough Riders was told and retold. The two were discussing the possibility of meeting the foe: "We'll be with you," said the colored soldier. "All right, old man," returned the cowboy, "but we'll lead you a hell of a hot dance." "Never you mind that, boy," said the colored man, displaying a whole quarry of gleaming teeth. "We can stand the heat, and we'll be right up there when the lead begins to sing."[31] And they were!

This first unordered advance proceeded up a small hill, located between the American army and San Juan Hill. Later, the men appropriately named it "Kettle Hill" because the first sight that met their eyes, on reaching the crest, was a number of large sugar kettles. The ascent of "Kettle Hill" progressed under deadly fire, and probably more men of the First United States Volunteer Cavalry lost their lives here than on San Juan—the hill which gave the battle its name. The men, tired and worn from the climb and the heat, broke ranks and straggled singly to the top—a prudent course of action which saved many lives since the Spanish fire was much more deadly to group formation.[32]

Their ears ringing with the words of Colonel Wood, "Don't swear, ——— ——— it, shoot!"[33] the troopers swarmed over "Kettle Hill," the Spanish gave ground, and Roosevelt and his men drove them down the declivity separating the two hills. Meanwhile, the charge of the Rough Riders had electrified the entire army, and at least a half-dozen regiments joined in the push. The sun, the din, the tremendous strain of muscle, and enemy fire all took their toll of the men's strength as they moved forward and upward, never halting until they reached their goal, the top of San Juan Hill.[34]

Death, backed by grim courage but futile determination, waited alone on the summit. The trenches were literally full of crushed defenders. But the foul apparition in its stark realism faded away in the background as the silken banners of the regiments and the Stars and Stripes unfolded and broke into the wind, while the cheers of the victorious troopers echoed and re-echoed through the hills and valleys.

The battle was over. The men relaxed and recounted their experiences, not only to one another but also in letters to the folks at home. And, in true soldierly fashion, in spite of the danger and tragedy involved, the volunteers had their souvenirs which in later years would adorn their walls and be objects of admiration for family and friends. "I have several relics which I will try to bring home: an officer's machete, pieces of Spanish money, neckties and even wine. We captured whole barrels of rum and wine, which the colonel ordered destroyed. . . ."[35]

NOTES TO CHAPTER XII

1. "Want To Be in the Fighting," *Chicago Daily Tribune* (Chicago, Illinois), June 3.

2. Marshall, *Rough Riders*, pp. 50-53.

3. Theodore Roosevelt, "The Rough Riders," *Scribner's Magazine*, XXV (February, 1899), 144-49; "Cowboy Cavalry Afloat," *Denver Republican* (Denver, Colorado), June 10. See *Letters from Theodore Roosevelt to Anna Roosevelt Cowles, 1870-1918* (New York: Charles Scribner's Sons, 1924), p. 216.

4. Marshall, *Rough Riders*, pp. 53-54.

5. Theodore Roosevelt, "The Rough Riders," *Scribner's Magazine*, XXV (February, 1899), 144-49; "Cowboy Cavalry Afloat," *Denver Republican* (Denver, Colorado), June 10.

6. "The Fight of the Rough Riders," *Outlook*, LX (September 3, 1898), 19.

7. Marshall, *Rough Riders*, pp. 56-57.

8. Richard Harding Davis, *The Cuban and Porto Rican Campaigns* (cited hereafter as Davis, *Campaigns*) (New York: Charles Scribner's Sons, 1898), p. 90.

9. "The Fight of the Rough Riders," *Outlook*, LX (September 3, 1898), p. 19.

10. *Santa Fe New Mexican* (Santa Fe, New Mexico), June 25. See "Rough Riders Win Their Spurs," *Denver Republican* (Denver, Colorado), June 25; "Full Details of Bloody Battle near Santiago in which Western Rough Riders Took Such a Prominent Part," *ibid.*, June 26; "Col. Roosevelt's Western Riders Show Their Mettle," *ibid.*; Richard Harding Davis, "The Rough Riders Fought Bravely," *ibid.*; "Heroic Fighting By the Rough Riders," *ibid.*; "The Battle of Las Quasina," *ibid.*, June 27.

11. *Rocky Mountain News* (Denver, Colorado), June 25.

12. *Denver Evening Post* (Denver, Colorado), June 25. See "Spaniards Fought Like Apache Indians," *ibid.*; "In to Death's Jaws Marched the Terrors," *ibid.*, June 26; "Dizzy from Heat and Famishing for Water," *ibid.*, June 27; Richard Harding Davis, "Americans Bluff Won the Day," *ibid.*, June 28; "Teddy's Terrors Talk of Their Baptism of Fire," *ibid.*, June 29.

13. "Engagement at Las Quasina," *Santa Fe New Mexican* (Santa Fe, New Mexico), June 29; "The Battle of Las Quasina," *Denver Republican* (Denver, Colorado), June 27.

14. "Las Quasina," *Santa Fe New Mexican* (Santa Fe, New Mexico), July 8.

15. James Morgan, *Theodore Roosevelt: the Boy and the Man* (New York: Grosset & Dunlap, 1919), p. 129.

16. "Las Quasina Battle," *Santa Fe New Mexican* (Santa Fe, New Mexico), July 8.

17. *Ibid.*

18. "The Fight of the Rough Riders," *Outlook*, LX (September 3, 1898), p. 20.

19. "Las Quasina Battle," *Santa Fe New Mexican* (Santa Fe, New Mexico), July 8.

20. *Ibid.*

21. *Ibid.*

22. Marshall, *Rough Riders*, pp. 132-33, 138.

23. *Ibid.*, pp. 127, 156, 158.

24. Davis, *Campaigns*, p. 177; Marshall, *Rough Riders*, pp. 158-59; "Spaniards Driven to Bay at Santiago," *Denver Republican* (Denver, Colorado), July 1.

25. Davis, *Campaigns*, p. 173; Marshall, *Rough Riders*, pp. 169-70.

26. Marshall, *Rough Riders*, p. 169.

27. *Ibid.*, p. 173.

28. *Ibid.*, pp. 174-75.

29. *Ibid.*, pp. 180-81.

30. *Ibid.*, pp. 185-86, 187. For criticism of General Shafter see Marshall, *Rough Riders*, pp. 180-88, 214-15; Richard Harding Davis, "Shafter Was Two Miles Away," *Denver Evening Post* (Denver, Colorado), July 7; "Some One Has Blundered," *Denver Republican* (Denver, Colorado), July 7.

31. "Colored Soldiers Are Brave Fighters," *Florida Times-Union & Citizen* (Jacksonville, Florida), July 8.

32. James G. Bennett, "Americans Assault Outworks of Santiago De Cuba," *Denver Republican* (Denver, Colorado), July 2; Davis, *Campaigns*, pp. 193-94.

33. "Don't Swear, But Shoot," *Denver Evening Post* (Denver, Colorado), July 2; "Colonel Roosevelt's Western Riders Show Their Mettle," *Denver Republican* (Denver, Colorado), June 26; [Editorial] *ibid.*, August 9.

34. "Friday's Desperate Fight," *Rocky Mountain News* (Denver, Colorado), July 3; "Harvest of Death on the Battle Field," *Denver Evening Post* (Denver, Colorado), July 3; "Shafter's Guns Still Pouring Shot and Shell into Santiago," *Denver Republican* (Denver, Colorado), July 3; Davis, *Campaigns*, pp. 197-98.

35. "Las Quasina Battle," *Santa Fe New Mexican* (Santa Fe, New Mexico), July 8.

CHAPTER XIII

TORREY SOJOURNS IN THE SOUTH

Down south, at Panama Park, Jacksonville, Florida, the Second United States Volunteer Cavalry was enjoying a well-deserved rest after the harrowing experiences of the trip from Cheyenne to the southern encampment. During those first days the troopers had considerable freedom, partly to restore their badly shaken morale resulting from the series of accidents encountered, and also to allow enough time for acclimation to the heat of midsummer in Florida.[1]

The camp was located in an attractive part of the park; tall pine trees towered overhead and, in all directions, magnolias and palms met the eye. The location, though five miles from the city, was only a half mile from the sea and afforded easy access for swimming. Each of the eight-foot, wall-type tents accommodated

four troopers; the circular tents, brought from Colorado, were used by the officers and as headquarters.
Shower baths were rigged up for each troop behind
the trees and bushes—a most welcome convenience
which added considerable comfort to camp life in the
sticky, hot climate. Artesian wells supplied drinking
water which, though practically impalatable because
of the sulphur taste, was considered very healthful.
Because of the extreme heat, orders were issued early
in July to dispense with the wearing of unnecessary
clothing, although a letter from Captain Davis reported
that the heat of the region did not have as bad an
effect on the men as had been expected; they were
getting along very comfortably and all were well. According to Surgeon Major Mortimer Jesurun, the
health of the Torrey cavalry was "singularly good."[2]

The fact that it was the rainy season in the South
soon dispelled these first favorable impressions, and
the rain came every day, with no perceptible change
of temperature. The slightest exercise caused the men
to perspire excessively, and, except for extreme down-
pours, the sides and the tent flaps were kept rolled
up to allow every possible breath of air. Fortunately,
the camp was located on sand, and the water disappeared as rapidly as it fell.[3]

At the end of the first week the men were drilling
three hours and a half a day. This was rather difficult because of the heat and the lack of first-class
drill grounds for cavalry work. Only a few places were
cleared of pine trees; stumps of fallen or burned trees,
which lay hidden in the bushes, proved to be dangerous obstacles. Yet, from a practical standpoint, the

situation offered an opportunity to work under conditions comparable to those in Cuba or Puerto Rico.[4] In the second week, conditions were no better; but the hearts of all grew lighter and the future looked rosier when it was announced that new canvas uniforms and the paymaster were coming.[5]

However, for those in command, affairs were not so pleasant. Many details evolved from the aftermath of the Tupelo wreck, all of which demanded immediate attention. Following the accident, Lieutenant Matt R. Root had remained with the injured until the serious cases were able to be moved to the railway hospital in Kansas City, while those who had recovered sufficiently rejoined the cavalry in camp.[6]

The bodies of those who lost their lives had been interred in burial plots in Tupelo. Relatives of the dead urged their respective congressmen to procure permission to move the bodies; consequently, two months after the accident, Representative John E. Osborne of Wyoming had completed the necessary negotiations with the authorities in Tupelo and now sought the approval of the Department of War.[7]

Colonel Torrey, however, had other plans. Originally, he had expressed his intention to erect a monument in memory of the men in the Tupelo cemetery, but later the following announcement was made:

The colonel has now concluded to have the bodies of the brave volunteers carried back to rest in the soil of their own western homes. In the late fall the bodies will be disinterred, placed in steel caskets and taken to Fort D. A. Russell, and there buried side by side in the Soldiers' cemetery. Over them the colonel will place a monument, on one side of which will be carved the names of the patriots, and on the other side an inscription reciting the manner of their death, and that they died without a murmur serving their country. In this inscription will not be forgotten the kind people of Tupelo, who did all humanity could to sooth them in their dying hours. Should relatives prefer to bury their own at any place other than Fort Russell, they will be at liberty to do so. In any event the monument will contain the names of all the dead.[8]

The railway company immediately began investigations in reference to adjustments and sent an agent who, with Colonel Torrey, interviewed all claimants.

. . . The highest amount agreed upon in any one case . . . was $150, and all who were confined to the hospital will not receive less than $100. All of these amounts are small, as it is a matter of compromise to avoid litigation. . . . Damages on account of deaths have not been yet touched upon, nor has there been any agreement as to individual property losses.[9]

Meanwhile, Colonel Torrey, who had been bruised and shaken up in the wreck, took rooms at the Windsor Hotel to facilitate medical care of his injuries. Here he granted an interview concerning his welfare:

It turns out that I had a most miraculous escape from death. When the shock came the caboose simply disappeared and the engine ran about two-thirds through my car. The part of the end where I stood was broken to pieces and carried forward. The noise of escaping steam and breaking timbers was simply awful. A portion of the side car fell out, allowing me to spring from the wreck and scramble up the embankment. There was a cut across my nose. My left hand and wrist were bruised and a piece of broken glass was taken from one of my fingers. My left arm was punctured in a couple of places. Slivers came so near piercing my neck that they made indentions on my collar. . . . Bruises and scars covered my feet and legs. The corps surgeon reported my condition to General Fitzhugh Lee and in a very considerate letter he recommended that I relinquish command and come to Jacksonville for treatment, which I did.[10]

Actually, his feet were so badly bruised and crushed by falling debris that he was unable to bear his weight upon them. His 230 pounds, in this respect, were a disadvantage. Later, X-rays showed that no bones had been broken but, on one foot, they were pressed tightly together. The capillaries were badly crushed and the ligaments were torn, the severity of which could not be determined by means of X-ray pictures. The swelling gradually disappeared, but, for several weeks, the Colonel was unable to walk. The physician, however, assured him of an ultimate complete recovery.[11]

On July 12 he was able to make his first visit to the cavalry. Accompanied in an ambulance by United States Senator George L. Shoup, Idaho, the party arrived at the camp in a downpour. When it was made known that Colonel Torrey was in camp, the troopers stormed Major Harbord's quarters and cheered lustily for their leader. One trooper, who had been injured at Tupelo, hobbled through the wet underbrush from the hospital to see him. Before returning to the Windsor Hotel, Torrey ordered the ambulance to be driven near the hospital tent where the men injured at Tupelo and other sick troopers rushed to the vehicle to greet him. "They seemed to forget their own injuries in their anxiety to learn of the Colonel's welfare."[12]

At various times the regiment was inspected and

reviewed by visiting army officers and United States officials. On one occasion when Major B. H. Cheever, general inspector of the United States volunteers, was expected to appear, the troopers spent considerable time in cleaning up their equipment, only to have it drenched by the heaviest rain that fell during their stay in camp. The Major, however, expressed sincere satisfaction with the appearance, discipline, and drill of the men, and "even went so far as to volunteer the information to Major Wheeler that it was the best regiment he had yet inspected."[13] On July 13 the Torrey regiment paraded through Jacksonville to be reviewed by General Fitzhugh Lee, Senator Shoup, and Colonel Torrey. The review point was the piazza of the Windsor Hotel, Lee's headquarters. Officers of the Seventh Division, members of the Cuban junta, and the elite of Jacksonville society were also in attendance. Immense crowds lined the streets. Led by a platoon of mounted police, the regiment, with drawn carbines, passed the reviewing stand and presented "a splendid appearance."[14]

Some time later, after reviewing the regiment, Brigadier General L. F. Hubbard, Third Division, Seventh Army Corps, issued the following statement:

I reviewed the Torrey cavalry to-day. I had four years' experience in the war of the rebellion and have seen very many cavalry regiments. I never saw as fine a body of cavalry as the Torrey regiment. Its maneuvering was perfect in every detail and their horsemanship is simply wonderful. There was nothing to call for the least adverse criticism and I have only words of praise for officers and men alike. It is an organization that, if opportunity offers, will, I am sure, do great credit to the volunteer army.[15]

Much concern was evidenced as to whether or not Torrey's men would have an opportunity to take part in the fighting. Two weeks earlier, information from Washington had caused the *Rocky Mountain News* to speculate concerning the future of both the Second and Third United States Volunteer Cavalries. While Roosevelt's Rough Riders had achieved victory and glory in Cuba, the Torrey and Grigsby regiments languished in camp without a prospect of getting into action. Speculating on the possbility of the Torrey regiment being sent to Puerto Rico, because it was rumored that the expedition for that war zone was to be made up of troops then in Jacksonville, the correspondent saw little hope that the Grigsby men would see war since they had been sidetracked in Camp Thomas. Prophetically, the *News* explained:

Letters received here from officers and men of both these cavalry commands show great impatience. They are fearful that all the honors of war for independent cavalry will go to the Roosevelt riders, and that the Second and Third regiments will never smell powder. The colonel of the First Volunteer cavalry has already earned the single star of a Brigadier. Roosevelt has become a full colonel and there have been promotions all along the line. The fact that the other cavalry regiments have had no chance and are not likely to get any, is proving very vexatious and earnest appeals have been made to senators and other influential public men to get these regiments ordered to Cuba. . . . But proofs are accumulating that the war depratment does not regard cavalry as essential, or even useful, at the front. It is pointed out that the Roosevelt regiment has done no work mounted, but has operated entirely as dismounted cavalry.[16]

Several days had passed without rain, and the weather continued to grow hotter as the summer advanced.

During the third week of July, even the natives complained of the insufferable heat, and finally the army physician advised less drill for both men and horses.[17] By this time the first wave of enthusiasm for Florida and camp life had receded, and letters written home by the troopers reflected the change in spirit. One trooper wrote: "This is the 'sunny south' sure enough. Sometimes I think there are two suns here. I would give a month's pay for just a breath of Wyoming air. You ask how far it is to hell, and they say, 'Just 2 blocks south.' " The drinking water which, he vowed, smelled like rotten eggs, brought forth this comment: "It may be healthy, but I can't go it. I have eaten about 2 dozen lemons to keep off chills and fever. . . . Oh, Lord, how we do sweat! And the horses look as if they had lost the last friends they had on earth. . . ." Concluding his letter, he added, hopefully, "We are all praying for an Indian outbreak so we can have a chance to fight savages in the cool mountains of the Rockies."[18]

The *Sun-Leader's* special correspondent bragged:

We are all well and happy. We have knocked out the infantry here entirely. The ladies . . . God bless them . . . just dote on the Torrey cavalry. In a contest of love, I'll back a common trooper of the Second United States volunteer cavalry against anything that goes afoot short of a brigadier general.[19]

J. T. Orr, a Wyoming boy, loyal to the fairest flowers of his state, wrote in a lighter vein: "The girls of the sunny south I have failed to see beauty in, so say all Torrey's rough riders. We have seen none to compare to Wyoming girls, and especially the university girls." In a more nostalgic mood he concluded, "While we are living on sowbosom and hardtack, bathing in salt water and sleeping in tents, we will think of you and our pleasant days in Wyoming."[20]

Another trooper mentioned the incessant rains, the leaking tents, the myriads of insects, and particularly tarantulas, but vouched that the boys were happy, regardless.

. . . Our horses are tied to a rope stretched in front of our line of tents, where they stand when not under the saddle, with their backs humped up to the rain. The "natives" look upon the "cowboy" regiment with much suspicion, and are in mortal dread of a pay day, for fear we shall shoot out the lights and kill or otherwise mutilate the whites and blacks.[21]

Like other volunteer regiments, the Torrey cavalry had the same opportunity to patronize the negro vendors of pies, fruits, and melons who infested the camps; however, by the time payday rolled around and they could afford such luxuries and commit the fatal error of indulgence, a canteen had been established and the competing vendors were shut out.[22]

Nevertheless, payday is a heyday, especially for the man in uniform:

The Saturday after pay day is the harvest in Jacksonville. The appearance of Bay street all afternoon and until late [that night] can be no better described than by liking it to an immense fair, with every store thrown wide open and blazing with lights. The boys in blue swarm the streets and jam the stores, anxious to part with their brand new scrip to supply their needs. To see a soldier with no packages under his arm denotes that he has not yet found the store he is after.

Most of the money spent goes for small articles of clothing

and to replenish the larder of private messes. Almost every one buys some small souvenirs to send home. Northern friends of soldiers at Jacksonville may view with just suspicion a small, narrow, perforated box which they receive by express. Ten chances to one it contains a live alligator, for baby "gators" are the favorite souvenirs. Many of the volunteers are sending home oranges, wood novelties, and Florida photographs. Drafts and express orders are flying by mail to all sections of the country, from New Jersey to Nevada. The Western cavalries have been conspicuously absent from the busy mart. Passes have been generally withheld from the riders all week, but it is believed half the regiment will walk the ancient streets of St. Augustine. . . .[23]

Many of the troopers made the trip to St. Augustine on the Sunday following the first payday, and subsequent excursions were made almost every day, for the railroads offered ridiculously low fares to the soldiers.[24] The excursions were leisurely and popular from the start. Although they were scheduled to leave at a late hour in the morning, any one "who came an hour and a half after that was in ample time to catch the train," and "the ticket office resembled the wheat pit of the Chicago board of trade on Black Friday."[25]

By this time railway accidents and Torrey's regiment were almost synonymous terms. On the return trip of this first excursion the inevitable accident occurred, slight, yet startling, especially to the men who remembered Tupelo. "A coupling broke and the train parted. . . . Considering the fact that the platforms were all packed with soldiers, an accident of this character might have been more serious. . . . It took the train crew something over an hour to solve the simple problem and proceed."[26]

In June a rumor made the rounds at Panama Park, purporting that the good people of Jacksonville had requested General Lee to withhold the soldiers' pay, lest they descend upon the city. Again in July, a similar source reported that the mayor of Jacksonville had requested Lieutenant Colonel Cannon, commander of the cavalry regiment, to refuse his men permission to visit the city because the citizens, though loyal, were not exactly fearless and were concerned about the rough character of the horsemen. This rumor finally reached the ears of the mayor, who emphatically denied it, branded it as false, and paid the Westerners the highest compliment:

I never was so surprised at anything in my life. The story is absurdly false, for I have the highest regard for the rough riders. Those I have seen have particularly impressed me with being troopers away above the average. I know that I voice public sentiment without a single exception, when I state that there are no soldiers more welcome to the city than the rough riders. No other troops here awaken more interest in the people than this gallant cavalry regiment, who, since they have been here, have not had a single man arrested by our police. In fact, these rough riders are a most splendidly behaved and disciplined regiment, and how such a cruel rumor could have gotten started I cannot comprehend.[27]

Soon after the arrival of the cavalry in Florida, a controversy developed over the relative merits of the saber and the revolver as weapons for the regiment. Earlier, Major B. H. Cheever had recommended the saber, although Colonel Torrey was opposed to its use since he felt that too much time would be necessary to acquaint the men with it and, seemingly, the need for such was highly improbable. The *News* aired both pro and con arguments:

In the last two wars, by which the present must be gauged, our civil war and the Franco-Prussian war, the saber is said to have demonstrated its effectiveness in modern warfare, furthermore it is a weapon for close fighting, and only cumbers when carried by men who have to fight an enemy armed with guns that carry a mile away with accuracy. Its opponents argue that in close quarters the reloading of six-shooters is too precarious to depend upon and the saber is always ready and a cavalryman is no cavalryman without one clanking by his side.[28]

However, in the *Florida Times-Union & Citizen,* the controversy waxed hot. A proponent of the flashing steel weapon, who wrote under the *nom de plume* "Sabreur," gave a long discussion on the value of the saber and scathingly concluded:

. . . And now to particularize—who knows the Second United States Volunteer Cavalry are all good shots when the rolls show clerks, lawyers, doctors, carpenters, engineers, sailors, reporters, teachers, and preachers among them, as well as range riders. Who supposes a horse will permit a revolver fired off of him and then object to a saber securely strapped to a saddle or held in the rider's hand, and as for the time, would not time be better employed in learning the saber than in facing kinetoscopes and cameras, or rehearsing for some theatrical performance with Government horses in violation of army regulations, and to the disgust of those who enlisted to go to war, and want to face something even more deadly than the camera, and as between sabers and typewriters favor the former.[29]

The argument continued for several days in the Jacksonville newspaper under the "People's Forum" column. Such responses as "A Word to Cowboy," "Revolvers vs. Sabers," "The Cavalry Saber's Use," "Cowboy Gets It Again," "War Clubs vs. Revolvers and Sabers" appeared almost daily; but, eventually, the subject became less interesting and gave way to other diversified bits of news concerning the regiment.[30]

The most interesting news that struck the camp in mid-July and reached major proportions in the Rocky Mountain Empire was the rumor that Colonel Torrey was negotiating to bring the onetime nationally famous Dodge City Cowboy Band to the camp. This illustrious group of musicians had originated in 1879 at Dodge City, Kansas, under the leadership of Chalk Beeson, and had enjoyed numerous appearances at various fairs and cattle conventions. In addition, invitations had taken the music-makers on a tour to St. Louis, Kansas City, Chicago, St. Paul, Minneapolis, Denver, and Pueblo, where they were so loudly acclaimed that they were invited to the national capital to take part in the inaugural parade in honor of President Harrison. For some twenty years, success and popularity rode high; then, at the turn of the century, headquarters moved to Pueblo, Colorado, under the direction of Jack Sinclair with whom Torrey now negotiated.[31]

Back in Cheyenne, Lieutenant Gracey, who had been left behind with a detail of men to round up more mounts for Torrey, probably welcomed the order from his chief to proceed to Pueblo and engage the band. The number of members was not to exceed twenty-four—the roster shows sixteen musicians, two principal musicians, a bandmaster, and the chief musician, Sinclair.[32]

The band had a royal send-off in Pueblo. Thousands of people attended the final public concert when the mustering took place, with Lieutenant Gracey administering the oath. Following this ceremony, a beautiful banner on behalf of Pueblo citizens was presented to the group. Later, showered with gifts and well provided with food—the ladies' speciality—the band waved farewell from the train platform, headed for their destination which was artistically displayed on the large floating streamers, "Going to Join Torrey's Rough Riders."[33]

The rousing reception that greeted the famous band upon its arrival in camp resulted in a spontaneous sample of music. The *Florida Times-Union & Citizen,* anticipating many more evenings of entertainment, commented as follows: "This band is one of the very few in the country which is able to furnish the best classes of music while mounted, and the novelty of such an entertainment will be not the least of the many attractions that have made the Second Cavalry a decidedly popular regiment."[34]

The first months of the southern sojourn of Torrey's Terrors were interspersed with much gaiety and merrymaking, which tended to keep the troopers in a happy frame of mind. Every day brought news of interest— the stampede of cavalry horses in Cheyenne, the arrival of Western horses in Jacksonville, the recruitment of additional troops, the court martial of Trooper Coffin, and continued praise of Torrey's Terrors. One particular incident in camp created considerable comment and much hilarity. Sergeant John A. Long, a Torrey volunteer, was tossed by a bronc and evidently removed his trousers to examine his bruises. A fellow trooper, opportunely equipped with a camera, snapped the "barefaced facts" of the victim, secretly made numerous prints, and passed them around in camp. Sergeant Long offered complaint and the pictures were confiscated, but he was arrested and faced court martial, as a result of which he was reduced to the ranks and fined twenty dollars. The *Rocky Mountain News* joshed the prisoner as a rival of Apollo Belvedere and the military court in a story headlined, "Is It Art Or Indecency?"[35]

NOTES TO CHAPTER XIII

1. "Western Boys Lambs," *Rocky Mountain News* (Denver, Colorado), July 1; "Col. Torrey Commands a Brigade," *ibid.*, July 2.

2. *Ibid.*; "Don't Mind the Heat," *Denver Republican* (Denver, Colorado), July 8; "Torrey's Terrors in Camp," *ibid.*, July 10.

3. "Torrey's Terrors in Florida," *Rocky Mountain News* (Denver, Colorado), July 7.

4. *Ibid.*

5. "Torrey Dislikes Sabers," *ibid.*, July 11.

6. "Col. Torrey Commands a Brigade," *ibid.*, July 2.

7. "Would Bring the Bodies Home," *ibid.*, July 8.
Charles Guemmer, Troop L; Samuel Johnson, Cornelius J. Lenihan, Henry S. Mapes, and William B. Wallace, Troop C, were killed in the train wreck at Tupelo. Henry Steltz, Troop C, was fatally injured and died later at Memphis. "Roll of Deceased Patriots," Colonel Torrey's annotated list, as found in his personal signed copy of *Torrey's Rough Riders, Historical and Biographical Souvenir of the Second United States Volunteer Cavalry* (Jacksonville, Florida: Vance Printing Co., 1898).

8. Shaft for Torrey's Dead," *Rocky Mountain News* (Denver, Colorado), July 17. See "Thanks for Tupelo's Aid," *ibid.*, July 18.

9. "Men Collect Damages," *Cheyenne Sun-Leader* (Cheyenne, Wyoming), July 21.

10. "Col. Torrey's Close Call," *Rocky Mountain News* (Denver, Colorado), July 27.

11. "Col. Torrey's Feet Badly Bruised," *ibid.*, July 3; "Torrey Sees His Own Bones," *ibid.*, July 22; "Col. Torrey Shows Improvement," *ibid.*, July 23.

12. "Colonel Torrey Visits His Men," *Denver Republican* (Denver, Colorado), July 13.

13. "Torrey's Men Show Up Well," *Rocky Mountain News* (Denver, Colorado), July 9.

14. "Torrey Cavalry on Parade," *Denver Republican* (Denver, Colorado), July 14.

15. "Praise for Torrey's Men," *ibid.*, July 30.

16. "Cavalry Gets No Gory Fight," *Rocky Mountain News* (Denver, Colorado), July 18

17. "Torrey Sees His Own Bones," *ibid.*, July 22.

18. "Camp Panama," *Cheyenne Sun-Leader* (Cheyenne, Wyoming), July 7.

19. "From Torrey's Cavalry," *ibid.*, July 11.

20. "A Wyoming Boy," *ibid.*, July 28.

21. "From Torrey's Regiment," *ibid.*, July 20.

22. "Western Boys Lambs," *Rocky Mountain News* (Denver, Colorado), July 1; "Torrey's Men Well Equipped," *ibid.*, July 16.

23. "Shaft for Torrey's Dead," *ibid.*, July 17.

24. "Torrey Dislikes Sabers, *ibid.*, July 11.

25. "Outing of Torrey's Men," *ibid.*, July 26.

26. *Ibid.*

27. "Rough Riders Popular," *Cheyenne Sun-Leader* (Cheyenne, Wyoming), July 30.

28. "Torrey's Men Show Up Well," *Rocky Mountain News* (Denver, Colorado), July 9; "Torrey Dislikes Sabers," *ibid.*, July 11.

29. "Cavalry Versus Cowboy," *Florida Times-Union & Citizen* (Jacksonville, Florida), July 20.

30. *Ibid.*, July 18, 19, 21, August 4.

31. Clifford P. Westermeier, "The Dodge City Cowboy Band," *Kansas Historical Quarterly*, XIX (February, 1951), 1-11; "Many Go with Torrey," *Denver Republican* (Denver, Colorado), July 20; *Torrey's Rough Riders, Historical and Biographical Souvenir of the Second United States Volunteer Cavalry* (Jacksonville, Florida: Vance Printing Co., 1898).

32. "The Cowboy Band," *Denver Republican* (Denver, Colorado), July 30; "Torrey's Regiment May Have Band," *Rocky Mountain News* (Denver, Colorado), August 1; "Horses Stampede," *Cheyenne Sun-Leader* (Cheyenne, Wyoming), August 1; "They Will Go," *Colorado Chieftain* (Pueblo, Colorado), August 4.

The membership of the band, as listed in *Torrey's Rough Riders, Historical and Biographical Souvenir of the Second United States Volunteer Cavalry* is twenty. Colonel Torrey's personal copy shows many corrections, in his handwriting, in the spelling of the names of the band members. He also reduces the number to nineteen.

33. "On Their Way to Jacksonville," *ibid.*, August 11.

34. "Cowboy Band," *Florida Times-Union & Citizen* (Jacksonville, Florida), August 4. "The average income of the . . . men in the band is $30 per week, which they have sacrificed in view of their patriotic desires to serve their country and to be with Colonel Torrey's Rocky Mountain Riders." "The Cowboy Band Here," *ibid.*, August 11.

35. *Rocky Mountain News* (Denver, Colorado), July 24, August 1.

CHAPTER XIV

IN CAMP WITH GRIGSBY

WHILE ROOSEVELT and his Rough Riders were climbing, not riding, to glory in Cuba, and the volunteers of the Second Cavalry were basking in the Florida sun, the Third Cavalry was "fenced in" in camp, impatient, restless, disappointed. At Camp Thomas, in Chickamauga, Georgia, Grigsby's men and horses, used to a life on open plain and prairie, suffered severely in the Southern heat, dampness, and the long, constant rains. Added to this discomfort was the lack of military attire. Upon arrival at the camp, only three troops had a semblance of uniforms; none was complete and, consequently, the cowboys of the North aroused the curiosity of the citizens of Chattanooga.[1]

By mid-June, information came that clothing and guns would arrive shortly. Although a requisition for uniforms had been forwarded to the quartermaster immediately, a whole month passed before the regulation attire was distributed. By this time, many of the men presented a sorry-looking lot of soldiers; their clothes were ragged and torn, their shoes barely still covered their feet. Finally, the regulation blue uniforms arrived, with added news of good cheer—white duck uniforms for service in Cuba were forthcoming, and "the cowboys will then probably make the finest appearance of any regiment in the park."[2]

Because of the intense heat, the camp in the woods soon proved to be a very unhealthy spot. A protest to the commanding general concerning the abuse of principles of military hygiene was countered with the reply that *all the open ground must be used for drill purposes.*[3]

It was only a question of days when it became obvious that typhoid fever was rampant and was rapidly reaching epidemic proportions. Herbert Lawrence, Troop E, was the first victim of the disease which the authorities refused to recognize as alarming until almost 50 per cent of the command had been stricken.[4] Naturally, rumors spread not only through the camp, but also throughout the nation. As the epidemic increased, so also did the immensity of rumors, only made more vivid and alarming by lurid and eye-catching headlines in the newspapers. During the last week in August, the *Times* in Chattanooga carried a frightful tale of neglect, suffering, and horror, supplemented by letters and statements from people which resulted in "a recital of facts that will sicken humanity."[5] Such headlines as OUTRAGEOUS NEGLECT, ALL SICK AT CAMP

THOMAS, EVIDENCES OF NEGLECT!, THE INHUMANE NEG-
LECT OF SICK SOLDIERS, were followed by an accumu-
lation of evidence which emphasized the enormity of
the "Criminal Neglect."[6] A gruesome story, one to
sicken and strike the hearts of soldier and civilian alike,
appeared under the headline CROWNING HOSPITAL
HORROR:

Nunns had been sick only five days. He died last Saturday,
and the corpse was given no attention until Monday. No
ice was used; an autopsy had been held, the man being split
open, the flaps of the stomach and bowels laid back. The
body was lying on a cot entirely naked, and was covered
with insects, horribly fly-blown, and maggots were crawling
over the body and out of the eyes and ears.[7]

On one occasion the *Times* gave a long list of the
causes of disease among the troops at Camp Thomas,[8]
and later an observer vehemently commented:

The volunteer hospital system is a disgrace to civilization.
The men are said to die from disease. I say they are being
murdered by this wretched system. I have seen fever patients
with their dry tongues hanging from their mouths, with flies
swarming over their faces, with maggots in their bed sores,
with no medical attention, with no water fit to drink, with
no milk, with no stimulant—simply left to die, and then
lie dead for hours alongside of other sufferers.
It's too horrible to talk about! Tell of Spanish atrocities,
of American massacres, of tortures at the stake, but for God's
sake don't imagine that anything can be more terrible than
the destruction of our volunteer army under the miserable
hospital system. It is even more fearful than Mauser bullets![9]

Major H. Gurdon Fish, the regimental surgeon, reported on several conditions which prevailed in the
camp. Since the water supplied to the camp by pipes

was contaminated, recourse was made to springs which offered a good supply. The officer did not, however, attach too much blame to the water as a carrier of the disease; he was much more concerned about the surrounding sinkholes as breeding places for flies. "Millions swarmed in these pest-holes and then gaily flew to the cook's quarter and fairly covered the juicy steaks and succulent pork being prepared for the table. Without any microscope, traces of fecal matter could be discovered in the tracks of these industrious fellows."

The climate was also considered as a contributory factor. According to Fish, the damp, sultry, hot climate of the South was too great a change for the men from the dry, high altitude of the Northwest. Nightly, a heavy mist enveloped the camp and lasted until sunrise. As one trooper said, "You could smell malaria in the mist." Fish's report also stated that "camp fever" of the malarial genus was one of the most difficult types of sickness which occurred in the park.

The lack of disinfectants and competent nurses was of great concern. Of the latter, he reported:

We had not one trained nurse. Men were detailed from the different troops for this important task and many instances of their fidelity was noticed. It was often a touching sight to see a rough-appearing "cow puncher" administering the tenderest care to the patients, and showing by face and actions almost the anxiety of a mother as she watches her child. Long vigils and most disagreeable work was [sic] required of them, and too much credit cannot be given these brave, rough men for their tireless attention to their "pards."[10]

The men were not only discouraged and downhearted; they were very bitter about the unsanitary conditions and the apparent reluctance on the part of those in command to give a true report. A few weeks later, the *Evening Post* (Denver, Colorado) published an interview with a returning volunteer, under the sensational headline, GAUNT WRECKS OF MAGNIFICENT MANHOOD. The soldier in question, ill, weak, and completely disillusioned about the glory that was never attained, talked freely about the "pest-grounds" at Chickamauga:

> The park is foul—it is offensive to the nostrils for miles in the vicinity. . . . The so-called hospital is filled to its capacity all the time. It's a dreary routine from morning to night and the finest feelings become brutalized. Liberty? We never know what it is. Kindness? We only get it outside of the camp.[11]

The horses and mules of the regiment also suffered from the heat and lack of proper equipment. Bridles and saddles had not yet arrived; this necessitated the use of crude halters, fashioned of wire, which proved dangerous to both the animal and his rider. Some of the horses were broncs that had never been ridden, and many amusing incidents accompanied the "busting" when attempts were made, bareback.

The animals that were brought from the West were affected by the climate, as were the men; those purchased in Eastern and Southern markets frequently had contracted catarrhal fever and distemper in the stockyards before shipment. Dr. Leslie C. Karn, the regimental veterinarian, discovered that one third of the twelve hundred animals under his care were afflicted with influenza, complicated by fever. To prevent an epidemic of the infection, he isolated the more serious cases and, as a result of this precaution, lost only thirty of approximately four hundred animals afflicted with disease. Dr. Karn had great praise for the hardy horse of the North, which, properly acclimated, was "worth two of the Southern horses for military purposes."[12]

Horse funerals were frequent sights during the month of July. The virulence of the disease made immediate burial imperative:

This duty was performed by the prisoners under the direction of the officer of the guard. The animals were dragged to a hole which had been prepared in the adjoining woods, and the carcass shoved in, the feet punched down and the dirt filled in on top. Thus did these poor, dumb brutes give their lives for their country.[13]

A common saying in time of war is, "beans kill more men than bullets." Again, rumors ran rampant, stating that the improperly cooked and tainted food was, in most cases, the cause of sickness and death in Camp Thomas. Complaints from the soldiers about their rations during the Spanish-American War were just as strong and vehement as in any war before or since. The food was "unfit to eat" and they were "half-starved." It was only natural that these "gripes" be expressed in letters to the folks at home, and soon they were echoed in the daily sheet of almost every nook and dell. Perhaps, in 1898, the United States could not boast of the "best fed army in the world"; but then, as now, there were other sources of food supply, and the commissary had to compete with food vendors and hucksters who overran the camps.[14]

To the south, at Fort McPherson, Georgia, two thousand recruits were deprived of their supply of pastries when the surgeon of the barracks recommended that this practice be discontinued.[15] A vast army of vendors infested Camp Thomas and brought in "wagon loads of fried chicken, hard-boiled eggs, ham sandwiches, pies, doughnuts, fruits of all kinds, lemonade and soda pop. Some even brought in large quantities of 'moonshine' whisky hidden under their wares. . . ." According to one report, tons upon tons of fruit and food were confiscated and destroyed by order of General John R. Brooke.[16]

Major Fish reported that the food served in the camp was, on the whole, good and wholesome. Occasionally, because of the dampness and heat, meat would get "ripe," but the disease prevalent in the camp could not be traced to spoiled meat, either fresh or the canned variety. He said, " a large proportion of our sickness was caused by the carelessness of the men and utter disregard of the instructions given them as to sanitation, etc."[17] He believed that the huge quantities of beer consumed at the canteen were responsible for much of the diarrheal difficulty experienced by the troopers. He hastened to add, however, that beer in moderation was at times more beneficial than water; also, he praised the sobriety of the members of the regiment, noting that there were not more than a dozen cases of acute alcoholism and only on one occasion was it necessary to dress a wound received in a drinking bout.[18]

The good doctor may not have been aware of all the extra activities, or he may have been loyal to his charges. July 8 was payday for the regiment and, the next day, the *Times* congratulated Colonel Grigsby and the officers of the regiment on the behavior of the cowboys. "The men received their money and seem to be enjoying it, although not an enlisted man or an officer has yet visited Chattanooga and become drunk and acted the general rowdy. The Rough Riders are showing themselves superior in every respect, and they are becoming familiarly known as the crack regiment of the park."[19]

A week later the *Times* had another story to tell. According to tales from Camp Thomas and Chattanooga, the boys with a "carousing tendency" had favorite haunts on East and West Ninth Streets which were lined with a number of cheap eating houses and, in all probability, other houses as well. One place in particular on West Ninth Street was operated by a Negro woman. While it may have appeared "uninviting and unappetizing" to the civilian, to the soldiers, who were probably the worse for drink, it was a haven where they could frequently be found, dispensing their generosity with a freedom so often associated with men in uniform.[20]

"Every time I come to town, . . ." said a Rough Rider yesterday, "I go around to the best eating joint in the town and order enough of good eating to offset the army fare until I come in again. Last night I was so hungry I ate two large suppers, drank two bottles of beer and wound up on the outside of the restaurant by eating three hot tamales. I then bought myself a cigar and started out to have a good time. Sometime during the night I got mixed up with the provost guard, and when I awoke the next morning I found myself at the police station without a sign of a shirt or coat. I guess I must have hocked my coat and shirt for booze, as I was broke that morning."[21]

Earlier, Colonel Grigsby had negotiated for a band and declared that "the regiment intended to have nothing but the very finest, and that when the band was fully organized it [would] be the finest in the entire park." A band leader was employed at eighty dollars per month; the musicians were carefully selected, and the band instruments were expected momentarily.[22]

There were no further developments concerning the band, but evidently a number of the troopers decided to make a big noise of their own. One evening, two members of this cowboy regiment were seriously wounded and a half-dozen more were badly beaten up in a fracas with the First Missouri provost guard and the First Illinois Cavalry. About fifty of the cowboys attempted to break down the doors of the Camp Thomas theater, and, when the lone guard refused them admittance, rocks and clubs were soon in evidence. At this point, the officer of the guard, Lieutenant Summers, with five sentries, appeared on the scene and demanded a halt to the action. His orders were ignored, whereupon one of the sentries reported to Lieutenant Murphy of the First Illinois Cavalry who rushed to the scene with a hundred armed men and surrounded the cowboys. Defiantly, the latter refused to surrender, and the guards charged with bayonets. Privates W. Coffman and T. C. Kimball suffered bayonet wounds and a dozen or more Westerners were tripped to the ground and beaten by the angry guards. Meanwhile, rocks and clubs flew wildly through the air, several pistol shots were fired, and, after an hour of rioting and free-for-all fighting, the cowboys were dispersed.[23]

The Third United States Volunteer Cavalry had fared poorly. These cowboys of the North who had been heralded as picturesque plainsmen, true men of the frontier, bold, fearless, and rugged, never had an opportunity to display their bravery. The lack of uniforms and equipment, the long weeks of fever and death, and the weary months of waiting while the First Cavalry was reaping laurels for heroic fighting in Cuba—all these distressing factors shook the morale of Grigsby's cowboys. In July their hopes were kindled anew by a rumor that they would be sent to Cuba as reinforcements, and many of the men packed at once. But the orders never came. The monotony and discomfort continued; day after day of drilling, constant sweating under the scorching sun, stinging insects night and day—"over forty of the boys reported on the sick list . . . after they received the disappointing news."[24]

Once it appeared that the fighting in Cuba was over, and rumors of surrender and peace swept the nation, a reaction set in among the states-side troops toward the entire adventure. Probably the surrender of Santiago (July 17) came at the right time, for the indecision on the part of American military leadership had almost brought disaster upon the invading army. Now the torrential, tropical rainy season had set in; malaria, yellow fever, and other illnesses, resulting from the aftermath of war, spread rapidly, and soon the army, both at the front and at home, was a vast hospital.

Back in the states, the volunteer army which had been created in a few months under difficult circumstances showed the manpower of the nation willing but untrained; poorly, if not completely lacking in proper equipment and arms; and with patriotic but inexperienced leadership. The general reaction toward the recent developments was one of dismay—a feeling of being cheated but, almost at the same time, one of relief. The morale, which had been so rapidly built up on the basis of immediate action, collapsed completely when no fighting was forthcoming, and the crushing blow took on various expressions. This blow was most shattering for the Second and Third United States Volunteer Cavalries who had been kept in camp while the Roosevelt Rough Riders had met the foe and fought with glory.

The rumors of surrender and peace which swept the front and ran on into the military camps were also rampant at Camp Thomas, where Grigsby's cowboys of the Third United States Volunteer Cavalry had waited for weeks for orders. They still wanted a chance to fight, even when it became obvious that the Cuban campaign was over. Their flagging spirits rose with expectation when encouraging reports stated that the Westerners were being considered as a likely selection for the Puerto Rico campaign.

General Brooke, who had been called to Washington for consultation concerning the new campaign, had looked with favor upon the cowboy regiment, but the final decision would be made in Washington.

When Colonel Grigsby learned that the prospects of his regiment joining the invading forces were growing dim, he was advised by General Brooke to make a formal plea of consideration to the War Department. He immediately forwarded his application but received no answer. Although he and his officers availed themselves of every influential contact in the capital, no satisfaction was gained.[25]

During the second week in August it became known that Spain was ready to cede the victory and hostilities ceased. The peace had not been decided, but it would come. Meanwhile, various rumors continued to flood the nation—the volunteers were being readied to be mustered out; the regiment would be sent to Cuba for garrison duty; it would proceed to Puerto Rico as a police force. All these rumors were possible but, with the exception of the first, proved improbable. The question of garrison duty or police action was extremely distasteful to the Westerners, for their original objective in enlisting was to fight Spain—to face action. Garrison duty anywhere was not to their liking; in their minds it was not the work of the volunteers.[26] Thus, by a process of elimination, the first of the rumors—mustering out—appealed to the men most of all.

Meanwhile, Colonel Grigsby went to Washington to plead his case—to keep the regimental organization intact and, especially, to fill the places of the men who desired to leave from the many applications he had received. Upon his arrival at the capital, he was deluged with letters, telegrams, and a petition from the regiment that it be mustered out since the war was over. Confronted with this evidence by the War Department, he acceded to the demands of his men.[27]

The internal dissension in the regiment did not escape the notice of the newspapers. The *Times* reported that nearly fifty of Grigsby's men who had been sick had left Chattanooga for the West on a thirty-day furlough to recuperate from their illnesses.[28] It also commented on the seriousness of the problem confronting the volunteers:

We do not believe it would be good policy to leave the question of muster out or stay in to the men in the ranks. Their wish in the matter should have great influence, but it ought not be conclusive. Regiments wherein a large majority should be very anxious to return home, would not be apt to render very good service if they were arbitrarily held. And it would be unfair to both, to muster out commands that wanted to remain and hold those that wanted to be discharged.

The greatest care ought to be exercised to get at the wishes of the men in the ranks, and while those wishes ought not be an absolute guide, they should generally turn the scale according to the soldiers' desire to stay or go.

And we can see no impropriety in allowing this wish to have great influence in carrying out the plan of trimming the army. These are citizen-soldiers. They entered the ranks of their own accord, to vindicate the honor and fight for the glory of their country. Both of these objects having been secured, they are none the less patriots if they say, "We would be best pleased to return to the homes we temporarily abandoned for a specific purpose, that has already been accomplished."[29]

This very weighty and fair statement also revealed that the desire to be mustered out came not only from the rank and file, but also from the officers of the Montana Squadron who had sent telegrams to their respective senators, requesting them to use their influence in the matter.[30]

In answer to, and in appreciation of, the stand taken by the *Times*, Corporal "A" wrote a letter which demonstrated the sentiments of the majority of the troopers:

The enlisted men of the park camp owe you a great deal for your manly stand in publishing letters expressing their sentiments with regard to being mustered out of the service. I think I may truthfully say that ninety-five per cent of the enlisted men in the park are very desirous of being allowed to return home to their various interrupted vocations, now that their duty to "old glory" (long may it wave) is well done.

. . . while a large majority have at one time or another been cowboys, we are or were at the time of our enlistment engaged in various vocations. In this regiment there are men who are serving as private soldiers who are large ranch owners, others who own and control immense mining interests, still there are others who are actuated in their desire to go home by a more sacred cause, the support and protection of wife and children. . . .

When the services of proficient men were required in Porto Rico, politics seems to have interfered with our going, although it has been admitted that we are one of the most efficient regiments in the park. We were not allowed to participate in the fighting when there were Spaniards to do battle with. But now that the battle with the "pick and shovel," and "broom" is about to be inaugurated we very respectfully beg to be excused. . . .

If peace negotiations were declared off and hostilities were again resumed our officers would learn without asking that we were willing to remain in the service. . . . Give us the chance to fight for our country against an honorable foe and we will march straight to the front and keep step with the bravest officer in the regiment.

. . . Let it be distinctly understood by citizens and all alike that we are soldiers and as long as we are such we will do our duty, and try and merit the love and respect of every man, woman and child in the United States of America. But we earnestly crave the meritorious privilege of doing our duty as citizens where we can now better serve our common country. We are men, not children.[31]

The strong efforts to keep the Third United States Volunteer Cavalry in service had failed, and, on August 28, orders were received at Camp Thomas that the regiment would be mustered out.[32] But rumors continued to spread, chiefly with respect to the date. One stated that the regiment would be mustered out September 3; another raised a question—would they muster out at Camp Thomas or be sent home?[33] Finally, all doubts were removed when orders were confirmed that the action would take place at the camp on September 8.[34]

A week of preparation was necessary to make up the muster and payrolls and to complete the medical examinations.[35] On September 5, Colonel Grigsby gave his last orders and delivered a farewell message to his men. He deeply regretted the fact that they did not have action in fighting; with words of praise he commented on their "soldierly appearance," "proficiency in drill," "perfect gentility," and "soldierly conduct"; and, most of all, he would always remember them with kind affection.[36]

Mustering out began and the cowboys took it with chins up. Their philosophy of the whole experience might have been summed up like this:

> I got a horse and got a gun,
> Show me a Spaniard, I'll make him run!
> Got no time to waste in camp and roam,
> Nothin' to do, so I'll go back home!

Troop L came first and engaged in one last fling.[37] They heaped the benches in Chickamauga Park into one large pile, set off a blazing bonfire and, amid loud Indian whoops, danced a war dance around the leaping flames. "The owners of the benches were complacent over the loss, being assured that Uncle Sam would pay for the fun the boys had."[38]

NOTES TO CHAPTER XIV

1. Sues, *Grigsby's Cowboys*, p. 22.

2. "Col. Grigsby's Brave Cowboys," *Chattanooga Times* (Chattanooga, Tennessee), June 3; "Col. Grigsby's Cavalry," *ibid.*, June 12; "Col. Grigsby's Boys," *ibid.*, June 25; Sues, *Grigsby's Cowboys*, p. 23.

3. Sues, *Grigsby's Cowboys*, p. 22.

4. *Ibid.*, pp. 36, 45.

5. "The Neglect of Sick and Suffering Soldiers," *Chattanooga Times* (Chattanooga, Tennessee), August 25.

6. See *Chattanooga Times* (Chattanooga, Tennessee), August 25-29.

7. *Ibid.*, August 30.

8. *Ibid.*, August 26.

9. *Ibid.*, August 30.

10. Sues, *Grigsby's Cowboys*, pp. 102-4.

11. *Denver Evening Post* (Denver, Colorado), September 13.

12. "Horses Die at Camp Thomas," *Chicago Daily Tribune* (Chicago, Illinois), June 16; Sues, *Grigsby's Cowboys*, pp. 25, 92.

13. Sues, *Grigsby's Cowboys*.

14. "Col. Grigsby's Rough Riders," *Chattanooga Times* (Chattanooga, Tennessee), August 10; "The Rough Riders," *ibid.*, July 30; Sues, *Grigsby's Cowboys*, p. 45.

15. "No More Pies for Volunteers in Georgia," *Denver Evening Post* (Denver, Colorado), May 25.

16. Sues, *Grigsby's Cowboys*, p. 118.

17. *Ibid.*, pp. 106, 107.

18. *Ibid.*, p. 103.

19. "Col. Grigsby's Boys," *Chattanooga Times* (Chattanooga, Tennessee), July 9.

20. "Stories of Soldiers at Camp Thomas," *ibid.*, July 17.

21. "Stories of Soldiers," *ibid.*, August 14.

22. "Col. Grigsby's Men," *ibid.*, July 7.

23. "Grigsby's Rough Riders Routed," *Denver Evening Post* (Denver, Colorado), August 5.

24. Sues, *Grigsby's Cowboys*, p. 38; "Grigsby's Rough Riders," *Chattanooga Times* (Chattanooga, Tennessee), July 27.

25. Sues, *Grigsby's Cowboys*, pp. 41-42.

26. *Ibid.*, p. 46.

27. *Ibid.*

28. "Rough Riders Go Home," *Chattanooga Times* (Chattanooga, Tennessee), August 21.

29. "The Cowboys," *ibid.*, August 22.

30. "Voice of the Rough Riders," *ibid.*, August 22.

31. "Grigsby's Rough Riders," *ibid.*, August 30. See Sues, *Grigsby's Cowboys*, p. 48.

32. "Grigsby's Cowboys," *Chattanooga Times* (Chattanooga, Tennessee), August 24; "Col. Grigsby's Cowboys," *ibid.*, August 31; "Col. Grigsby's Boys," *ibid.*, September 1.

33. "The Rough Riders," *ibid.*, September 8.

34. Sues, *Grigsby's Cowboys*, p. 48.

35. *Ibid.*, p. 18.

36. *Ibid.*, pp. 48-49.

37. *Ibid.*, p. 49.

38. "The Cowboy Regiment," *Chattanooga Times* (Chattanooga, Tennessee), September 9.

CHAPTER XV

TORREY'S CAVALRY OF WOE

DISAPPOINTMENT likewise struck hard in the ranks of Torrey's regiment when the war, in which they had eagerly volunteered and ardently hoped to fight, came to an end while they were still in camp. The fact that Grigsby's men were the first to be mustered out, plus the rapidity with which this action was executed, caused little or no public comment. However, previous to the release of the Second Regiment late in October, widespread publicity of military graft, sharp criticism of officials, and heartbreaking pleas to bring the sick men home had reached a sensational point in the press.

Torrey's men had had national interest from the beginning. The wild chase over Western territory for suitable horses and the hospitality offered the troopers at Fort Russell had not escaped notice. The tragedy which they encountered en route to Jacksonville only increased this interest and aroused the sympathy of the nation. Theirs was a regiment whose popular leader, incapacitated in a railway wreck, gave orders from a sick bed; theirs, the long weeks of drilling under adverse conditions only to learn that it had all been in vain; then, epidemics of disease; and, finally, the weary waiting in uncertainty when the fighting was over and the other regiments were mustering out.

In time of war, the spirit soars high; but, with the descent of peace, the glory fades, man grows normal, and army life loses its gleam. It is little wonder that in the War of 1898, as in every war, opinions long suppressed were aired, exaggerated, and enumerated. The countless letters of complaint which were printed in every local newspaper, the published interviews with sick, embittered, returning volunteers added more fuel to the already blazing fires of a press avid for sensational news. Excerpts from a typical letter set the tone for thousands:

Well, my friend, many of the boys, myself included, can truthfully assert that soldiering in the volunteer service is not so pleasant as we anticipated. Our military duties are not so bad, but oh, the country we are in and the worse one we are liable to be ordered to. I wouldn't trade our beautiful city park in Cheyenne for the entire state of Florida or one Cheyenne girl for 50 down here. I can have more fun in Cheyenne in one hour than in six months in this country. But we have a good camp and are slightly enjoying camp life. I guess because we have to. We are seven miles from town, but the boys go there, just the same. But you know how I like to work, especially in a place where it is hot. It's cool today, only 100 degrees in the shade. An order has been issued for the men not to do a thing between 9 a. m.

and 4 p.m. We get up at 4 a. m. and are out drilling at 6
o'clock and drill in a swampy place, and the rest of the day
lay [sic] in the shade and perspire. The nights are cool and
we all sleep, myself included. We have good eating, two
fine colored cooks. Say, Joe, this would be a good place for
you to reduce in, and there are some fine colored girls down
here.[1]

Other letters all reveal that the men were tired of
war and anxious to return home; many were sick, and
the food was terrible.[2] "The heat and change of water,
plus green and overripe watermelons, pink lemonade
and hoky poky galore seemed to have proved too much
for our wild rough riders."[3]

Various rumors only intensified the feeling of dissatisfaction. In mid-August, the men heard that they
would be part of the army of occupation in Cuba;
then word was passed around that they would be among
100,000 volunteers to be mustered out; camp gossip
ruminated that the entire regiment would be moved
to another site.[4] Constantly, the officials at the camp
made every effort to keep up the spirits of the troopers.
They issued passes for excursions to near-by cities,
they encouraged amateur theatrical performances and
exhibitions of riding and roping, and the portrayal of
typical scenes from the West of cowboys and Indians.
The celebrated cowboy band held bi-weekly concerts,
known as the "Colonel's Serenade," interspersed with
dances, speeches, and songs. Such diversion helped
"to make the evenings most lively and pleasant, and
a very decided change from the usual tedium of camp
life."[5]

Nevertheless, letters complaining about camp life,

the weariness of being "tin soldiers," the desire to return to home, friends, and occupations continued to reach the West and were published in local newspapers. When a semiofficial announcement stated that Grigsby's cavalry had received orders to prepare for mustering out, Torrey's men immediately speculated as to the time when they would receive a similar order, and the *Rocky Mountain News* poignantly observed: "Nostalgia, as well as swamp fever, has converted every member of the Torrey regiment to a peace footing."[6]

During these days of rumor, gossip, indecision, and ennui, reports of trouble in the Second United States Volunteer Cavalry came to Denver. The following extract from a letter, written by a member of Troop B, Denver, attests the pointed dissatisfaction over the proposal that the regiment should perform garrison duty in Cuba:

There is a deuce of a row in the regiment. All the men wish to go home and the officers want to go to Cuba. The regiments have the option of going or not, just as they decide. The officers tell every one that the men wish to go, and so it gets into the papers that the regiments are all eager for Cuba. A petition has been gotten up and signed by over 700 men, which shows you about how the wind blows. Major Wheeler made an address to his squadron and said that the men were babies, etc. He afterwards made a speech to our troop and said he would publish the name of the first man that signed the petition from our troop throughout Colorado. He so bluffed our men that no one from B Troop signed it, but all wished to go home. The officers stopped one petition but the other has, I guess, gone through. There is a mighty good chance of the regiment being mustered out. Of course Wheeler wants to stay. He never saw so much money in a year before in his life. He gets $4,000.[7]

It appears that the men, convalescing from various illnesses or from injuries sustained at Tupelo, could, if they were able to travel, obtain furloughs and return to their homes. Early in September, men from this regiment, en route westward, were interviewed in several Western cities and expressed themselves freely concerning conditions in Panama Park. In the Chicago railway station, members of the Red Cross and the Army and Navy League provided refreshments for such a group of fifteen volunteers, who highly praised their leader but complained bitterly about the lack of care for the patriots in the army hospital in Jacksonville.

"If it was [sic] not for Colonel Torrey," said Sergeant Miller, "half of the boys in the regiment would be dead. As it is, 300 of the 1,000 men in the regiment are on the sick list and other regiments are worse off than we are.

"It seems good to get back to God's country once more. There is a big difference between the way we have been treated in the North and in the South. The people of Cincinnati met us at the depot and provided us with everything we could ask, just as the people of Chicago are doing. All the boys on this car are sick but convalescing and we will be all right as soon as we reach our homes."[8]

A correspondent of the *Evening Post*, Denver, Colorado, dipped his poetic pen deep into a sympathetic fluid and prepared his readers for an interview with members of this same group of "ill-treated" volunteers:

Coughing in the drizzle and cold wind blowing down the wet tracks, five troopers of Torrey's cavalry, all ill and half starved, made their way from this morning's early train into the depot. . . .[9] When questioned about his experiences, Trooper Linderfelt replied: "They treated us very kindly when we were on our journey. Going through the South they held us up and we couldn't get a square meal for under 50 cents. At Cincinnati, Chicago, and Omaha we had a regular ovation. Ladies and gentlemen with lunches and fruit meet every train at the depots and seek out the soldiers. At Chicago they had oyster soup for us."[10] Regarding the actions of Major Wheeler the trooper informed the interviewer that he had been ill on that day and had not talked to any one who had heard the Major's remarks, but—he added hesitatingly— "A man cannot say all that he wants to until he is discharged, and there are many things I could tell that would be surprising, . . ."[11]

By September Colonel Torrey had recovered sufficiently enough to take over the command of the regiment and made a short speech to his men in which he pointed out that the outcome of the regiment was still in a stage of uncertainty; however, he emphatically stated that those men who wanted to return home "real bad" would have an opportunity to do so.[12]

At this time and thereafter, the newspapers of the Rocky Mountain Empire were filled with letters which voiced the terrible conditions at camp and the sentiments of the troopers.

You ask me if I was disappointed in not getting to the front. Disappointed is not the word. I am disgusted with the way things are being run here. We were to go direct to Cuba when we left Fort Russell, but when the colonel got hurt at Tupelo we were side-tracked here, and now the officers want us to stay as peace soldiers. They go so far as to send telegrams to Washington stating that we are all anxious to do garrison duty, but about 99 per cent of us want to be sent home. You can't blame the officers because they never had such a snap before—this getting anywhere from $135 to $400 per month with a nigger or two to wait on them.

The food we get is something terrible. More than half the time our meat is tainted, the bread is always sour, and the coffee weak. The horses do not get enough to eat, but you can see government hay and oats in every station in Jacksonville. Sugar, of which we don't get half enough, you can find in every store and stand in the country. Somebody is getting a rake-off, and don't forget it!

The sick are objects of pity and subjects of charity. If it were not for the Red Cross society they would all be dead. It furnishes nurses and good things for them. It seems strange that in a country like ours, so big and so rich, that even the sick, if not the well, cannot be better taken care of than they are.

I am feeling first rate but am so thin that I have to look twice before I can see my shadow. . . .[13]

And in the same town:

It is a perfect outrage for this government to keep the regiment of cavalry here in this filthy death trap. We have been in this camp longer than the law allows and I should think the government would be liable for the deaths caused from remaining in this filthy camp. I cannot describe to you how heartless men are treated who are sick. They are treated like brutes and many of them ordered to report for duty who are hardly able to stand on their feet. Be sure and do not let anyone publish these things in my name for they would make me smoke for daring to expose their cruelty. Nevertheless I speak the truth and nothing but the truth.[14]

A letter to C. W. Bond, Denver, revealed some startling facts:

The men are dying at the rate of from five to nine a day. Last night there were nine straight volleys fired, indicating that three more souls had passed away to the happy hunting grounds, when they might just as well have been home if it was [sic] not for the many sharks that run the whole affair to suit themselves, regardless of the poor soldiers.[15]

In Cheyenne, Leo Leffler, on sick leave, spoke freely:

There are scarcely any men in the regiment who can be called well. In the morning drills it is noticeable that the troops on the average are composed of from 10 to 20 men, while in a full troop there are from 70 to 80 men. . . . Ninety-nine per cent of the boys want to come home. In fact, dissatisfaction is noticeable on all sides. In the hospital the state of affairs is terrible. I was in the hospital 15 days and could not get half enough to eat. Dr. Fields ordered that we should have all to eat that we desired, but when I complained that I was hungry he said that there had been a mistake in the commissary department somewhere, but he did not know where it was.

You ought to be with us at dinner. Every plate is emptied and everybody goes away hungry. The cooks tell us, "I would like to give it to you boys, but I haven't got it. . . ." In the last two weeks the boys have begun to look worse than ever before. Some take yellow jaundice, others liver and kidney diseases, there are typhoid and malarial fevers, and the boys generally are broken out with boils and look emaciated.[16]

And another trooper, returning to Denver, said in an interview in Kansas City:

The condition of things in the big camp at Jacksonville is terrible. . . . The country has been so flooded with the stories of suffering and death from Chickamauga and Montauk Point that the real condition of Jacksonville has been hidden. . . . A week ago yesterday there were twenty-four funerals in camp and several times lately there have been as many as twenty a day. The hospital service is good, what there is of it, but when I tell you that in many instances 150 sick men, some of them at the point of death, are left to the care of two trained nurses and one assistant nurse, you may judge for yourself whether or not they receive proper care.[17]

The appearance of such statements, interviews, and

letters in the newspapers aroused sharp and tense indignation throughout the West. Some newspapers suppressed unfavorable criticism. The *Rocky Mountain News,* upon learning that the above-mentioned Private Leo Leffler, in behalf of his comrades in camp, had attempted to "tell his story" to the press in Cheyenne only to be refused, declared that public interest had reached such a point that the truth must come out and the boys must be heard.[18]

At this point the chief executive of the state of Colorado moved to get information and action and, on September 14, sent the following telegram to the Secretary of War:

Colorado is much exercised over the reports from our soldiers at Jacksonville concerning health and hospital conditions. Many are very young men, and if there is to be no active service, their families would like them sent home, where they are needed.[19]

In reply, Governor Adams was informed that 569 men were under treatment in the three division hospitals, but only a few were seriously ill—with typhoid. Ailments of a less serious nature were treated in quarters. Furthermore, it was asserted that Jacksonville was one of the healthiest army grounds in the United States.[20]

Toward the end of September and throughout October, conflicting reports on life in camp appeared. Not all of the furloughed men returned with tales of horror, neglect, and death. One recruit maintained that nine-tenths of the stories sent out by soldiers were exaggerated;[21] another said the regiment was in

the healthiest camp in the country, rations were sufficient, but there was considerable sickness in the
camp;[22] a third reported that "nearly every man in
the regiment has had a more or less severe attack of
the fever";[23] a fourth felt that from the standpoint
of health the Torrey camp was "above the average
of other camps in Florida, although fully 70 per cent
of the men of the regiment are sick either in quarters,
in hospitals or at home."[24]

This letter was of a not too critical nature:

The boys are in pretty bad shape, and there is ample reason.
When we reached Jacksonville the regiment was assigned a
space about 5,000 yards long and 350 yards wide. In that
limited boundary not only the men, but the horses, have
been kept ever since.

When Secretary of War Alger visited the camp only 276
out of the 1,028 members of the regiment were able to participate in the review. The medical service is good and the
food is all right, but the climatic and sanitary conditions
are not what they might be. The division hospital is over-
crowded, but the doctors manage to take good care of all
the sick men.[25]

Of a more interesting nature is an observation by
one of the few men who returned from the adventure,
satisfied with the treatment he received:

"There are a lot of natural grumblers," he said, "who cannot go any place without finding fault with everyone and
everything. Now, we had as hard a time as any regiment,
I think, and yet we all came home devoted to Torrey and
satisfied that we were well treated. The only thing we did
growl about was the inactivity of our camp life, and how
we did growl about that. . . . It was hard on us to lay [sic]
in camp from June 28. . . .[26]

A former steward of the regimental hospital of the Torrey cavalry was bitter in his denunciation and incriminated everyone from Colonel Torrey to the medical staff of the hospital:

Col. Torrey is a nice man, socially, but he has no idea of military discipline, and this practically disorganized the camp. He was anxious to obtain political influence and wanted to be a good fellow. When the captains of a troop would refuse to give a man a pass the man would simply go to Col. Torrey and tell him he had worked hard for several days and wanted to go to town.

The latter would slap him on the back and exclaim, "Patriot, certainly you may go."

The hospital service was not adequate to the wants of the regiment, either supplies or nurses. Before the acceptance of the regiment by the government Dr. Clayton Parkhill of Denver recommended female nurses. Gen. [George M.] Sternberg would not listen and men nurses were sent for the first four months. These nurses were the riff-raff of the regiments. When a company had a man who was no good for anything else he was put on nurse duty. . . .[27]

As a conclusion to the evidence offered by letters arousing criticism and indignation, the following covers every phase:

We had 1,000 men and their horses camped on the same ground for four months without a single move. . . . We were on the right side of the railroad tracks. . . . Commencing with the tracks, our vaults were only eighteen feet away; eighteen feet further south was the horse line; twelve feet further was the kitchen; another twelve feet the mess tents, while only twelve feet from that were the sleeping tents, pitched right in the wet sand. . . . The dews were something terrible, and we had no dry clothes. The hard tack was mouldy and musty, the meat had skippers in it, while the potatoes and onions were kept in barrels and soon became half rotted. Our rations consisted of this kind of stuff, with a change from beans to rice, then back to beans again. We had the very poorest grade of Mexican coffee, while such things as butter and milk were not known in camp unless brought in by citizens and presented to the men. . . . We didn't have a single doctor that was competent. Diarrhoea was prevalent and the one dose was a blue pill in the morning and salts at night. . . . Barton & Conners ran a stand on the outside of the grounds for awhile, and there the boys could get something good to eat. Colonel Durbin conceived the idea of making a stake for himself by abolishing this enterprise and opening one on his own account which he did, but the boys refused to patronize him. After he started his stand no one dared bring anything into the camp. If you did it would be taken away from you and thrown upon the ground. Barton & Conners and several others have filed suit against Colonel Durbin. When the boys started a petition Major Wheeler took them all out on the drill ground and said: "I shall publish every man in the Denver papers who signs that petition." Consequently no one signed.[28]

The uppermost question in the minds of all concerned was the fate of the Second United States Volunteer Cavalry. Would it be retained in service, and if so, would it be assigned to duty in this country or in Cuba? A news dispatch, special to the *Rocky Mountain News,* revealed that some time earlier the War Department had decided to muster the regiment out of service. However, influential friends of the officers of the regiment, anxious for action, made efforts to demand that the unit be retained and employed. Senator Shoup of Idaho and three other Western senators pressed the matter in Washington, and it appeared that Torrey's cavalry would be retained. At the same time prominent citizens and political figures used their pressure to urge the release of the men. At the time of the special dispatch, indications favored the group demanding retention of the regiment which, in all probability, would be sent with the army of occupation to Cuba in November.[29]

Shortly thereafter, the public learned that Colonel Torrey was in Washington to explain to the War Department "the conditions that made it desirable to discharge a considerable number of men who had important business interests at home or who had left educational institutions before completing their courses, etc." He proposed to Secretary Alger that the regiment be brought up to its full strength by enlistments or transfers from other regiments. When he had finished his convincing oratory, Alger reluctantly informed him that the department had decided to muster out the whole command.[30]

This news was a welcome relief to the Rocky Mountain Empire. For a few days there was some concern over the point of operation—Jacksonville or Cheyenne —but soon the former city was confirmed as the scene of the occasion. Each man was to receive travel pay, approximately one hundred dollars.[31]

Late in October a week was devoted to physical examinations; then the men were discharged. According to reports received in Denver, at least 50 per cent had physical defects, resulting from the hardships in the Southern camp. Of the 1,100 strong, healthy men who comprised the regiment, only about 300 were now fit for service; over 400 were qualified for a pension; the other 400 faced a long period of convalescence. The death toll of the regiment numbered 40, including those who died at Tupelo. The select horses, sought out after a long and intensive hunt on western mountain and plain, and involving a tremendous expenditure of money, were transferred by the government to the Seventh and Eight Cavalry, in camp at Huntsville, Alabama.[32]

The Second United States Volunteer Cavalry was the last of the three regiments to be mustered out,[33] but this is not the last heard of them. In the remaining two months of the year, newspapers continued to keep up with them. First of all, there was a controversy over the matter of travel pay. The men who were sent home on sick furlough demanded the same traveling expenses as those who were mustered out at Jacksonville. The officials at the paymaster's office contended that since the men on furlough had already received their transportation costs from the government they were not entitled to additional pay.[34] Colonel Torrey was called upon as arbitrator. Major Sniffen, chief paymaster of the Department of Colorado, in adherence to orders from the War Department, was rightfully reluctant about paying the 210 men who had made claims. Considerable correspondence evolved between Torrey and the War Department; however, after two weeks, a settlement was reached which favored the troopers.[35]

The press followed Colonel Torrey long after his regiment disbanded. Early in December, he was collecting evidence relative to the wreck at Tupelo and was preparing to bring suit against the railroad company on behalf of the relatives of the victims.[36] Two years later, back in "wonderful Wyoming," he announced his plans to establish a rough riders' school at his ranch at Embar for the benefit of former members of his regiment who wished to gain a practical education and qualify for better positions than range riding.[37]

With gusto, guns, and horses galore,
Torrey led his Terrors off to war;
He marched them up and marched them down,
But only round the camp and town;
Never a glimpse of Spanish foe,
But days, weeks, and months of woe;
No battles to fight, no laurels to win,
So, he marched them home again.

NOTES TO CHAPTER XV

1. "Not for All Florida," *Cheyenne Sun-Leader* (Cheyenne, Wyoming), August 4.

2. "Torrey Boys Tired of War," *Denver Republican* (Denver, Colorado), August 14.

3. "From Torrey's Terrors," *Cheyenne Sun-Leader* (Cheyenne, Wyoming), August 3.

4. "Will See Cuba," *ibid.*, August 15; "From Torrey's Cavalry," *ibid.*, August 19; "Torrey's Troopers," *Florida Times-Union & Citizen* (Jacksonville, Florida), August 21; "Troopers to Leave," *ibid.*, September 29; "Second Cavalry," *ibid.*, October 5.

5. "Outing of Torrey's Men," *Cheyenne Sun-Leader* (Cheyenne, Wyoming), July 26; "Rough Riders on Stage," *ibid.*, July 15; "Riders from the Rockies," *Florida Times-Union & Citizen* (Jacksonville, Florida), August 5.

6. "Tired of Being Tin Soldiers," *Denver Republican* (Denver, Colorado), August 24; "Torrey's Cavalry Tired of War," *ibid.*, August 29; "Torrey's Rough Riders To Be Mustered Out," *Rocky Mountain News* (Denver, Colorado), August 30; "Volunteers Anxious To Be Sent Home," *ibid.*, August 31.

7. "Trooper Allen Voices the Sentiment of Torrey's Rough Riders," *Denver Evening Post* (Denver, Colorado), September 11; "Want To Come Home," *Denver Republican* (Denver, Colorado), August 31.

8. "Torrey's Rough Riders Met," *Chicago Daily Tribune* (Chicago, Illinois), September 9.

9. "Torrey's Men," *Denver Evening Post* (Denver, Colorado), September 10.

10. *Ibid.*

11. *Ibid.*

12. "Troop H Did Not Sign," *Denver Republican* (Denver, Colorado), September 12.

13. "Two Letters from Privates of Torrey's Cavalry," *Denver Evening Post* (Denver, Colorado), September 13.

14. *Ibid.*

15. "The Dread Sound Soldiers at Jacksonville Hear," *ibid.*, September 14.

16. "Torrey Boys Go Hungry," *ibid.*, September 15.

17. "Terrors of Camp Panama," *Rocky Mountain News* (Denver, Colorado), September 16.

18. "Are Begging for Relief," *ibid.*, September 18.

19. "Want the Boys Back from Jacksonville," *Denver Republican* (Denver, Colorado), September 15.

20. "Few Colorado Boys Are Sick at Jacksonville," *ibid.*, September 27.

21. "Torrey's All Right," *Cheyenne Sun-Leader* (Cheyenne, Wyoming), October 7.

22. "How the Torrey's Fare," *ibid.*, September 28.

23. "Torrey Cavalry Reports," *Denver Republican* (Denver, Colorado), October 1.

24. "Camp Cuba Libre in Bad Shape," *ibid.*, October 5.

25. "Torrey's Men Cooped Up in Too Small Space," *ibid.*, October 7.

26. "Is Grateful to Uncle Sam," *ibid.*, October 29.

27. "Horror of Camp Life Told by Torrey Men," *ibid.*, October 28.

28. "Inside Facts from Colonel Jay Torrey's Camp," *Rocky Mountain News* (Denver, Colorado), October 22.

29. "Shall Torrey's Men Go to Cuba," *ibid.*, October 3.

30. "Torrey's Men Coming Home," *ibid.*, October 12.

31. *Ibid.;* "Torrey's Men Go Home," *Denver Republican* (Denver, Colorado), October 11; "Mustered Out," *Cheyenne Sun-Leader* (Cheyenne, Wyoming), October 11; "Torrey's Regiment," *ibid.*, October 12; "Left in Doubt," *Florida Times-Union & Citizen* (Jacksonville, Florida), October 13.

32. "The Breaking Up of Torrey's Regiment by the Government," *Denver Evening Post* (Denver, Colorado), October 24.

33. "To Muster Out Torrey's Cavalry," *Florida Times-Union & Citizen* (Jacksonville, Florida), October 12.

34. "Torrey Men Await the Colonel's Coming," *Denver Republican* (Denver, Colorado), November 2.

35. *Ibid.;* "Torrey Claims Pay for His Men," *ibid.*, November 5; "Trooper Doubts of Travel Money," *ibid.*, November 4; "Not Yet Has Colonel Torrey Relief for His 210 Men," *ibid.*, November 6; "Troopers Will Be Paid," *ibid.*, November 16.

36. "Rough Riders Buried," *ibid.*, November 28; "Col. Torrey Prepares Case," *ibid.*, December 12.

37. "Torrey's School for His Cowboys," *ibid.*, September 23, 1900.

CHAPTER XVI

HAIL AND FAREWELL—ROUGH RIDERS

THE BATTLE OF San Juan was followed by long and weary days in the trenches before the surrender of Santiago was negotiated. These were difficult for the men of the First United States Volunteer Cavalry—a life of idleness was neither their habit nor liking. As one of the Rough Riders said, "We have got those Spaniards corralled; why in h—— don't we brand them."[1] Recurring tropical rain and blazing midsummer sun only aggravated the situation. Supplies were wanting; food was scarce and poor. At this crucial moment, no one was more concerned than the gallant leader, Theodore Roosevelt, who was well aware of an impending crisis and spoke in encouraging words of praise and good comradeship. He recalled and recounted for them various incidents that typified the courage and spirit of each and all. Singling out one individual, he said, "You should have seen him one morning just below the bombproof, where the shrapnel kept cracking over his hat. They couldn't reach him, and he knew it. Though they touched the brim of his hat at times he sat perfectly placid, breaking the beans of his coffee with the butt of his revolver, and minded the bullets no more than if there had not been any."[2]

As always, in letters home, troopers vividly described existing conditions:

In the first place I have no underclothing on, no socks on; in fact, nothing but a pair of shoes, trousers, a shirt and a hat. . . . Up to this morning I had not had a wash for ten days. I am tanned a fine chocolate color and look like a Spanish pirate. . . . Food is scarce and hunger a pretty constant companion. Tobacco is selling at $10 a pound. For a $1 army hat you have to give $10 to $15, and a pair of trousers are worth their weight in gold. A correspondent whom I know came into camp a couple of days ago and gave me some cigarettes. May Allah reward him![3]

Eventually, numerous letters and reports of a similar nature which reached the War Department indicated that much of the hardship was unnecessary. Later it was revealed that the fault lay not on the supply department, but rather on the inadequate means of transportation and the inexperience of the volunteer officers in the use of provisions and requisitions. This latter failure came to light in a complaint by Brigadier Leonard Wood who was informed that the First United States Volunteer Cavalry was without subsistence. An investigation revealed that the regular troops had sufficient food for several meals, while the Rough Riders had none. Results of further inquiry indicated that the same amount of food had been issued to all, but only a part of the rations for Roosevelt's men had been used and the remainder thrown away. Besides this unwarranted waste of food, sufficient evidence proved that the volunteer officers not only were unfamiliar with the procedure of securing provisions, but also were not careful in the use of them.[4]

Under such dire circumstances, it was only a question of days before the tired, dirty, underfed men fell victim to diseases brought on by fever-breeding jungles and weakened bodies. As the diseases ravaged, the lack of medicine and poor facilities for proper care only added to the discomfort and made the men more vulnerable. Thousands of soldiers afflicted with malarial and typhoid fevers justified the prompt removal from the island—the army doctors in charge were unable to cope with the infectious diseases which daily increased at an alarming rate; the entire regiment was debilitated and consequently unfit for duty. In this precarious situation, Theodore Roosevelt realized that action must be taken to salvage what life remained in the death-besieged camp and fearlessly, though overstepping his authority, he took the initiative.[5] In a private letter to Secretary Alger, he expressed the imperative need of a change to a more healthful location and explained the desperate situation which confronted the army:

SANTIAGO, CUBA, July 23, 1898—

MY DEAR MR. SECRETARY:

I am writing with the knowledge and approval of General Wheeler.

We earnestly hope that you will send us—most of the regulars, and at any rate the cavalry division, including the Rough Riders, who are as good as any regulars and three times as good as any State troops—to Porto Rico.

There are 1,800 effective men in the division. If those who were left behind were joined to those, we could land at Porto Rico in this cavalry division close to 4,000 men, who would be worth easily any 10,000 National Guard armed with black powder, Springfields, or other archaic weapons.

Respectfully,
THEODORE ROOSEVELT.[6]

After a ten-day period of deliberation, and probably of "cooling off," Secretary Alger cabled the following reply:

WASHINGTON, D.C., August 4, 1898

COLONEL THEODORE ROOSEVELT:

Your letter of the 23d is received. The regular army and volunteer army and the Rough Riders have done well, but I suggest that unless you want to spoil the effect and glory of your victory, you make no invidious comparisons.

The Rough Riders are no better than other volunteers. They have an advantage in their arms, for which they ought to be grateful.

R. A. ALGER
Secretary of War[7]

Immediately the *Daily Tribune* of Chicago branded this as a "demagogue's tricky misconstruction of a sentence in the Colonel's letter, and yet Secretary

Alger had the effrontery to hand it to the reporter of the Associated Press for publication." Was Roosevelt questioning the bravery of the regular soldier or was he finding fault with the inferior old Springfield muskets and black powder? The *Daily Tribune* interpreted his criticism as directed toward the latter.[8] Nevertheless, this reproach from the "lordly Secretary of War" did not daunt "bold Teddy"—he wrote directly to General Shafter. The letter was to the point, as the following excerpt indicates:

MAJOR GENERAL SHAFTER

SIR: In a meeting of the general and medical officers called by you at the palace this morning we were all, as you know, unanimous in our view of what should be done with the army. To keep us here, in the opinion of every officer commanding a division or a brigade, will simply involve the destruction of thousands. There is no possible reason for not shipping practically the entire command North at once. Yellow-fever cases are few in the cavalry division, where I command one of the two brigades, and not one true case of yellow fever has occurred in this division, except among the men sent to the hospital at Siboney, where they have, I believe, contracted it.

But in this division there have been 1,500 cases of malarial fever. Not a man has died from it, but the whole command is so weakened and shattered as to be ripe for dying like rotten sheep, when a real yellow-fever epidemic instead of a fake epidemic, like the present one, strikes us, as it is bound to do if we stay here at the height of the sickly season, August and the beginning of September. Quarantine against malarial fever is much like quarantining against the toothache.

All of us are certain that as soon as the authorities at Washington fully appreciate the conditions of the army, we shall be sent home. If we are kept here it will in all human possibility mean an appalling disaster, for the surgeons here estimate that over half the army, if kept here during the sickly season, will die. . . .

I write only because I cannot see our men, who have fought so bravely and who have endured hardship and danger so uncomplainingly, go to destruction without striving so far as lies in me to avert a doom as fearful as it is unnecessary and undeserved.

Yours respectfully,
THEODORE ROOSEVELT[9]

The ball was now rolling. Before the effect of this missive could lose its potency, three major generals, four brigadier generals, and Colonel Roosevelt formulated and signed a "round robin" letter. Major M. Wood, the chief surgeon of the First Division, emphatically stated: "The army must be moved or it will be unable to move itself." General Ames sent the following cable to Charles H. Allen, Assistant Secretary of the Navy, Washington, D.C.: "This army is incapable, because of sickness, from [sic] marching anywhere except to the transports. If it is ever to return to the United States it must do so at once." In an interview with a correspondent of the Associated Press, the General said: "If I had the power I would put the men on the transports at once and ship them north without further orders. I am confident such action would ultimately be approved. A full list of the sick would mean a copy of the roster of every company here."[10]

The round robin was ready to go but the matter of speeding it on its way caused a problem, which even the ingenious Teddy could not solve. The estimated cost by cable, along with a copy of Roosevelt's letter to Shafter, was about $1,500, and by regular mail a week or more would elapse—too long a period both for effect and for existing conditions. An Associated Press correspondent, eager for news of the day, happened by and learned of the predicament. He immediately offered to assume the expense; the statement was prepared and left on a table in a tent. Shortly thereafter, it was telegraphed to the United States at a cost of approximately $1,700! Once this information of an impending disaster reached President McKinley, he issued immediate orders that the fever-stricken army be removed to Montauk Point, Long Island.[11]

Meanwhile, news concerning the experiences and adventures of four troops of the First United States Volunteer Cavalry who had been left behind at Tampa with the horses also appeared in the newspapers. One evening, shortly after the invasion force had left the states, six hundred horses and some mules stampeded, broke down the corrals, and overran the countryside. Fortunately, the incident occurred at a time when the neighborhood was deserted, and only two soldiers were badly bruised in the melee—others saved themselves by climbing fences and trees. It was rumored that some discharged Mexicans were the instigators of the affair.[12]

On another occasion some of the mule packers and Rough Riders visited a disreputable house and raised a row. "Alice May, who lived in the house, was shot several times by the soldiers and one of the soldiers was shot by an inmate of the house." This resulted in the arrest of three mule packers and two Rough Riders who were expected to have a difficult time with the law, and Major Henry B. Hershey "expressed the hope that this would be the case, believing that the punishment of the culprits would have a good effect upon the troops generally."[13]

Kurtz Eppley, a member of the Essex Troop, New Jersey National Guard, commented thus on the general character of the troopers:

If anybody thinks that Colonel Roosevelt got up this outfit to parade with, that person is a fool. No doubt we have some "Willies" with us, but they soon find out that unless they tackle down and work they catch it. The Riders are the toughest set of men I have ever met. Many of them are outlaws and I might venture to state that 70 per cent of them are "man killers" of some note in one part or another of the wild and woolly West. They drink, gamble and raise the devil generally. Their language is beyond description and they are always fighting and ready to shoot at the first chance that offers. They all carry 45-calibre six-shooters and knives and when they get in Tampa on a good time they make things howl.

On the other hand, they always stand ready to help a fellow out of any difficulty, and will share their last cent with you.[14]

These Rough Riders, tarrying in Tampa, may have looked like "man killers," drank, gambled, cussed, and whored, but they were not guilty of every charge brought against them. A false rumor accused Troop H of instigating a riot with colored soldiers, in which Captain Curry and Lieutenant Ballard of the troop were injured. An account of the affair had been printed in the *Headlight,* Deming, New Mexico, which was promptly "put in its place" and informed by a letter from Tampa that "the only colored soldiers the boys have seen were from car windows."[15]

These days and nights of escapades and masculine frivolity were numbered. On August 8 the four troops received orders to join their companions at Montauk Point, and, figuratively, Tampa "kissed the boys good-bye."[16]

The sea voyage from Cuba to the States took nine days. When the eight troops of the First United States Volunteer Cavalry landed at Montauk Point on August 15, some were too weak to walk, many were suffering from dysentery—a few in a critical condition—consequently, all were held in a detention camp for at least three days for observation.[17]

Roosevelt, when quizzed about his health, exclaimed with characteristic heartiness, "I'm as strong as a bull moose."[18]

Information received from Washington on August 25 indicated that the Rough Riders were to be mustered out before the end of the month. Governor Otero requested that this be accomplished as quickly as possible, and Colonel Roosevelt, in an urgent telegram, heartily supported the move.[19] In appreciation of the volunteers from New Mexico, the Colonel sent a warm letter of praise to Governor Otero. In part he wrote:

I write you a line just to tell you how admirably the New Mexican troopers in the battalion of the "Rough Riders" which I have commanded before Santiago have behaved. Three of the eight troops with me were from New Mexico, being commanded by Captains Muller, Luna, and Llewellen. All three captains, and all three troops, distinguished themselves. As for the troopers themselves, I cannot say too much for their daring and resolution in battle, their patient endurance of every kind of hardship and labor, and their discipline, ready obedience and order in camp—these last qualities being as indispensable to soldiers as courage itself. I am more than proud to be in the same regiment with them; I can imagine no greater honor than to have commanded such men.[20]

Shortly thereafter, Governor Otero visited Camp Wikoff and brought the troopers personal greetings from families and friends.[21]

According to flying rumors, the mustering out of Roosevelt's victorious volunteers was to be a glorious affair. Tentative plans called for a grand parade in New York City; however, this was canceled, and a cowboy tournament was arranged under the auspices of the women representatives of the National Relief League.[22] Twenty of the Rough Riders were scheduled to perform, but again the event did not materialize. Finally, a bronc-riding contest was staged at Camp Wikoff, which was won by Troop H.[23]

The program for the final farewell was elaborate in every detail. On September 13, the long-anticipated day arrived and the mustering out proceeded smoothly, except for the confusion in regard to those men who, earlier, had been given a sixty-day furlough.[24]

In the afternoon the gallant troopers presented their more gallant leader with a bronze figure, "Bronco Buster," fashioned by Frederic Remington.[25] The beloved Colonel paid his men a glowing tribute in acceptance:

It is an American regiment because it has in it men who represent all the classes who have given to America its honor and glory and its free institutions; men who have made the American country theirs by adaptation and inheritance. No matter whether a man has a dollar or a hundred thousand dollars, here he treats his brother trooper as his equal and fights shoulder to shoulder with him. I have learned to love and respect you because of the way you have treated me. You shared your blankets with me and gave me a part of your hardtack when I had none.[26]

Civilians once more, many of the volunteers decided to see a bit of the country for which they had fought before they returned home. Still they were pursued by the press:

Some of Teddy's Terrors fired a few volleys from their revolvers on Brooklyn Bridge, but, the dispatches say, the policemen allowed them a good deal of latitude. That is just the most proper thing to do when [a] . . . cowboy gets to slashing around with his gun.

In their sight-seeing, the Rough Riders were not presented with keys by the city fathers but, nevertheless, according to the headlines, they "owned New York City."[27] Earlier in the month, however, when the able and well volunteers had been granted furloughs, the press wrote in a different note. The *New York World* reported that twelve Rough Riders, with home-bound tickets but no money in their pockets, went to the East 35th Street Police Station with a sad tale that "they went into the Army Building to draw $4.50 each to which they were entitled. There they were told that they had been docked $1.50 for something or other and only received $3 apiece."[28]

Another account of the "down-and-out" soldier appeared in the same newspaper:

Six of Colonel Teddy Roosevelt's rough riders and tough fighters; sick, very weak and stranded, penniless in this city overnight, were glad to accept the hospitality of Harry Jackson, night manager of an undertaker's concern, and when it was found that three of them filled all the regular sleeping accommodations of the place the other three promptly filled three partly made coffins with excelsior and then cuddled down in the beds thus formed and in a trice were fast asleep. And Jackson, who had surrendered his bed besides providing a feast of coffee, potted ham, pies and cakes, is very proud of his hospitality to his fighting guests.[29]

By the third week in September, the territorial newspapers reported that volunteers were arriving home daily. Some, however, had remained in the East to visit and to continue their sight-seeing; one group visited Washington, D.C., where several were presented by Delegate Fergusson to President McKinley, who greeted them with warm words of praise: "Your record is one of which the entire nation is proud. . . . You have not only done well . . . but I have no doubt you would be willing to again serve your country in an emergency."[30]

Theodore Roosevelt had much to say about his mounted fighters and he has been quoted innumerable times, most often, probably, in regard to his farewell address, on which he himself comments in *The Rough Riders:*

One Sunday before the regiment disbanded I supplemented Chaplain Brown's address to the men by a short sermon of a rather hortatory character. I told them how proud I was of them, but warned them not to think that they could go back and rest on their laurels, bidding them remember that though for ten days or so the world would be willing to treat them as heroes, yet after that time they would find they had to get down to hard work just like everyone else, unless they were willing to be regarded as worthless do-nothings. They took the sermon in good part, and I hope that some of them profited by it. . . .[31]

Much had been written about the cowboy, the cavalryman, the Rough Rider—some of the criticism was derogatory, but much of it was favorable. Already early in the war a controversy had developed over the relative merits of the cowboy as a soldier. An old cavalryman, J. D. Dillenback, expressed his opinion about the cowboy as a cavalryman:

. . . seriously, I am inclined to doubt that cowboys, as a class, are likely to make superior cavalrymen. At the outset they have two apparently important points in their favor: they are accustomed to the hardships of an outdoor life in all kinds of weather, and they know how to ride. My experience has been that these qualifications are not such important factors in the make-up of a cavalryman as many suppose. Both can be acquired in a few weeks by any set of healthy and intelligent young men.

The average cowboy, as I know him, is given to drink and hard to discipline. Doubtless Teddy Roosevelt can make a valuable scout, if not a thorough soldier out of him. But I cannot help believing that Teddy's cowboys and rough riders will prove the least valuable part of his regiment. It will be difficult to make the cowboy police his camp, set his tent properly, keep himself clean and take care of his health.

Riding a bucking bronco and throwing a lariat are not the highest soldierly accomplishments. The habit of keeping clean and obeying orders is decidedly preferable.[32]

In opposition to this, an item entitled "Cowboys Make Best Cavalrymen," quoted the words of a high military authority: "To be a perfect cavalryman the man must have learned to ride before he learned to walk."[33] Richard Harding Davis wrote: "The grit of the cowpuncher has never been doubted."[34] On innumerable occasions, Theodore Roosevelt voiced the highest praise for the cowboys of his regiment:

Ninety-five per cent of my men had at one time or another herded cattle on horseback or had hunted big game with the rifle. They were, therefore, natural riders and good shots, used to out-of-door life, a dead game lot and intelligent—so we could discipline them. The groundwork of the regiment is the cowpuncher. . . .[35]

In a reprint article, the *Republican,* Springfield, Massachusetts, revealed the scope of information concerning the volunteer:

People are getting ruffled at hearing so much about the Rough Riders. . . . Not about the "Rough Riders," but about a few members of the regiment. There are, perhaps 980 odd cowboys from the west in the organization, and from ten to 20 eastern college graduates and New York society men. One might think from reading the New York newspapers that these ten or 20 easterners, brave as they are, made up the entire force.[36]

A leading editorial in the *Denver Republican* highly acclaimed the leader and the men of the volunteer regiment:

Col. Roosevelt never tires of lauding his regiment of Rough Riders, the basis of which, he says, is the cow puncher. There are ex-policemen, Harvard men, country doctors, dudes and heirs to millions in his regiment, but the framework of the organization that won fame in Cuba is the cowboy, bronzed, daredevil, loud and unveneered.[37]

On another occasion Roosevelt said, "The grand work of the regiment is due largely to the cowpuncher —the man who has herded cattle on the plains for a living—and next to him comes the Rocky Mountain miner, who has also usually been a small ranchman.[38]

Several months later, Roosevelt was more conservative and inclusive in his estimation of the mounted cavalry:

Our men behaved very well indeed—white regulars, colored regulars, and Rough Riders alike. The newspaper press failed to do full justice to the white regulars, in my opinion, from the simple reason that everybody knew that they would fight, whereas there had been a good deal of question as to how the Rough Riders, who were volunteer troops, and the Tenth Cavalry, who were colored, would behave; so there was a tendency to exalt our deeds at the expense of those of the First Regulars, whose courage and good conduct were taken for granted.[39]

In an appraisal of past heroics, the Rough Riders join other immortal fighters in history—Xenophon's Ten Thousand, Caesar's Tenth Legion, the Light Brigade, Napoleon's Imperial Guard; their names have become fragments of romance, but their deeds, magnified and gilded, have thrilled many a fireside circle in the past half century.

NOTES TO CHAPTER XVI

1. "Tired of White Flag," *Sun* (Baltimore, Maryland), July 14.
2. "Roosevelt Praises His Men," *Chicago Daily Tribune* (Chicago, Illinois), August 18.
3. "Rough and Tough Riders," *Denver Republican* (Denver, Colorado), August 7.
4. "Blame for Volunteers," *Chicago Daily Tribune* (Chicago, Illinois), August 13.

5. "Alger and 'Teddy' Roosevelt," *ibid.*, August 9; "What Alger Said," "Alger's Reply," *Florida Times-Union & Citizen* (Jacksonville, Florida), August 5.

6. "Army In Cuba to Flee From Yellow Fever," *Chicago Daily Tribune* (Chicago, Illinois), August 5; "Alger and 'Teddy' Roosevelt," *ibid.*, August 9.

7. "Alger and 'Teddy' Roosevelt," *ibid.*, August 9.

8. *Ibid.*

9. *Ibid.*

10. "Officers Tell of the Danger," *ibid.*, August 4; "Roosevelt's Round Robin," *Florida Times-Union & Citizen* (Jacksonville, Florida), August 7; "Shafter on the Round Robin," *ibid.*, August 9; "Teddy Shakes Up Things," *ibid.*, August 9; "The Round Robin," *ibid.*, August 10.

11. "Roosevelt's Round Robin," *Rocky Mountain News* (Denver, Colorado), September 4; "Alger and 'Teddy' Roosevelt," *Chicago Daily Tribune* (Chicago, Illinois), August 9.

12. "Charged the Camp," *Denver Evening Post* (Denver, Colorado), June 17.

13. "Rough Riders in a Scrape," *Sun* (Baltimore, Maryland), June 23.

14. "Rough Riders Are Terrors," *Rocky Mountain News* (Denver, Colorado), July 26.

15. "New Mexico Notes," *Denver Republican* (Denver, Colorado), July 13.

16. "Torrey's Rough Riders off for Montauk Point," *Denver Evening Post* (Denver, Colorado), August 8; "Torrey's Rough Riders Now at Montauk Point," *ibid.*, August 11. Evidently a typographical error was made by the *Denver Evening Post*—there were at no time any of Torrey's regiment at Tampa.

17. [News Item] *Santa Fe New Mexican* (Santa Fe, New Mexico), August 15, 16; "Rough Riders Land with Roosevelt and 'Joe' Wheeler, in a Storm of Cheers," *New York World* (New York, New York), August 16; "Rough Riders Reach Home," *Chicago Daily Tribune* (Chicago, Illinois), August 15. See Theodore Roosevelt, "The Rough Riders," *Scribner's Magazine*, XXV (June, 1899), 686, 688; "Cavalry First to Leave Cuba," *Rocky Mountain News* (Denver, Colorado), August 8; "Rough Riders on the Sea," *Denver Evening Post* (Denver, Colorado), August 8; "Rough Riders at Montauk," *Denver Republican* (Denver, Colorado), August 15; "Rough Riders Are Well," *ibid.*, August 19.

18. "Roosevelt at Long Island," *Chicago Daily Tribune* (Chicago, Illinois), August 16.

19. [News Item] *Santa Fe New Mexican* (Santa Fe, New Mexico), August 25.

20. *Ibid.*, September 3.

21. "Gov. Otero Visits the Rough Riders," *Denver Republican* (Denver, Colorado), August 22; "Invalided Rough Riders," *ibid.*, August 26. See Otero, *My Nine Years as Governor*, etc., pp. 56-58.

22. "Now for the Soldiers," *Chicago Daily Tribune* (Chicago, Illinois), August 24; "Rough Riders not to Parade," *Denver Times* (Denver, Colorado), September 2; "No Parade of Rough Riders," *New York World* (New York, New York), September 2.

23. "Rough Riders Will Hold a Tournament," *Rocky Mountain News*

250 WHO RUSH TO GLORY

(Denver, Colorado), September 20; "Rough Riders Fight a Fire in the Rear," *New York World* (New York, New York), September 20; "Rough Riders Sport in Camp," *Rocky Mountain News* (Denver, Colorado), September 18.

24. "Rough Riders To Be Mustered Out," *Denver Republican* (Denver, Colorado), September 1; "Rough Riders Granted Sixty Days Furlough," *Rocky Mountain News* (Denver, Colorado), September 1; "Mustering Out of Rough Riders," *Denver Evening Post* (Denver, Colorado), September 2; "Cold Wave at Camp Wikoff," *Denver Republican* (Denver, Colorado), September 12; "Rough Riders Quit Uncle Sam To-Day," *New York World* (New York, New York), September 13; "Are Getting Soldiers Away from Camp Wikoff," *Denver Republican* (Denver, Colorado), September 15; "Volunteers Wonder as to Standing," *Rocky Mountain News* (Denver, Colorado), September 19.

25. "Rough Riders Mustered Out," *Denver Republican* (Denver, Colorado), September 18.

26. "Roosevelt Given a Present," *Chicago Daily Tribune* (Chicago, Illinois), September 14; "Rough Riders' Farewell," *New York World* (New York, New York), September 14. See Marshall, *Rough Riders,* pp. 247-54.

27. "Rough Riders Own New York City," *Rocky Mountain News* (Denver, Colorado), September 15; [Editorial] *Denver Republican* (Denver, Colorado), September 15; "The Rough Riders Having a Good Time," *Denver Evening Post* (Denver, Colorado), September 25; "Rough Rider in Trouble," *New York World* (New York, New York), September 18; "Pranks and Pleasantries of Our Rough Rider Visitors," *ibid.*

28. "Rough Riders Fed by Police," *Rocky Mountain News* (Denver, Colorado), September 4.

29. "Rough Riders Sleep in Coffins," *ibid.;* "Living Soldiers Sleep in Coffins," *Chicago Daily Tribune* (Chicago, Illinois), August 25.

30. Teddy's Men at Capital," *Denver Evening Post* (Denver, Colorado), September 20; "Rough Riders Call on McKinley at White House," *ibid.,* September 21; "Greeted the Rough Riders," *Denver Times* (Denver, Colorado), September 21; "New Mexico Rough Riders Visit President McKinley," *Denver Republican* (Denver, Colorado), September 22; "Soldiers Call On McKinley," *Chicago Daily Tribune* (Chicago, Illinois), September 23; "McKinley Praises Rough Riders," *New York World* (New York, New York), September 22; "Rough Riders at the White House," *Santa Fe New Mexican* (Santa Fe, New Mexico), September 26.

31. Roosevelt, *Rough Riders,* p. 225. See "Roosevelt's Sermon," *Rocky Mountain News* (Denver, Colorado), September 10; "Roosevelt's Adieu; Nine Die At Wikoff," *New York World* (New York, New York), September 5; H. E. Armstrong, "Roosevelt As a Volunteer Soldier," *Independent,* LIII (September 26, 1901), 1901, 2281; Paul E. Cunningham, "Rough Riders' Reunion," *New Mexico,* XXVII (June, 1949), 42.

32. "Cowboy Cavalry and Rough Riders," *Denver Republican* (Denver, Colorado), June 19.

33. *Rocky Mountain News* (Denver, Colorado), August 14.

34. "Dashing Bravery of Rough Riders," *Denver Republican* (Denver, Colorado), July 18.

35. "Col. Roosevelt Lauds His Men," *ibid.,* August 20.

36. [News Item] *Santa Fe New Mexican* (Santa Fe, New Mexico), July 5; *ibid.*, July 22. See "Virile Young Society Men," *Denver Republican* (Denver, Colorado), June 26; "The Gallant Dude," *ibid.*, July 17.

37. "Teddy's Terrors," *ibid.*, August 21.

38. "Teddy Roosevelt Praises His Men," *Rocky Mountain News* (Denver, Colorado), August 16.

39. Theodore Roosevelt, "The Rough Riders," *Scribner's Magazine*, XXV (March, 1899), 275.

CHAPTER XVII

RETROSPECT

And this bright story of your bold
Exploits, when centuries have rolled,
By abler poets shall be told
In ringing rhyme, Rough Riders.[1]

AT CAMP WIKOFF the Rough Riders made ready to lay aside the raiment of war and to return to a life of normalcy. But, in the final days of anticipation, a note of nostalgic longing for the days that were gone ran through the ranks; theirs was too glorious a regiment to die away only to be revived in history's pages; even fifty years ago "old soldiers didn't die" and, consequently, they brought into being the organization of Roosevelt's Rough Riders "to perpetuate the name and fame of this remarkable cavalry regiment." Unfortunately, a number of the troopers had already departed, but they were to be informed by mail. Two officers were elected, Lieutenant Colonel Brodie, president, and J. D. Carter, secretary.[2]

In the months following, plans were made to hold the first reunion at Las Vegas, New Mexico, in June, 1899, on the anniversary of the Cuban victory. Theodore Roosevelt, the illustrious leader, who had ridden back from battle into the gubernatorial office of New York State, wholeheartedly approved the plans and made known his intentions to attend the celebration —to which the committee on arrangements replied that there would "be no padlock on the door."[3]

When it was generally made known that Las Vegas had been named "convention city," other towns in the Southwest that had also provided volunteer troops contended for the honor role of host. Santa Fe, as the capital and official residence of Governor Otero, who himself was a Las Vegan, longed to hang out a banner of welcome, and Albuquerque, farther south, boasted its accommodations. Both cities bowed to the persuasive forces of Las Vegas but loudly censured, in the press, the tactics employed by the latter town.[4]

These intercity differences faded, however, and New Mexicans banded together in protest when a report stated that negotiations were afoot to lure the Rough Riders to El Paso, Texas. Again, bombastic blasts of disloyalty and unfair play appeared in the newspapers of the towns concerned. Captain George Curry, a member of Troop H from New Mexico, finally calmed the tense situation by informing the general public through the press that he had suggested New Mexico as a centrally located site to the president of the association.[5]

Shortly thereafter, El Paso dropped her efforts, and, as a final blow to the Texan neighbor for her "unethical" procedure, the *New Mexican* printed a statement, allegedly made by an El Paso citizen: "I am about as patriotic as the average American and I appreciate the fact that the rough riders fought gallantly in Cuba. But I don't know what we would do with them in El Paso. While in New York they raised cain, and would do the same thing in this city."[6]

Las Vegas made elaborate plans for a hearty welcome of the delegates. The Santa Fe Railway cooperated in full by offering attractive low-rate fares, and, immediately, the office of the reunion committee was flooded with requests for information and accommodations from Rough Riders in neighboring states. Reliable estimates from the various key sources revealed that the attendance would by far exceed the number anticipated.[7]

At long last, the day of the reunion arrived. A heavy rainstorm practically ruined all the elaborate decorations which gave a festive air to the city. Unfortunately, they could not be replaced because all available bunting for miles around had been used in the original grand display. The train bearing Theodore Roosevelt southward stopped at various towns in New Mexico to permit the guest of honor to greet advance welcoming committees of the troopers. At Raton he remarked, "I am mighty glad to see you, boys, and to be able to be with you. I wouldn't have missed this for anything. If the reunion had been

held in Alaska I would have gone there to see you."[8]
Later at Wagon Mound, where he was greeted by
Captain Luna, he ejaculated heartily, "I'm glad to
see you. It does me good to shake your paw. How
are you?"[9]

The Rough Riders poured into the city. The heavy
rain did not dampen the spirit of these men who only
a year ago had been the victors in Cuba. Friendships
were renewed, experiences recounted; laughter and
joy prevailed, except for moments of stillness when
the names of missing comrades were mentioned. Hardship of travel meant nothing to the rough and ready
ex-troopers; the call of the reunion pulled as strong
at the heartstrings as the fighting spirit in time of
battle. A loud cheer rang through the air when one
enthusiastic Rough Rider drove his mule-drawn wagon
into the gala city. With his bride he had spent ten
days on the road because he wanted her to see Colonel
Roosevelt and could not afford railway fare. "I've had
a hell of a time getting here. I don't think there is
a strap on that old harness that hasn't broke at least
once since I started and the wagon broke three times,
but I ain't sorry that we started."[10]

An elaborate three-day program had been arranged.
Business of the association got under way the first
morning in Lincoln Park, where the regiment was
reviewed and Governor Roosevelt and Lieutenant
Colonel Brodie made appropriate speeches. The election of officers resulted in Brodie's re-election as president; Captain Llewellen and Lieutenant Goodrich,
first and second vice presidents, respectively; and Lieutenant Dame, secretary. Oklahoma City was selected

as the meeting place for the next reunion. Amid loud
ovations and rousing cheers, Governor Roosevelt was
made honorary president of the organization for life.[11]
Governor Otero, who had worked so loyally in the
formation of the regiment and had just recently proclaimed June 24 as "Rough Riders' Day," was deeply
moved when Roosevelt presented him with a copper
regimental medal indicative of an honorary membership. Otero was the only person who had not been
in Cuba during the war to receive such a distinction
and, in acceptance, lauded the aims of the association "to keep warm the fires of patriotism and nourish
the love of country and devotion to its flag, which
has ever marked the true American."[12]

A large parade with five military bands moved
through the crowded streets at midmorning; in the
afternoon another of expert horsemen participated in
a tournament of races, roping, and bronc busting. For
the citizens there were numerous foot, bicycle, and
horse races with cash awards as prizes and gold and
silver medals for first- and second-place winners. A
grand evening reception in the Duncan Hotel climaxed
the first day of celebration.

The second day (Sunday) was marked by a memorial service and a grand concert by the military
bands. On the final day, the program reverted to
more entertainment of races, cowboy sports, and a
baseball game. The finale, a grand ball at the Montezuma Hotel and a magnificent display of fireworks
depicted the Battle of San Juan, concluded the first
reunion of the Rough Riders.[13]

As the years passed by, the War of 1898 faded into the past on history's pages, and World Wars I and II took their toll of American youth. But still, every summer, the Rough Riders, older now and in ever-dwindling numbers, looked forward to their reunion; and, in 1949, came their Golden Jubilee celebration. Fittingly, this took place in Las Vegas, New Mexico, on the same dates that marked in memory the glorious battle. The same men who, fifty years ago, had rushed to glory, moved more slowly now—they were bent with age, their eyes were dim and their steps uncertain. The ranks grew ever smaller; through the years, many had joined their illustrious leader as "riders in the sky." In the meantime, those volunteers of 1898, now gathered in Las Vegas, had seen the doughboys and the G.I.'s—more powerful in numbers and better equipped, but certainly not more loyal—march off to more distant shores than Cuba. In those two wars there were no cowboy cavalry regiments; but the cowboy, too, with millions of others, had received the official letter with greetings; so, he had fondly patted "old Paint," waved farewell to the ranch and grazing herds of cattle, and joined the ranks in uniform.

About fifty members of the original Rough Riders' Association were able to attend the half-century celebration and, with nostalgia, recalled the days that were gone.

William J. Love, in charge of the arrangements, reminisced freely:

Teddy first started out to enlist the whole regiment from

New Mexico . . . but a lot of Arizona and Oklahoma boys raised such a holler to get in, that the regiment was finally made up of three squadrons, one each for New Mexico, Arizona and Oklahoma, though as near as I can remember there was [sic] about 550 of us enlisted from New Mexico. So some of us got assignments to other squadrons to fill them out. Around 1,200 men altogether, a big lot of us cowboys, but we also got among us young lawyers, preachers, doctors, railroaders, miners and I don't know what all. Maybe even a few outlaws, but all a-rarin' to fight.[14]

Frank C. Brito, of Silver City, related in very frank words the filial respect which had brought about his enlistment: "My father sent for us and said, 'Did you know the United States is at war with Spain?' When we answered no, he said, 'I want you boys to go to Silver City and enlist and fight for your country.' Them days you did what your father told you to do."[15]

Frank S. Roberts, who had contracted typhoid fever and dysentery while in service, said the "goat's milk which he drank in Cuba probably saved his life."[16]

"The worst mis-handled war there ever was," said George F. Murray, who recalled with vivid memory the rations of hardtack and canned "goat" meat and said "they were given green coffee beans, which they roasted in their canteens and then took the butts of their pistols to grind the beans before coffee could be made." Fighting for one's country in those days was not especially glamorous at $13.60 [$15.60] per month!"[17] Ben H. Colbert commented that he had gone through the war as a "buck private and was never reduced;" however, later he was honored by

Roosevelt with an appointment as United States marshal of the territory of Oklahoma.[18]

The Cowboy Volunteers of 1898, a spontaneous
expression of Western enthusiasm and patriotism,
were organized to meet the emergency of war. The
mounted cavalry grew out of the need for a particular
individual, adept in horsemanship and marksmanship,
at the same time endowed with the physical endurance associated with outdoor life. These qualifications
were best found among the young men of the last
and rapidly disappearing frontier of the states and
territories of the United States.

The Volunteers came from all walks of life, although enlistments revealed a preponderance of individuals engaged in the cattle industry. The vast and
rugged areas of the West necessitated travel on horseback, regardless of the individual's occupation. Because of the dangers of frontier life—the bandit, out-
law, and desperado, and the pilfering which occurred
on the frontier border—any man, be he miner, herder,
cattleman, railroader, cowboy, government scout, me-
chanic, clerk, or stenographer, needed skill with firearms to protect his life and property. This was an
era when, and a place where, men were engaged at
one time or another in several pursuits in order to
make a livelihood. Therefore, it was not uncommon
to find the former cowboy working for the railroad
or in the mines, or the one-time clerk or stenographer
engaged in governmental scouting activities — their
common ground, because of environment, was horsemanship and marksmanship.

As all volunteers, they lived to learn that a nation is never fully enough prepared to meet the needs of its soldiers in order to avoid the adjustment from civilian to military life. Difficulties and hardships which consequently arose were taken in their stride with good humor and the normal amount of complaining.

The colorful background and personalities gave the three cowboy volunteer cavalry regiments much publicity and notoriety. As warriors, Teddy's Rough Riders were the most popular of the three and probably received far greater acclaim than they deserved. They were not self-seeking, but their leadership was in the hands of a young, prominent, aggressive, dashing, up-and-coming man—Theodore Roosevelt. The aura of publicity, which at this time was beginning to surround him, and which continued to do so throughout his life, was bound to include the men under his command. Yet, despite their publicity and that of their leader, when they came to test under fire, his volunteers proved to be sturdy, capable, and brave.

It was the cowboy's day—his sunset, glorious, lurid. Like the bison and the Indian he had reached the trail leading over the Great Divide; here, he turned in his saddle, waved a last farewell, and through the cloud of dust there came back a faint "So long!"

The assembling of the cowboy volunteer cavalry regiments was the apotheosis of the plainsman of the old range days. For a brief moment, his carefree cry triumphed over the roar of civilization; for a moment, he broke through the encircling barbed wire and the mesh of railroads which throttled his existence and staked out a claim on fame's eternal camping ground. The last thing he painted red was a page in history.

NOTES TO CHAPTER XVII

1. "Welcome Rough Riders," *La Voz del Pueblo* (East Las Vegas, Neuvo Mexico), 24 *de Junio de* 1899.

2. "To Perpetuate the Name and Fame of the Rough Riders," *Denver Evening Post* (Denver, Colorado), September 1; "Rough Riders Held First Reunion in Vegas Fifty Years Ago This Month," *Las Vegas Daily Optic* (Las Vegas, New Mexico), June 21, 1949.

3. *Denver Field And Farm* (Denver, Colorado), April 22, 1899, p. 8; " 'Teddy' Is Coming," *Santa Fe New Mexican* (Santa Fe, New Mexico), May 27, 1899.

4. *Santa Fe New Mexican* (Santa Fe, New Mexico), May 8, 1899.

5. *Ibid.*, May 10, 1899.

6. *Ibid.*

7. *Ibid.*, June 5, 6, 1899.

8. *Ibid.*, June 24, 1899.

9. *Ibid.*

10. [News Item] *Las Vegas Daily Optic* (Las Vegas, New Mexico), June 26, 1899.

11. "Association Business," *Santa Fe New Mexican* (Santa Fe, New Mexico), June 26, 1899.

12. Otero, *My Nine Years as Governor*, etc., p. 65.

13. "Programee Revisado de los Festividas," *La Voz del Pueblo* (East Las Vegas, Neuvo Mexico), 24 *de Junio de* 1899; "*La Gran Celebracion*," *ibid.*, 1 *de Julio de* 1899; "*Los Rough Riders de Roosevelt*," *ibid.*, 24 *de Junio de* 1899.

14. Omar S. Barker, "Rough Riders Gather Here Again for Reunion Friday, Saturday," *Las Vegas Daily Optic* (Las Vegas, New Mexico), June 22, 1949.

15. "Each Rider Has Story About Life with T. R.," *ibid.*, June 24, 1949.

16. "Rough Riders To End Session with Mabry as Guest Tonight," *ibid.*, June 25, 1949.

17. *Ibid.* The $13.60 is probably a typographical error, or perhaps veteran Murray does not quote the entire congressional increase.

18. *Ibid.*

BIBLIOGRAPHY

NEWSPAPERS

Albuquerque Daily Citizen (Albuquerque, New Mexico), 1898.

Bismarck Tribune (Bismarck, North Dakota), 1898.

Chattanooga Times (Chattanooga, Tennessee), 1898.

Cheyenne Sun-Leader (Cheyenne, Wyoming), 1898.

Chicago Daily Tribune (Chicago, Illinois), 1898.

Colorado Chieftain (Pueblo, Colorado), 1898.

Daily Argus-Leader (Sioux Falls, South Dakota), 1898.

Daily Oklahoma State-Capital (Guthrie, Oklahoma), 1898.

Daily Oklahoman (Oklahoma City, Oklahoma), 1898.

Dakota Huronite (Huron, South Dakota), 1898.

Denver Evening Post (Denver, Colorado), 1898.

Denver Field And Farm (Denver, Colorado), 1898.

Denver Republican (Denver, Colorado), 1898.

Denver Times (Denver, Colorado), 1898.

Florida Times-Union & Citizen (Jacksonville, Florida), 1898.

Fort Collins Courier (Fort Collins, Colorado), 1898.

Herald (St. Joseph, Missouri), 1898.

Las Vegas Daily Optic (Las Vegas, New Mexico), 1898-1899, 1949.

La Voz del Pueblo (East Las Vegas, Neuvo Mexico), 1899.

New York World (New York, New York), 1898.

Rocky Mountain News (Denver, Colorado), 1898.

Salt Lake Herald (Salt Lake City, Utah), 1898.

San Antonio Daily Express (San Antonio, Texas), 1898.

Santa Fe New Mexican (Santa Fe, New Mexico), 1898-1899.

Sun (Baltimore, Maryland), 1898.

Yankton Press and Dakotan (Yankton, South Dakota), 1898.

BOOKS

COWLES, ANNA ROOSEVELT. *Letters from Theodore Roosevelt to Anna Roosevelt Cowles, 1870-1918.* New York and London: Charles Scribner's Sons, 1924.

COZE, PAUL. *Rodeos de cow-boys et les yieux du lasso.* Paris: Société française de librarie et d'éditions, 1934.

DAVIS, RICHARD HARDING. *The Cuban and Porto Rican Campaigns.* New York: Charles Scribner's Sons, 1898.

HAGEDORN, HERMANN. *Roosevelt in the Bad Lands.* New York: Houghton Mifflin Co., 1930.

——. *The Rough Riders: A Romance.* New York: Harper & Brothers, 1927.

MARSHALL, EDWARD. *The Story of the Rough Riders: 1st U. S. Volunteer Cavalry.* New York: G. W. Dillingham Co., 1899.

MORGAN, JAMES. *Theodore Roosevelt: The Boy and the Man.* New York: Grosset & Dunlap, 1919.

OTERO, MIGUEL ANTONIO. *My Nine Years as Governor of the Territory of New Mexico, 1897-1906.* Albuquerque: University of New Mexico Press, 1940.

RIIS, JACOB A. *Theodore Roosevelt the Citizen.* New York: Outlook Co., 1904.

ROOSEVELT, THEODORE. *The Rough Riders.* New York: Charles Scribner's Sons, 1899.

SUES, OTTO L. *Grigsby's Cowboys.* Salem, South Dakota: Privately printed, 1900.

Torrey's Rough Riders, Historical and Biographical Souvenir of the Second United States Volunteer Cavalry. Jacksonville, Florida: Vance Printing Co., 1898.

VINCENT, GEORGE E. *Theodore W. Miller, Rough Rider, His Diary as a Soldier together with the Story of His Life.* Ohio: Privately printed, 1899.

Wyoming Volunteers, Seven Companies of Second Regiment, Torrey's Rough Riders. Privately printed, n.d.

ARTICLES

ALLEY, JOHN. "Oklahoma in the Spanish-American War," *Chronicles of Oklahoma*, XX (March, 1942), 43-50.

ARMSTRONG, H. E. "Roosevelt as a Volunteer Soldier," *Independent*, LIII (September 26, 1901), 2277-81.

CUNNINGHAM, PAUL E. "Rough Riders' Reunion," *New Mexico*, XXVII (June, 1949), 22, 41-42.

JOHNSON, J. R. "Nebraska's 'Rough Riders' in the Spanish-American War," *Nebraska History*, XXIX (June, 1948), 105-12.

ROOSEVELT, THEODORE. "The Rough Riders," *Scribner's Magazine*, XXV (January, 1899), 3-30; (February, 1899), 131-51; (March, 1899), 259-77; (June, 1899), 677-93.

"The Rough Riders Ride Again," *Life*, XXXIII (August 25, 1952), 43-45.

THOMPSON, ALBERT W. "I Helped Raise the Rough Riders," *New Mexico Historical Review*, XIV (July, 1939), 287-99.

VIVIAN, WALTER. "Return of the Rough Riders," *New Mexico*, XXXI (June, 1953), 13-15, 37.

WESTERMEIER, CLIFFORD P. "Teddy's Terrors: The New Mexican Volunteers of 1898," *New Mexico Historical Review*, XXVII (April, 1952), 107-36.

———. "The Dodge City Cowboy Band," *Kansas State Historical Quarterly*, XIX (February, 1951), 1-11.

WINTER, JR., JOHN G. "The Fight of the Rough Riders," *Outlook*, LX (September 3, 1898), 19-20.

DOCUMENTS

"Roll of Deceased Patriots," an annotated list by Colonel Jay L. Torrey, found in his personal signed copy of *Torrey's Rough Riders, Historical and Biographical Souvenir of the Second United States Volunteer Cavalry*. Jacksonville, Florida: Vance Printing Co., 1898. Courtesy of William B. Hodge, West Plains, Missouri.

INDEX

Accidents (train), 127, 128-129, 130, 131-132, 194; burial of victims, 187-188; compensation, 188

Adams, Alva, 35, 36, 99, 137, 138, 162, 226

Adams, "Girlie," 136

Aguadores River, (Cuba), 179

Alabama, 133, 231; *see also* individual cities

Albuquerque, N. Mex., 50, 51, 52, 54, 57, 253

Albuquerque *Daily Citizen*, 27, 50, 51, 52

Albuquerque *Democrat*, 52, 53

Alger, R. A., 27, 28, 29, 30, 32, 33, 35, 42, 43, 44, 90, 226, 227, 230, 236, 237, 238

Allen, Charles H., 239

America, 79, 243

American (s), 79, 84, 95, 96, 174, 243, 254, 257; army, *see* United States Army

Ames, Adelbert, 239

Amusements, *see* camp, recreation

Anderson, Ed, 25, 26

Anderson (railroad clerk), 125

"Antelope" (name of horse), 106

Appelget, A. M., 41

Ardmore, Okla., 58

Arizona, 28, 36, 40, 57, 80; troops, 57, 58, 59, 258; *see also* individual cities and towns

Army and Navy League, 222

"As We Go Riding With Torrey," 156-157

Austin, Henry H., 107

Austin, Tex., 25

Bacon, John Mosby, 116

"Ballad of Teddy's Terrors, The," 153-155

Ballard, C. L., 50, 241

Baltimore *American,* 143

Barton & Conners (Jacksonville, Fla.), 229

"Battle Cry of Freedom, The" (melody of), 164

Battle yell (s), 102

Battles: casualties, 174, 177, 181; Las Guasimas, 175; San Juan, 179-182, 234, 256

Beeson, Chalk, 197

Belle Fourche, S. Dak., 118

Bergere, A. M., 50

Big Horn, Wyo., 90

Billings, Mont., 116

Birmingham, Ala., 133

Black Hills Squadron, 117

Bocock, John Paul, 151
Bond, C. W., 224
Brighton, Colo., 100
Bristol, Albert, 131
Brito, Frank C., 258
Brodie, Alex (Alexander O.), 40, 43, 57, 253, 255
"Bronco Buster, The," (Remington sculpture), 243
Brooke, John R., 207, 211, 212
Brooklyn Bridge, 244
Brown, Henry A., 245
Buffalo, Wyo., 64, 90
Buffalo Bill, 44, 45, 46, 78; rough riders, 119; Wild West Show, 34
Burch, George, 34
Butte, Mont., 116

Cadiz fleet, 128
"Cake Day" (Cheyenne, Wyo.), 141
Calverley, Robert, 107
Camp food, 76, 79, 83, 91-92, 173, 178, 193, 206-207, 220, 224; complaints of, 225, 258
Camp life, 74-75, 76, 80, 92, 133-134, 192; conditions of, 74, 75, 171, 172, 178, 179, 185-186, 187, 193, 220-229; incidents in, 82-83, 92, 122, 134, 209-210, 216; recreation and amusements, 82, 110, 193-194, 208-209, 220; routine, 80, 111, 134; sickness and disease, 85, 202-205, 210, 224, 225, 226, 258
Camps (military): Adams, 96; Thomas, 191, 201, 202-203, 206, 207, 208, 209, 211, 215; Wikoff, 243, 252; Wood, 79.
Cannon, John Q., 107, 195
Capital Pharmacy (Cheyenne, Wyo.), 139-140
Carrizo Springs, Tex., 24
Carson City, Nev., 90
Carter, J. D., 253
Carter, Thomas H., 70
Casper, Wyo., 90, 92
"Cavalry Charge, The," 82
Chadron, Nebr., 136
Chase, John, 69
Chattanooga, Tenn., 121, 201, 208, 213
Chattanooga Times, 118, 121, 202, 203, 208, 213, 214
Cheever, B. H., 190, 195
Cheyenne, Wyo., 63, 67, 68, 69, 88, 89, 90, 91, 92, 93, 96, 97, 98, 100, 101, 105, 111, 112, 113, 124, 125,

127, 140, 162, 185, 197, 198, 219, 225, 226, 230
Cheyenne Sun-Leader, 40, 45, 63, 64, 92, 95, 131, 192
Chicago, Ill., 116, 118, 197, 222, 223
Chicago Daily Tribune, 59, 117, 170, 237, 238
Chicago Inter Ocean, 34
Chickamauga, Ga., 116, 118, 121, 205, 225
Chickamauga Park, 72, 215
Cincinnati, Ohio, 222, 223
Civil War, 147
Cody, William F., see Buffalo Bill
Coffin, Stanley D., 198
Coffman, W., 209
Colbert, Ben H., 258
Coleman, Sherrard, 175, 177
"Colonel's Serenade, The," 220
Colorado, 32, 43, 44, 60, 69, 78, 99, 100, 101, 105, 107, 137, 138, 146, 160, 161, 186, 221, 226; cowboys, 37; State Horticultural Society, 137; troops, 37, 90, 93, 96, 97, 98, 99, 101, 138, 142, 162; see also individual cities and towns
"Colorado's Battle Song," 162-163
Colt revolver, 65, 77, 83, 109, 118, 120, 195-197
Columbus, Nebr., 126
Commissary Department, 78
Congress of the United States, 23, 28, 39, 41, 42, 43, 51, 111
Cooper, C. L., 53
Coutant, C. G., 65
Cowboy (s), 32, 33, 34, 37, 38, 39, 40, 41, 43, 45, 46, 50, 54, 55, 58, 63, 64, 65, 66, 68, 70, 71, 75, 79, 81, 83, 89, 96, 106, 107, 117, 119, 129, 130, 134, 136, 148, 150, 156, 158, 162, 165, 181, 201, 202, 208, 209, 210, 215, 220, 244, 246, 256, 259, 260
Cowboy volunteers, 32, 40, 41, 43, 47, 109, 110, 120, 259; appearance of, 57, 118, 119, 120, 259; characteristics of, 54, 59, 60, 118-119, 121, 122, 133; escapades of, 242, 245; occupations of, 54, 68, 75, 76, 117, 118, 196, 214, 247, 258, 259; qualifications for, 52, 67, 72, 89, 97-98; unfitness for service, 52, 53, 71
"Cowboy Volunteers, The," 161-162
"Cowboys' Battle Song," 166-167
Cowgirls, 137

Cox, William L., 107
Craig, Nebr., 129
Cripple Creek, Colo., 44
Cuba, 29, 42, 49, 52, 55, 57, 72, 78, 84, 85, 97, 99, 109, 116, 126, 133, 137, 146, 149, 156, 160, 163, 164, 165, 171, 172, 173, 174, 176, 187, 191, 201, 202, 210, 212, 220, 221, 223, 229, 230, 242, 247, 254, 255, 256, 257, 258
"Cuba Libre Song," 55, 148-149
Cuban (s), 25, 46, 64, 77, 84, 139, 147, 149, 156, 163, 167, 168, 174, 175, 177, 253; invasion, 99, 175
Cuban campaign, 33, 180, 211; camp conditions, 173, 235; food supplies, 234, 235, 236; sickness and disease, 236, 238
Cuban junta, 190
Culver, Jacob H., 116
Curry, George, 50, 60, 231, 253
Cussick, James, 121

Daily Oklahoma State Capital, 35, 59
Daily Oklahoman, 82
Daiquiri, Cuba, 174, 175
Dame, William E., 255
Daniels, William Cooke, 142
Daughters of the American Revolution, 138
Davis, Louis G., 107, 186
Davis, Richard Harding, 84, 247
Day, Dave, 44
Deadwood, S. Dak., 118
Deming, Headlight, 241
Denver, Colo., 35, 36, 68, 78, 89, 90, 93, 100, 101, 104, 107, 108, 137, 142, 162, 197, 221, 224, 225, 229, 230
Denver Evening Post, 35, 137, 205, 222
Denver Republican, 32, 100, 247
Denver Times, 34, 112
Dewey, George, 102, 112, 148, 167
Diario, 78
Dillenback, J. D., 246
Dodge City, Kans., 60, 197
Dodge City Cowboy Band, 197-198, 220
Douglas, Wyo., 90
"Dudes Before Santiago, The," 151
Duncan Hotel (Las Vegas, N. Mex.), 256
Durbin, Winfield T., 229

East, the, 68, 69, 75, 113, 245
East Indies, 109
East St. Louis, Ill., 130, 131
Easterner (s), 74, 76, 117, 150, 151
Eggleston, Frank W., 139
El Caney, Cuba, 151
El Heraldo de Madrid, 78
El Paso, Tex., 50, 253, 254
El Poso, Cuba, 179
Embar, Wyo., 90, 232
Emerson, Edwin, Jr., 153
Epidemics, see camp life, sickness and disease
Eppley, Kurtz, 241
Equipment (military), 77, 98; see also Colt revolver, Krag-Jörgensen carbine, Mauser (firearms), and saber, use of, 195-197
Evanston, Wyo., 90

Farewell demonstrations, 60, 99-100, 101, 113, 115, 142
Fargo, N. Dak., 116
Fergusson, H. B., 28, 50, 51, 245
Fields, Doctor [Field, Peter Conover?], 225
First Reunion of Rough Riders, see Reunions (Rough Riders')
First United States Volunteer Cavalry Regiment, 30, 33, 55, 57, 59, 72, 74, 76, 99, 117, 124, 126, 138, 155, 170, 174, 179, 181, 191, 210, 234, 235, 240, 242
Fish, H. Gurdon, 203, 204, 207
"Flag of the Torrey Men," 157-158
Flags (regimental), 137-138, 157
Flagstaff, Ariz., 28
Florida, 83, 84, 143, 159, 171, 173, 185, 192, 195, 201, 219, 227; see also individual cities and towns
Florida Times-Union & Citizen, 196, 198
Forts: Bayard (N. Mex.), 27; Brown (Tex.), 25; Keogh (Mont.), 116; McPherson (Ga.), 207; Ringgold (Tex.), 25; Russell (Wyo.), 67, 88, 90, 91, 92, 93, 96, 98, 100, 101, 105, 108, 109, 124, 125, 140, 141, 143, 157, 187, 188, 223; Wingate (N. Mex.), 27
Fox, George W., 37, 66, 67
French, Leigh H., 121; ('s) Squadron, 116

Galveston, Tex., 83
Geronimo, 33

Gill, James, 93, 96
Globe, Ariz., 25
Golden, Henry G., 91
Golden Jubilee Celebration, see Re-
  unions (Rough Riders')
"Good-bye, My Lover, Good-bye"
  (melody of), 55, 148
Goodrich, David, 255
Goulding, George L., 104, 108
Governors' Day (Cheyenne, Wyo.),
  138
Gracey, Robert C., 125, 197, 198
Grand Island, Nebr., 164
Greeley, Colo., 101
Green River, Wyo., 90
Griffin, William E., 177
Grigsby, Melvin, 33, 35, 36, 37, 39,
  41, 42, 43, 69, 70, 71, 72, 99,
  115, 119, 208, 209, 212, 215, 218
Grigsby's cowboys, 33, 121, 122; see
  also Grigsby's regiment
Grigsby's Cowboys, 41, 120, 211
Grigsby's regiment, 117, 118, 145,
  164, 191, 201, 210, 213, 221; see
  also Grigsby's cowboys
Guemmer, Charles, 133
Guthrie, Okla., 57

Hamburg, Nebr., 129
Hansborough, Henry C., 70
Harbord, James G., 189
Harris, Bert, 108
Harrison, Benjamin, 197
Hartzell, Ike, 111
Harvard University, 56, 247
Havana, Cuba, 147
Helena, Mont., 119
Henderson, Mrs. H. B., 140, 141
Herald, The (St. Joseph, Mo.), 182
Hershey, Henry B., 241
Hill, Mrs. Nathaniel P., 142
Hoadley, Willis F., 107
Holcomb, A. A., 105
Holcomb, Silas A., 137
Horse (s), 50, 59, 64, 66, 72, 80, 81,
  88, 89, 97, 98, 104-109, 150, 156,
  158-159, 171, 196, 198, 205, 224,
  228, 230, 240; care of, 127, 129,
  133; cost of, 68, 81, 104, 105, 106,
  108; gear, 205, 206; funerals, 205-
  206; specifications of, 68
Horsemanship, 63, 64, 66, 67, 69,
  72, 259
Hospital system, 203, 225, 226, 227,
  228
Hoyt, Percy S., 68, 105

Hubbard, L. F., 190
Hughes, Thomas, 54
Humphries, Colonel [Humphrey,
  Charles F.?], 78
Huntsville, Ala., 231

Idaho, 36, 44, 69, 89, 90, 94, 138,
  160, 188, 229; see also individual
  cities and towns
Illinois, 38, 78, 130; First Cavalry
  of, 209; see also individual cities
  and towns
Indian (s), 45, 46, 79, 117, 176, 216,
  220, 260; campaigns, 33, 44, 59,
  107; uprisings, 27, 28; wars, 44
Inman, Henry, 45
Inter-Dakota Squadron, 117
Inter Ocean Hotel (Cheyenne,
  Wyo.), 69
"Irish Fusiliers" (melody of), 155
Iron Mountain, Wyo., 90
Isleta, N. Mex., 57
Ivey, Jack (John), 110

Jackson, A. H., 111
Jackson, Harry, 245
Jacksonville, Fla., 109, 112, 124, 125,
  133, 160, 189, 190, 191, 193, 194,
  195, 196, 198, 219, 222, 224, 225,
  226, 227, 230, 231
Jesurun, Mortimer, 186
Juragua, Cuba, 175

Kane, Woodbury, 76
Kansas, 36, 60; see also individual
  cities and towns
Kansas City, Mo., 124, 187, 197, 225
Karn, Leslie C., 205, 206
Kemmerer, Wyo., 90
Kentucky, 130
Kerr, H. B., 69
"Kettle Hill" (Cuba), 181, 182
Kilburg, Charles, 111
Kimball, T. C., 209
Knickerbocker Club (New York),
  56
Krag-Jörgensen carbine, 77, 109
Kyle, James H., 42, 70

"Ladies' Day" (Fort Russell), 141
Lander, Wyo., 90
Laramie, Wyo., 37, 68, 69, 89, 91,
  94, 104, 131-132, 139
Las Cruces, N. Mex., 50
Las Guasimas, Cuba, 175
Las Vegas, N. Mex., 253, 254, 257

Lawrence, Herbert, 202
Lead City, S. Dak., 118
Ledgwidge, T. P., 77
Lee, Fitzhugh, 189, 190, 195
Leffler, Leo, 225, 226
Lemmen Brothers' Circus, 110
Lincoln, Nebr., 116
Lincoln County, N. Mex., 54
Lincoln Park (Las Vegas, N. Mex.), 255
Linderfelt, Carl E., 222
Llewellen, W. H. H., 60, 142, 242, 255
Long, John A., 199
Love, William J., 257
Luna, Max (Maximiliano), 52, 53, 60, 148, 149, 242, 255

McCord, Myron H., 40
McHenry, Blanche, 137
McIntire, Albert W., 43
McKinley, William, 32, 33, 40, 42, 66, 78, 240, 245
MacNutt, Charles H., 107
Maghee, Morgan M., 107
Maine, the, 24, 49, 146, 147, 152, 157, 160, 164, 166
Malaria, 204, 225, 236, 238
Manardi, John B., 107
Mapes, Henry S., 133
"Marching T h r o u g h Georgia" (melody of), 148, 156, 162
Marshall, Edward, 173
Marti, Joaquin, 24, 25
Maryland, 33
Mauser (firearms), 152, 176, 203, 237
Meek, Sam Cary, 147
Memorial Day (1898), 99, 100, 101
Mexican (s), 64, 229, 240; border, 24, 26; troops, 27
Mexico, 25, 26
Miles, Nelson A., 40, 45, 65
Military Affairs Committee, 42
Military departments: Dakota, 116; Colorado and Missouri, 91.
Miller, Harry H., 222
Minneapolis, Minn., 197
Mississippi, 134; see also individual cities and towns
Missouri, 38, 126, 127, 128; see also individual cities and towns
Montana, 70, 105, 108; squadron, 117, 213; troops, 116; see also individual cities and towns
Montauk Point, L.I., 225, 240, 242; escapades at, 245; illness of troopers, 242
Montezuma Hotel (Las Vegas, N. Mex.), 256
Mules, 80, 81, 107, 121, 171, 205, 240
Muller, Frederick, 60, 242
Murphy, Lieutenant, 209
Murray, George F., 258
Mustering out, 212-215, 220, 229-231, 242, 243

National Guard, 38, 237, 241
National Livestock Association, 107
National Relief League, 243
Navy, Department of the, 56
Nebraska, 27, 37, 70, 126, 138, 146, 163; see also individual cities and towns
Needle cases, 140-141, 142
Negro (es), 130, 134, 143, 180-181, 193, 208, 220, 223, 241, 248
Nevada, 36, 69, 90, 94, 107, 160, 194
Newcastle, Wyo., 90, 105
New Jersey, 194, 241
New Mexico, 24, 28, 36, 49, 52, 54, 57, 59, 76, 80, 138, 139, 147, 148, 242, 253, 254, 258; cowboys, 76; National Guard, 24, 51; volunteers, 27, 29, 50, 59, 60, 81, 174, 242, 258; see also individual cities and towns
New Orleans, La., 25, 83
New York (state), 78, 247, 253
New York City, 56, 78, 243, 244, 254
New York *Press,* 34
New York *World,* 24, 54, 244
New Yorker (s), 75-76
Ninth regiment (colored), 180-181
Norfolk, William H., 107
Norris, Private, 163
North, the, 206, 210, 222
North Dakota, 36, 70; see also individual cities and towns
Northwest, the, 33, 70
Nuevo Laredo, Mex., 24
Nunns (trooper), 203

"Ode to Grigsby's Cowboys," 164-166
O'Donnell, Thomas W., 128, 129
Ogilvy, Lyulph G. S., 101
Ohio, 78, 222, 223
Oklahoma, 36, 57, 59, 146, 259; troops, 58, 59, 80, 255; see also individual cities and towns

Oklahoma City, Okla., 60
Old Santa Fe Trail, The, 45
Omaha, Nebr., 72, 115, 127, 128, 223
"On to Cuba," 146-147
Orr, J. T., 192
Osborne, John E., 187
Otero, Miguel A., 24, 27, 28, 29, 30, 49, 50, 51, 54, 147, 242, 243, 253, 256

Pais, 79
Palace Pharmacy (Cheyenne, Wyo.), 139
Panama Park (Jacksonville, Fla.), 133, 134, 159, 185, 195, 222
Parkhill, Clayton, 228
Patriotism, display of, 50, 51, 57, 60, 64, 70, 118, 125, 127-128, 198, 222, 223
Pay (military), 85-86, 111, 223, 230, 231, 244, 258
Payday escapades, 193-194, 195, 208-209
Paymaster, 85, 111
Pettigrew, Richard F., 36
Philippine Islands, 91, 99, 112, 138
Phoenix, Ariz., 25, 137-138
Pierre, S. Dak., 41
Pittsfield, Ill., 38
Platteville, Colo., 101
Poems (patriotic: "Ballad of Teddy's Terrors, The," 153-155; "Cowboy Volunteers, The," 161-162; "Dudes Before Santiago, The," 151; "On to Cuba," 146-147; "Rough Riders Afoot," 158-159; "Rough Riders at El Caney," 151-152; "Rough Rider's Lament, A," 168; "Throughout the world two things retain" (first line), 167; "Torrey Boys' Lament," 160-161; "Torrey's Tigers," 159-160; "We Are Coming, Governor Otero!" 147; "We Are the Boys of Company M," 163-164
Prescott, Ariz., 25
President of the United States, see McKinley, William
Press: Associated, 238, 239, 240; interviews, 92-93; rivalry, 95-96
Prince, Mrs. L. Bradford, 138
Protectors, abdominal, 138-140, 141
Pueblo, Colo., 197, 198
Puerto (Porto) Rico, 109, 112, 113, 129, 187, 191, 211, 212, 214, 237

Quartermaster Department, 68, 93

"Rally Round the Flag, Boys," (melody of), 157
Raton, N. Mex., 254
Rawlins, Wyo., 90
Red Cross Society, The, 143, 222, 224
Remington, Frederic, 243
Reunions (Rough Riders'): first, 254-256; golden jubilee, 257-259
Revolver, see Colt revolver
Richards, William A., 40, 64
Rio Grande River, 24, 26
Roberts, Frank S., 258
Rock Springs, Wyo., 90
Rocky Mountain Empire, 32, 44, 55, 118, 174, 197, 223, 230
Rocky Mountain News, 36, 37, 93, 95, 96, 97, 98, 99, 191, 196, 199, 221, 226, 229
Rocky Mountains, the, 39, 133, 248
Roosevelt, Theodore, 29, 33, 34, 35, 39, 43, 54, 56, 57, 72, 77, 78, 80, 124, 150, 151, 152, 153, 154, 155, 175, 179, 180, 182, 191, 201, 234, 236, 237, 238, 239, 241, 242, 245, 246, 247, 248, 253, 254, 255, 256, 257, 259, 260
Roosevelt's Rough Riders, 58, 77, 78, 79, 82, 83, 85, 100, 101, 124, 137, 139, 145, 153, 172, 173, 174, 176, 177, 179, 180, 181, 182, 191, 201, 211, 234, 236, 237, 240, 241, 242, 243, 244, 245, 246, 247, 248, 252, 253, 254, 255, 257, 260; nicknames for, 34
Root, Matt R., 187
Rough Riders (applied to cowboy volunteers), 32, 33, 39, 41, 195
Rough Riders, The, 39, 54, 245
"Rough Riders Afoot," 158-159
"Rough Riders at El Caney," 151-152
Rough Riders' Day (June 24), 256
"Rough Rider's Lament, A," 168
Rough Riders' Organization (Roosevelt's), 252, 257
Rough Riders' Roundelay," 155-156
"Round robin" letter (military), 239

Saber, use of, 195-197
Sackett, Archie A., 130
Saint Augustine, Fla., 194

St. John's River (Fla.), 134
Saint Joseph, Mo., 128, 129, 131
Saint Louis, Mo., 38, 78, 107, 124, 126, 129, 197
Saint Louis *Globe Democrat,* 38
St. Paul, Minn., 197
Salmon City, Ida., 90
Salt Lake City, Utah, 90, 107
Salvation Army, 121
San Antonio, Tex., 55, 56, 57, 58, 60, 72, 74, 75, 76, 81, 83, 84, 85, 99, 138, 148, 171
San Antonio *Daily Express,* 58, 75
San Francisco, Calif., 72, 116, 127, 138
San Juan, Cuba, 178, 180, 234
San Juan Hill, 181, 182
Santa Fe, N. Mex., 23, 30, 50, 51, 53, 54, 57, 59, 60, 80, 138, 174, 253
Santa Fe *New Mexican,* 28, 30, 51, 52, 53, 59, 60, 78, 138, 254
Santiago, Cuba, 152, 153, 154, 174, 179, 210, 234, 237, 242
Scott, William E., 44
Scribner's Magazine, 39
Second United States Volunteer Cavalry Regiment, 35, 66, 68, 72, 88, 109, 117, 124, 126, 133, 185, 191, 192, 196, 198, 201, 211, 218, 221, 229, 231
Secretary of War, *see* Alger, R. A.
Seminole scouts, 25
Shaffer, Fred C., 162
Shafter, William R., 153, 238, 240
Shanton, George R., 107
Shely, Wash W., 24
Sheridan, Philip, 158
Sheridan, Wyo., 41, 105, 106, 110
Sherman, Horace E., 149
Shoup, George L., 189, 190, 229
Shute, Mrs. (Colorado State Horticultural Society), 137
Siboney, Cuba, 155, 238
Silver City, N. Mex., 28, 258
Sinclair, Jack (John B.), 197, 198
Sioux Falls, S. Dak., 36, 70, 71, 115, 116
Sitting Bull, 46
Six-shooter, *see* revolver
Smith, Robert E., 71
"Smoked Yank, The" (Grigsby), 164
Smokeless powder, use of, 176
Sniffen, Culver C., 231
"Sobre las Olas," 81
"Soda Day" (Laramie, Wyo), 139

Solomonsville, Ariz., 28
Somerset Club (Boston), 56
Songs (patriotic): "As We Go Riding with Torrey," 156-157; "Colorado's Battle Song," 162-163; "Cowboys' Battle Song," 166-167; "Cuba Libre Song," 148-149; "Flag of the Torrey Men," 157-158; "Good-bye, My Lover, Good-bye," 148; "Ode to Grigsby's Cowboys," 164-166; "Rough Riders' Roundelay," 155-156
South, the, 99, 186, 203, 222, 223
South Dakota, 36, 70, 116, 119; *see also* individual cities and towns
South Omaha, Nebr., 127
Southwest, the, 33, 40, 54, 253
Spain, 49, 67, 147, 160, 164, 212, 258
Spaniard (s), 26, 35, 79, 84, 92, 125, 149, 152, 154, 156, 159, 164, 165, 166, 174, 176, 177, 214, 215, 234
Spanish, 45, 46, 98, 153, 155, 157, 163, 165, 166, 167, 175, 178, 179, 180, 182, 183, 203, 232, 235
Spanish-American (s), 24, 36; War, 40, 206
Springer, John W., 107
Springfield *Republican,* 247
Squadrons, 116-117
Starr County, Tex., 24, 25
Sternberg, George M., 228
Stewart, Robert W., 116
Stockle, G. E., 105
Story of the Rough Riders, The, 173
Sturgis, S. Dak., 118
Sues, Otto, 41, 43, 119, 120
Summers, Lieutenant, 209
Sumner, E. V., 91
Sumner, Samuel S., 105, 179
Sundance, Wyo., 90

Tampa, Fla., 55, 72, 83, 84, 85, 139, 170, 171, 172, 240, 241, 242
"Teddy's College Terrors," 149-151
Teddy's Terrors, 34, 44, 68, 77, 84, 155, 174, 244
Tedrow, Harry B., 126
"Teethadore," 34
Tennessee, 127, 130
Tenth cavalry (colored), 248
Texas, 24, 25, 26, 80, 82, 101, 162; cowboys, 75; horses, 59; Rangers, 27, 64; *see also* individual cities and towns

"There Will Be a Hot Time in the Old Town Tonight" (melody of), 164

Third United States Volunteer Cavalry Regiment, 37, 70, 71, 72, 99, 115, 117, 124, 126, 191, 201, 210, 211, 215

"Throughout the world two things retain" (first line), 167

Thurston, John M., 70

Tiffany, J. H., 28

Tiffany, William, 76

Tombstone, Ariz., 25

Torrey, Jay L., 32, 33, 37, 38, 39, 40, 41, 42, 43, 65, 66, 67, 68, 69, 72 88, 89, 90, 92, 93, 94, 95, 97, 98, 99, 105, 106, 107, 109, 110, 111, 112, 113, 124, 127, 128, 131, 133, 138, 142, 157, 160, 161, 187, 188, 189, 190, 195, 197, 218, 222, 223, 227, 228, 230, 231, 232

Torrey Bankruptcy Bill, 39

"Torrey Boys' Lament," 160-161

Torrey's Terrors, 94, 111, 126, 129, 134, 139, 198

"Torrey's Tigers," 159-160

Torrey regiment, 67, 68, 91, 92, 95, 96, 97, 100, 102, 105, 110, 113, 129, 130, 138, 145, 156, 157, 164, 186, 190, 191, 192, 194, 208, 221, 222, 228, 229

Transportation of troops, 57, 112, 124-125, 126, 173-174

Tucson, Ariz., 25

Tupelo, Miss., 131, 132, 187-188, 189, 194, 222, 223, 230, 231

Uniforms (military), 76-77, 84-85, 98, 109; lack of, 201-202

Union Pacific Railroad, 112, 124

United States, 45, 52, 67, 79, 215, 226, 239, 240, 242, 258, 259; Army, 35, 95, 97, 143, 177, 179, 181, 243; government, 50, 78, 107, 143

Utah, 36, 69, 89, 90, 107, 138, 160

Varnum, Charles A., 68, 104

Volunteer Aid Societies, 137, 142

Volunteer Army Bill, 42, 43, 63, 64

Wagon Mound, N. Mex., 255

War, Department of, 35, 36, 38, 45, 66, 67, 69, 70, 98, 187, 191, 212, 213, 229, 230, 231, 235

War of 1898, 111, 143, 219, 257

Warren, Francis E., 40, 42

Washington, D.C., 32, 33, 35, 36, 37, 39, 40, 42, 45, 51, 56, 63, 66, 67, 68, 78, 99, 191, 211, 212, 223, 229, 230, 237, 238, 242, 245

Washington University (St. Louis), 38

"We Are Coming, Governor Otero!" 147

"We Are the Boys of Company M," 163-164

West, the, 32, 41, 45, 56, 59, 68, 74, 75, 89, 117, 118, 121, 130, 133, 149, 155, 160, 205, 213, 220, 241

West Indies, 109

West Point, 40

Western, 35, 36, 42, 63, 69, 137, 194, 218, 222, 229, 259

Westerner(s), 59, 64, 89, 133, 134, 195, 209, 211, 212

Weyler, y Nicolau, 147, 165

Wheatland, Wyo., 90

Wheeler, Joseph, 179, 237

Wheeler, William G., 90, 98, 107, 190, 221, 223, 229

Wild West Show, 107, 137

Wiley, John A., 121

Wilhelm, Thomas, 113

Williams, A. H., 69

Wind River Region, Wyo., 106

Windsor Hotel (Jacksonville, Fla.), 188, 189, 190

Women volunteers, 136-137

Women's activities, 122, 125, 127, 128, 129, 132-133, 136-143

Women's Relief Corps, 137

Wood, Leonard, 29, 32, 33, 34, 39, 79, 154, 170, 171, 174, 179, 182, 235

Wood, M. W., 239

Wood's Weary Walkers," 85

World Wars I and II, 110, 257

Wynkoop, Harman, 60, 138, 139

Wyoming, 36, 37, 38, 39, 40, 44, 64, 65, 66, 67, 69, 89, 90, 91, 95, 97, 105, 110, 112, 138, 139, 140, 142, 143, 156, 157, 160, 161, 192, 193, 231; cowboys, 40, 156, 161; University of, 68, 69; volunteers, 37, 93, 131, 138, 145; see also individual cities and towns

Yale University, 56

Yankee(s), 78, 100, 153, 154

Ybor City, Fla., 171

Young, Samuel B. M., 179

Yucatan, 172

61-31484